Mexico and the United States, 1821 - 1973:
Conflict and Coexistence

AMERICA AND THE WORLD

EDITOR: Robert A. Divine

Mexico and the United States, 1821 - 1973:

Conflict and Coexistence

KARL M. SCHMITT
University of Texas

John Wiley & Sons, Inc.
New York • London • Sydney • Toronto

Library of Congress Cataloging in Publication Data:

Schmitt, Karl Michael, 1922-
  Mexico and the United States, 1821-1973.
  (America and the world)
Bibliography: p.

  1. United States—Foreign relations—Mexico.
2. Mexico——Foreign relations—United States.
I. Title.

E183.8.M6S35   1974   327.72'073   73-20327
ISBN 0-471-76198-2
ISBN 0-471-76199-0 (pbk.)

Printed in the United States of America

10 9 8 7 6 5 4 3 2 1

To Alberto Casares Ponce
who introduced me to Mexico

Foreword

"From the halls of Montezuma . . ." is the beginning of the U.S. Marine Corps hymn, an all-too familiar reminder of the lowest point in this country's relations with its neighbor to the south. Mexico has been very important in the diplomatic history of the United States. In the first half of the nineteenth century, Americans stripped the Mexicans of nearly one-half of their national domain, first by the annexation of Texas in 1845 and then by the forceful acquisition of California and the vast New Mexico territory in 1848. Two decades later, Americans watched sympathetically as Mexico valiantly resisted French intervention and finally redeemed her sovereignty by overthrowing Emperor Maximilian. Relations steadily improved over the next half century as American entrepreneurs reaped huge profits in Mexico under the complaisant rule of Porforio Díaz. Conflict and tension returned when Woodrow Wilson blindly attempted to direct the Mexican Revolution along democratic lines and succeeded only in uniting all factions within Mexico against him. Armed intervention at Veracruz in 1914 and Pershing's futile efforts to capture Pancho Villa in 1916 nearly resulted in war between the two nations again. In the 1920s and 1930s, wiser United States diplomats gradually closed the wounds Wilson had opened up and ultimately solved the problems stemming from Mexico's determination to control her own economic resources. World War II brought the two neighbors close together, and ever since they have displayed an admirable ability to deal with the complex issues of migration, water rights, and border disputes in a harmonious spirit.

Karl Schmitt offers a broad overview of this changing relationship from the perspective of a detached observer. Avoiding either a partisan United States or Mexican viewpoint, he traces the interaction of the two young nations that began with relatively equal power on the international scene and gradually moved further and further apart in political prestige and economic development. Although he never ignores the cultural and intellectual differences, he places major emphasis on the power differential that became the main source of tension between the two countries. United States-Mexican relations thus become a fascinating case study of the way in which a great power and a small power interact, moving from rivalry and conflict to a grudging respect for each other's distinctive position in the international community.

This book is one in a series of volumes tracing the history of American foreign policy toward those nations with which the United States has had significant relations over a long period of time. By stressing the continuity of diplomatic themes through the decades, each author will seek to identify the distinctive character of America's international relationships. It is hoped that this country-by-country approach will not only enable readers to understand more deeply the diplomatic history of their nation but make them aware that past events and patterns of behavior exert a continuous influence on American foreign policy.

ROBERT A. DIVINE

Preface

Mexicans are seldom at a loss for words to express their feelings and emotions—eloquently and at length. A few years ago, however (so the story goes), a group of dignitaries and leading citizens were left virtually speechless by a visiting delegation from Turkey. Having been wined, dined, and properly impressed with Mexico's economic and political accomplishments, the Turks effusively thanked their hosts for their hospitality. Moreover, they also congratulated Mexico for its good fortune (so superior to their own) for being blessed with a friendly although rich and powerful neighbor, the United States. The precise Mexican response has not been recorded, but there was a moment of pause and some embarrassment. After all, many of these Mexican leaders had long been lamenting their misfortune of being so close to the Colossus of the North. They had also been advocating closer ties with the Soviet Union and its associated states to lessen their economic dependence on the United States. The Turks, of course, had long been victims of Russian imperialism, and had joined NATO after World War II in self-protection.

The story may well be apocryphal, but it points up the first major axiom of international relations: foreign policy positions and attitudes, that is, the definition of the national interest, are based on personal and individual perceptions of reality. In this particular instance, geography played a major role in conditioning perceptions. Other conditioning factors are relative size in territory and population, state of wealth and technology, capabilities of the armed forces, ideological-philosophical doctrine, and various combinations of these. In most countries with a press as free as Mexico's the political leadership engages in spirited and sometimes acrimonious debate over foreign policy. And not just over projects, programs, or approaches, but also over fundamental positions. We have recently seen such debate in the United States. But the Mexican leadership appears substantially united on basic issues: a detachment from power blocs, adherence to international organizations, nonintervention, the absolute sovereignty of states, and a settlement of all disputes by peaceful means.

Whatever the official definition of the United States national interest at any one time, it has run almost always at variance with that of Mexico at least since World War II. The United States has attempted to establish and lead regional power blocs around the world and has obviously resorted to force to settle disputes. In the process, its armed forces have intervened in the affairs of other states and have disregarded their claims to absolute sovereignty. These actions have angered and frightened Mexicans who as a militarily undefended people have a long memory of United States troops occupying parts of their country. They are further disturbed by the tightness of the bonds that tie their economy to that of the United States.

This leads to the second axiom of international relations: foreign policy is concerned with defending national interests (however defined), and "defending" implies conflict or at least competition. Even the friendliest of states have conflicting interests from time to time. Conflicts between Mexico and the United States have been severe in the past: one major war and territorial seizure; various United States attempts to acquire additional territory through purchase or threat; several major incursions of United States forces to defend or protect United States persons, property or national honor; acrimonious disputes over property rights; and enormous inflows of United States capital that have led many Mexicans to fear that United States entrepreneurs would control the country through their investments. Presently relations are basically harmonious but include an element of tension over the questions of United States interventions in the Caribbean and United States direct and indirect participation in the Mexican economy. The major purpose of this study is to examine these tensions, that is, to understand the nature of the disagreements, the source of the feelings of fear, frustration, greed, pride, or power that underly the disputes, and the alternatives and options open to the parties for peaceful and mutually beneficial compromises.

We now come to the third axiom of international relations: foreign policy is seldom in its overall effects a zero-sum game between two states. In some types of interchange both parties lose heavily and in others both score substantial gains. Perhaps the Mexican War approached a zero-sum game, but almost all other major transactions between Mexico and the United States resulted in some costs and benefits to both sides. Admittedly Americans have won more often than Mexicans, but they have also suffered serious losses both in lives and property. At the same time it would be mistaken to identify conflicts of interest as between rich Americans and poor Mexicans. Seldom, it is true, is there a conflict of any magnitude between poor Americans and rich Mexicans (although incidents occur on a local, personal level) but there have been major disagreements that confront poor Americans and poor Mexicans, for example, the question of Mexican labor in the United States that displaces workers of United States citizenship, many ironically of Mexican descent. More often the disputes pit rich Americans against rich Mexicans. In the economic conflicts over trade, investments, loans, technology transfer, it is often difficult to know precisely who gains, who loses, and who comes out even in any given transaction. This study is not sufficiently detailed to examine particular cases for answers, but it hopes to make the reader aware of the complexities involved.

Two themes run through this story. The first is that the economic dependency of Mexico on the United States is of relatively recent origin. It dates from the mid-to-late 1880s and has not developed in a straight-line pattern. The two countries began their independent lives relatively equal in resources and expectations. The United States quickly passed Mexico in population and wealth, but despite the War of 1846, economic and political relations between them remained rather unimportant until the end of the nineteenth century. At that time United States investments flowed heavily southward, and by 1910 Mexico had become a virtual economic satellite of the United States. This dependency was lessened somewhat between 1910 and 1940 but was never reduced substantially. Today Mexico's economy is tied to that of the United States in many ways.

The second theme is that United States threats, armed incursions, and pressures to sell territory or to grant concessions have occurred whenever Mexico as a small power was least able to defend itself, that is, when it was rent by internal conflict or disorder. On the other hand whenever peace prevailed, United States economic penetration occurred, and on the two occasions when this has taken place—1880 to 1910 and 1945 to the present —Mexico's internal peace and stability have been threatened partly by the consequences of that process. The only moment when United States and other foreign influences were reduced occurred when political stability and unity had been achieved under a revolutionary leadership that was willing to pay the economic costs, that is, during the administration of Lázaro Cárdenas (1934 to 1940), when lands were seized and the oil industry expropriated.

I am convinced that at the present Mexico has little to fear from the United States in the way of armed incursions. I see United States political leadership today as basically reoriented from an earlier era. Not only is there no great American interest in naval bases and transit rights on Mexican territory, for example, but there is much less American apprehension over the cold war issue of Communist "penetration and subversion" into our southern neighbor. Third-party rivalry vis-à-vis Mexico is seen as economic competition, and no responsible leader in the United States has suggested limiting that with armed force.

As long as Mexico remains politically stable and as long as Mexicans retain control of their own destinies, the United States leadership will regard Mexico as a secure bulwark on the southern frontier. Should Mexico fall again into disorder (which is improbable short of a serious economic collapse) or should any foreign power attempt to intervene in Mexican political affairs (which is highly improbable under any foreseeable circumstances), the United States might then feel threatened. In the economic area my own judgment is that Mexican leadership will slowly extend national control over foreign economic interests without driving them from the country, that tensions between the two countries will continue at about their present level or at a somewhat higher level, and that local problems such as the salinity level of the Colorado River will be handled through compromise and adjustment. I perceive the present Mexican leadership as a basically satisfied new elite that profits from the current arrangements. Although it wants to control the economic game and would like eventually to possess all the chips, it is not willing to risk great losses by adventuresome tactics.

One final word. All the goodwill, understanding, and knowledge in the world will not of themselves solve these conflicts. Disagreements, disputes, and conflicts of interest exist and will continue; new ones will replace the old. United States leaders know Mexico, and Mexican leaders know the United States very well indeed. The problem is not so much one of understanding and education (although on occasion these may help); today the problem is to acknowledge national differences and to work out practical compromises based on the political and economic realities in both countries. That is not easy to do, but if neither country feels severely threatened by the policies of the other, it is not impossible either.

Let me acknowledge my own debts:

To Robert A. Divine, William P. Glade, Stanley R. Ross, Francis Beer, and Gilberto Ramírez of the University of Texas at Austin; Romeo Flores Caballero of El Colegio de México; Mary Chapman and Stephen Kane of the Department of State; Lyle Brown of Baylor University; Robert Freeman Smith of the University of Toledo; Charles Hale of the University of Iowa; Annette Fox of Columbia University; Michael Meyer of the University of Arizona; David Pletcher of the University of Indiana; and Warrick Edwards of the Mississippi Southern University—for their comments and criticism on the manuscript.

To Ann Kerry, Rexene Haynes, Mark Szuchman, Michael Hennen, and Rainer Godau—for assistance in research;

To Shirley Burleson, Ann Bragg, Helena Cunningham, and Kathy Corbett—for typing and proofreading;

To the Institute of Latin American Studies at the University of Texas at Austin—for a grant to initiate this study.

All interpretations and errors of facts are my responsibility alone.

Austin, Texas, 1973   KARL M. SCHMITT

Contents

INTRODUCTION

An Exchange of Views

APART FROM INTELLECTUAL CONTACTS, individual friendships, and tourist exchanges, Mexico and the United States have never become particularly "good neighbors." Linguistic, religious, ethnic, and other cultural predispositions have made it exceedingly difficult for these two peoples to communicate easily and readily. Moreover, they have on occasion confronted each other in conflicts of interest that could not be compromised. These clashes included armed conflict over domains of imperial extent and the utter defeat of one by the other, two subsequent military interventions, numerous threats of intervention, economic conflicts, and an ever-increasing disparity in military and economic strength. Given these factors, one can readily understand the continuation of distrust and suspicion by the defeated and weaker party and of a negotiating stance of superiority and dominance by the stronger.

For many Mexicans, the country's current status as a "small power" in the world community is particularly galling because Mexico emerged in 1821 as an independent state with bright hopes and prospects for playing a major role in the Western Hemisphere if not in all of Western Christendom. During the eighteenth century the Bourbon monarchs of Spain introduced economic and administrative reform measures to the Spanish Empire that produced a new flowering of prosperity, elegance, and intellectual ferment. Foremost among the beneficiaries in the Spanish world was Mexico (or New Spain as it was then called). On the eve of its independence, the Kingdom of New Spain enjoyed greater economic prosperity and cultural flowering than

1

it had ever known before. The arts—music, drama, science, and painting—flourished. Construction was booming, mining output reached an all-time high, land productivity increased substantially, and the royal revenues from the colony supported a series of imperial wars with Great Britain.[1] Although the struggle for independence, in part a product of this very ferment, destroyed much of the wealth of the country, created a heavy outflow of Spanish capital and reduced productivity sharply,[2] no one believed that the damage was irreparable. Independence was achieved in the clear expectation that Mexico would soon take its place among the great powers.

After all, one could argue that not only had New Spain exerted a kind of leadership among Spain's other colonies in America, but that it had in fact supported the mother country itself. No less an authority than the famous German scientist, Alexander von Humboldt, had written glowingly just before independence of the wealth and splendor of the country. The dream of greatness lasted about 15 years. After a shaky experiment with monarchy, a republic was created, a president elected and inaugurated, and several years of peace ensued. The economy in some sectors demonstrated remarkable abilities to recover, but by the late 1820s recurrent political quarrels, accompanied by military uprisings, forced loans, and armed depredations prevented the general economic growth and development from matching that of the eighteenth century, let alone any modernization and innovation in the use of machinery and other technology. With the loss of Texas in 1836, and the disaster of the war with the United States in the 1840s, the dream vanished utterly; thus Mexicans had to resign themselves to the view of their country as a small power.[3] Since that time Mexico's attitude toward the outside world has been cautious and reserved. One Mexican

---

[1] Hugh M. Hamill, Jr., *The Hidalgo Revolt: Prelude to Mexican Independence* (Gainesville: University of Florida Press, 1966), p. 1.

[2] Jan Bazant, *Historia de la Deuda Exterior de México (1823–1946)* (México: El Colegio de México, 1968), pp. 10–14.

[3] Mario Ojeda Gómez, "The Role of Mexico as a Middle Power," in J. King Gordon, *Canada's Role as a Middle Power* (Toronto: The Canadian Institute of International Affairs, 1966), pp. 129–130.

diplomat has characterized his country's international stance as "hermetic, nationalistic, distrustful, and defensive."[4]

Official and private views and attitudes toward the government and people of the United States have ranged over a broad spectrum. These have included fear and respect, hatred and admiration, and resentment and envy, combined in almost every conceivable combination and often within the same individuals. Americans have expressed fewer ambiguities in their views of Mexicans. Considerable ambivalence was evident, however, in the early years of Mexico's independence among the handful of intellectuals and political leaders who were aware of events in Spanish America. On the one hand there still persisted the long enmity mixed with contempt that most Englishmen felt for Spaniards. On the other hand there was satisfaction because their neighbors seemed to be following the United States road to independence and political liberalism. Implicitly the contempt surfaced, however, in their frequent requests that Mexicans relinquish some of their border territories on such ludicrous grounds that political administration would be eased as a consequence.

Odd as it may seem in the late twentieth century, the first signs of admiration for the United States in independent Mexico came from the then most radical political group, the federalists (or Liberals) of the 1820s who modeled the Constitution of 1824 in part upon that of the United States. They also accepted into their counsels the first United States Minister to Mexico, Joel Roberts Poinsett, and followed his lead in establishing York Rite Masonry as a political base. The opposition group, the centralists (or Conservatives) thoroughly detested Poinsett and deeply distrusted the United States government on the grounds that it had designs for territorial expansion at Mexico's expense. The Conservatives also tended to harbor the traditional Catholic Spanish hostility toward the Protestant English-speaking world, a hostility that had its roots in imperial and religious rivalries stretching over three centuries. While the federalists recognized the land hunger of their northern neighbor, they believed that the United

---

[4] Jorge Castañeda, "Revolution and Foreign Policy: Mexico's Experience," *Political Science Quarterly*, Vol. 78 (September 1963), No. 3, p. 391.

States would not use force to achieve this end. Apparently they were blinded by the sympathy expressed by Poinsett for their domestic political views. With the Conservatives in the ascendancy by the late 1820s, the Mexican government requested Poinsett's recall. Never again was an American diplomat to have such influence on or entrée into Mexican political life.

At the time of Poinsett's return home, the Texas question was beginning to arise, and finally culminated in war between the two countries. In the intervening years, Mexico's distrust of the United States continued to grow and the Mexican-American War, with its attendant losses of immense territories, provided Mexico with a permanent focus of xenophobia. However, the war produced neither an immediate sentiment for national unity nor a crusade to recover the lost territories. Instead, Mexican intellectual and political leaders resumed their domestic conflicts once the war was over and within 10 years were engaging in a fratricidal civil strife that led to another foreign invasion, this time by the French. Notable too is the absence of any particularly vitriolic attacks on the United States in the novels of the period about the war. Manuel Payno's *El pistol del diablo*, published serially during the war with the United States, blamed not the invaders for Mexico's ills, but the generals and their followers who had plunged the country into chaos and disorder. In *El monedero* (1861) Nicolás Pizarro, a staunch Liberal, portrays Americans in the War of 1846 in an unfavorable light, but the overall conflict remained largely incidental to his story, which is concerned primarily with the plight of the Indians and the struggle for political liberalism. Even less anti-United States, Manuel Martínez' *Julia* (1868), while treating the war at great length, appears more concerned with expressing the author's basic pessimism about humanity in general than in attacking Yankees specifically.[5] For the United States, the 30 years prior to the outbreak of its Civil War was marked first by the growth of wide popular feelings of antipathy and impatience toward Mexico for not recognizing the independence of Texas. The war, when it came in 1846, was also greeted with general approbation,

---

[5] John S. Brushwood, *Mexico in Its Novel. A Nation's Search for Identity* (Austin: University of Texas Press, 1966), pp. 73–99.

although considerable resistance appeared. The leadership of the Whig Party, north and south, criticized the war as unjustified and aggressive. Antislavery politicians, whether Whig or Democrat, denounced it as a scheme to extend slavery. And intellectuals like Ralph Waldo Emerson, Henry David Thoreau, James Russell Lowell, and William Ellery Channing condemned it as immoral. New England constituted the primary center of dissent, but strong voices were also heard in the West and South. Despite this criticism, however, Congress overwhelmingly voted for war and supported legislation in behalf of the war effort. Among ordinary people the war was popular, and sentiment was strong among some groups to absorb all of Mexico.[6] As soon as the war was over most Americans, secure in a sense of superiority over their immediate neighbors, turned their attention to internal matters. A few newspaper editors and local politicians, hungering for more Mexican territory, continued to alarm their southern neighbors, but general interest declined after 1848.

With the freeing of the slaves in the United States, with the presence of the sympathetic figure of Abraham Lincoln in the presidency, and with the moral support of the United States government and people for Juárez against the French, Mexican attitudes shifted to a somewhat more favorable view of the United States. Old fears of invasion and territorial seizures revived in the mid-1870s when United States armed forces crossed the border in pursuit of Indians and bandits. In addition, old resentments flared when the Grant and Hayes administrations delayed recognition to Porfirio Díaz when he seized the presidency in 1876. But once these issues were settled and United States investments began to pour into Mexico upon official and private invitation, mutual attitudes and views between the two peoples improved immeasurably. Business opportunities in Mexico were announced throughout the United States, paeans of praise were sung to the dictator, the Mexican ambassador in Washington became a leading foreign personage along the United States eastern seaboard, and visiting groups of United

---

[6] Frederick Merk, "Dissent in the Mexican War," in *Dissent in Three American Wars* by Samuel Eliot Morison, Frederick Merk, and Frank Freidel (Cambridge: Harvard University Press, 1970), pp. 35–63.

States officials and businessmen received royal treatment in Mexico. On the whole, Mexican leaders during the last two decades of the nineteenth century, influenced by a positivist, scientific perspective, voiced little criticism of the United States, and seemingly had forgotten the lost territories. Those few "malcontents," whether of the left protesting sellouts to the northern colossus or of the right condemning the encroachments of materialism, Protestantism, and atheism, gained little attention from Mexico's economic and political elites. In fact they were fortunate if they were not repressed or imprisoned. At the same time the new elite retained some of the old caution toward the North. Díaz tried to balance United States investments with European investments (but not too successfully); and once he perceived the vital economic role played bv the railroads, the Mexican government began the process of nationalization. Justo Sierra, the leading intellectual of the Díaz period, warned around the turn of the century that the "financial object of the Americans in extending their railroad network to Mexico was to dominate our markets. . . ."[7] Only in the last decade of the dictatorship (1900–1910) did serious criticism of the United States again appear. It tended to be coupled with a general dissatisfaction with the Díaz dictatorship over the degree of involvement permitted foreign interests in Mexico's economy, the narrowness of the social base participating in the national prosperity, and the persistence of an authoritarian regime. At the same time some doubts arose in the United States about the benevolence of the Mexican regime, particularly with the appearance of John Kenneth Turner's critical magazine articles in 1909 and his book *Barbarous Mexico* in 1910. In general, however, both official and private relations between Mexicans and Americans appeared sound and harmonious at the opening of Mexico's centennial year of 1910, a year that ended with a revolution underway.

The Great Revolution that began in 1910 marked a major turning point both in official and private United States-Mexican attitudes. Not only did it unseat Díaz and produce a decade of

---

[7] Justo Sierra, *The Political Evolution of the Mexican People*, translated by Charles Ramsdell (Austin: University of Texas Press, 1969), p. 361.

armed conflict, but it brought drastic social and economic changes that vitally affected United States private interests in the country. And at that time private interests became very much the official interests of the United States government in terms of extending protection to the lives, welfare, and property of United States citizens. Conflicts arose over revolutionary laws and decrees expropriating land, mineral rights, and utilities. The anticlericalism of the Revolution had long troubled United States Catholics, and when the revolution turned virulently anti-Catholic in the 1920s, that powerful minority demanded United States intercession for their coreligionists.

Despite some temporary softening of differences and quarrels at various times between 1910 and 1940, United States-Mexican relations remained basically at odds. Accusations of "Red Mexico," thievery, banditry, atheism, and murder were hurled by United States opponents of the Revolution, while countercharges of intervention, assassination, domination, racism, and reaction were tossed back against the United States. Although all Mexican political and military leaders during the period sought recognition and at least tacit support of the United States government for their factions or regimes, most were probably motivated by practical necessities. Only Francisco Madero, the initiator of the Revolution, seemed actually to desire friendly relations, as a result of his belief in free elections and the democratic representative process of government. Popular bitterness against the United States became particularly exacerbated by General Pershing's military expeditions against Villa, but even more importantly by President Wilson's occupation of Veracruz in 1914, allegedly over a slight to some United States sailors at Tampico, but in reality as a measure to unseat the dictator Victoriano Huerta who had overthrown Madero.

The Revolution unleashed a veritable torrent of Mexican literature, serious and popular, attacking the United States. Books and plays produced during the fighting phase of the Revolution portray the United States as a predator intent on destroying Mexico's national independence, as an implacable and unalterable enemy, or as a decadent society to be shunned. Later Diego Rivera painted greedy Yankees into his murals of social commentary, while filmmakers depicted exploiting Yankees mistreating Mexican farm laborers, and novelists attacked United States economic, military, and political interventions of the past. Among the intellectuals these themes have persisted to the present and, in fact, the condemnation of the War of 1846 became more intense and bitter after 1910 than before. Interestingly, among some of the sharpest critics of the United States some of the old ambivalence remained. José Vasconcelos, one of the great reforming educators in the 1920s, who wrote a history of Mexico in the following decade that showed great disillusionment over the Revolution, saw the evil hand of the United States in Mexico's misfortunes. However, he also had harsh words for many of his country's leaders and compared them unfavorably with nineteenth century United States political leaders, many of whom he openly admired.[8]

By the late 1950s, however, as the Revolution stabilized, one can detect a new emphasis in the Mexican critique of the United States. The old grievances were not forgotten, but they were bypassed for criticisms of Mexican society itself for imitating American fashions, whether in the drive to accumulate wealth and power or in the popular acceptance of Coca-Cola, and of the Mexican government and private entrepreneurs for opening the country to a new flood of United States capital in Mexican industry and commerce.[9] Recent governments have shown themselves much more alert to this kind of criticism than did the Díaz dictatorship. Official pronouncements have emphasized the necessity of Mexican control over national economic life, and governmental decrees have slowly limited and restricted foreign investments. In the United States the once bitter attacks on the Revolution subsided after World War II. Mexico's political stability, growing economy, and protection of foreign capital, however restrained, made the country once more respectable in the eyes of United States investors and government officials. Disagreements with United States foreign policy, and divergences in practice, produced some annoyance and impatience but did not

---

[8] José Vasconcelos, *Breve Historia de México*, 5th edition, (México, D. F.: Ediciones Botas, 1944), p. 344.

[9] For an excellent discussion of political themes in Mexican art and literature, see Frederick C. Turner, *The Dynamics of Mexican Nationalism* (Chapel Hill: University of North Carolina Press, 1968).

mar official relations. And hundreds of thousands of tourists began to flock to Mexico annually in ever-increasing numbers. Although United States visitors showed some residue of unease toward the remaining revolutionary rhetoric, most of them seemed unaware that Mexico was once feared as a foothold for Red Bolshevism in the hemisphere. United States scholars dealing with Mexico were for the most part sympathetic with the Great Revolution and deplored the interventions of their government in Mexican affairs. Some recent United States scholarly criticisms have arisen, not this time from the right, in condemnation of the Revolution and its goals, but from the left in questioning whether the Revolution has failed to continue the pursuit of its proclaimed goals.[10]

At the present time Mexican attitudes toward the United States are again mixed. On the one hand, government and business leaders desire warm and amicable relations to attract capital and to widen the United States market for Mexican goods. At the same time they are wary of too much foreign control over the economy, especially in key sectors. Businessmen, moreover, wish to avoid destructive competition with foreign firms and therefore support government policy to restrict foreign capital. The primary anti-United States sentiment comes from the Marxist left, but the left has been so fragmented in recent decades that it has failed in efforts to mount a sustained and effective campaign. Beyond these loosely organized groups there is a large substratum of resentment against the United States for past injuries and for present racial discrimination.[11] Tourists who have flooded Mexico since World War II have at times added to the stereotype of the uncouth Yankee. In addition to vulgar

---

[10] See Stanley R. Ross (ed.), *Is the Mexican Revolution Dead?* (New York: Knopf, 1966) and Kenneth F. Johnson, *Mexican Democracy: A Critical View* (Boston: Allyn and Bacon, 1971). A revised and expanded edition of the Ross work has appeared in Spanish: *¿Ha muerto la Revolución Mexicana? Causas, Desarrollo y Crisis*, 2 vols., (México: Secretaria de Educación Pública, 1972).

[11] As an example of a tendency to think the worst of the United States, note the accusation in a clandestine publication that CIA agents gave money to Mexican Communists to sabotage the Olympic games in Mexico City in 1968 in order to divert them to Detroit. Cited in Johnson, *op. cit.*, p. 7.

behavior, some Americans have angered Mexicans by smuggling archaeological treasures out of the country.

At the same time, some of the general resentment appears to be dissipating. Certainly it does not seem to be strongly propagated in the public or private schools. School textbooks are not particularly xenophobic in general or anti-American in particular. In a recent survey of the political attitudes of Mexican children from the fifth to the ninth grades inclusive, an overwhelming and surprising majority listed the United States as the country most friendly with Mexico. The United States also ranked highest among primary school children as a place of residence if they had to leave Mexico, and second only to Western Europe among secondary school students. Revealingly, among children from working-class or campesino families, the United States remained the first choice of residence outside Mexico through all grades.[12] Moreover, no less an authority than Pablo González Casanova recognized this changing attitude in his concluding remarks on United States influences in Mexico, which by the way he deplores: "In the midst of difficulties and pressures, Mexico is one of the most stable countries in Latin America and perhaps the only one in which 'anti-American' sentiment has given way to a strategy of national independence and development."[13]

---

[12] Rafael Segovia, "Nacionalismo e Imagen del Mundo Exterior en los Niños Mexicanos," *Foro Internacional*, Vol. XIII (October-December, 1972) No. 2, pp. 287–289.

[13] Pablo González Casanova, *Democracy in Mexico*, translated by Danielle Salti (New York: Oxford University Press, 1970), p. 64.

CHAPTER I

The Inheritance

O<small>N</small> D<small>ECEMBER</small> 12, 1822, Secretary of State John Quincy Adams presented José Manuel Bermúdez Zozaya to President James Monroe in the White House. By this action the United States officially recognized the independence of Mexico, and the newly created empire of Agustín Iturbide (Agustín I). These formalities, however, were not concluded in an historical vacuum. Centuries of rivalry between Englishmen and Spaniards in Europe and in America over trade, empire, and religion on both public and private levels had conditioned all participants in their respective roles. Although leading citizens of the United States could identify in some way with the aspirations for political freedom among the inhabitants of New Spain, they also held certain misconceptions about the Mexican struggle for independence, labored under a massive ignorance about the area and its people, and harbored certain prejudices and stereotypes about Spaniards and Spanish culture in general, views collectively known as the "Black Legend." The leaders of New Spain were similarly ambivalent about their northeastern neighbor. Interested in United States experiments with republicanism and constitutionalism, they knew virtually nothing of the practical side of United States politics. Remembering tales of British pirates and freebooters (and North Americans were not easily distinguishable), and faced with recent United States expansionism in Louisiana and Florida, Mexicans could only look to the north with some apprehension. Beyond these concrete threats, Mexicans were imbued with their own prejudices and stereotypes about Englishmen and Anglo-Americans, that is, their own

"Black Legend." In other words, although some of the omens were favorable, there were serious obstacles to cordial relations and smooth cooperation between the two governments and their peoples.

I

Although much has been made of the religious side of the conflict between England and Spain in the sixteenth century, it is unquestionable that overseas imperial questions predominated in the mind of Philip II when he launched his ill-fated Armada against Elizabeth I. Religion may well have increased the fighting fervor of the rank and file on both sides of the conflict, but the leaders understood the game in different terms. By the late sixteenth century the English were not only exploring the coasts and making minor settlements in North America, but they were also beginning to encroach on the trading monopoly that Spain was attempting to impose on her new world dominions. The defeat of the Armada badly damaged Spanish military prestige and emboldened English merchants, freebooters, and would-be colonists to press ahead with projects in the Americas. One by one the English acquired firm footholds, not only along the Atlantic coast of present-day United States, but also on Caribbean islands and the coast of Central America. Simultaneously English pirates on numerous occasions had struck fear and hate into Spanish administrators and colonials with their attacks, raids, and ransom demands along the Spanish main. By the outbreak of the American Revolution, British sea power was threatening Spanish control of the Gulf of Mexico and British American frontiersmen, having pushed their settlements over the mountains, were threatening Spanish territories west of the Mississippi River.

Trade and commerce constituted another arm of British imperial advance. Paradoxically English (or British) merchants were often welcomed into the same ports that had first attracted the pirates. In time they replaced the marauding freebooters as the primary Spanish-British contact. Although all such trade was illicit until the early eighteenth century, enforcement of Spanish navigation laws remained lax, not only because the British enjoyed a price advantage over Spanish-authorized merchants, but also because at times the British supplied goods unavailable through legal sources. Spanish colonials were eager to acquire British goods, and Spanish administrators often winked at the illegal transactions. In 1722 when the British finally gained a minor trade concession in the Caribbean, they simply used it as a bridgehead to expand still further their illicit traffic.

After the Bourbon replaced the Hapsburg dynasty at the beginning of the eighteenth century, Spain and its empire experienced a revival. Military capabilities improved, administrative and fiscal reorganization strengthened royal controls over the far-flung domains, and internal economic reforms led to a new burst of growth and prosperity. A new push along the rim of the empire between 1760 and 1800 accompanied the imperial reforms. Spanish diplomats, priests, soldiers, and engineers acquired Louisiana, although somewhat reluctantly, recovered the Floridas from the British, constructed forts in the Mississippi Valley, and established missions in Upper California. In fact, this renewal of expansion and ambition finally brought Spain into war against Great Britain in 1779 at the height of the American Revolution. It is symptomatic of Spanish caution and distrust of the Americans (read "British-Under-a-Different Flag") that Spain refused to enter into an alliance with the rebels, although France had done so. Thus the Spaniards delayed attacking Britain for almost two years after France had entered the war, although war preparations had begun as early as the spring of 1776. Spanish drives to recover Florida, Minorca, and Gibraltar, to wipe out British posts in the Gulf of Mexico and the Caribbean Sea, to cut off contraband trade, and to close the Mississippi were tempered by the realization that a defeat of Great Britain would mean independence for the British Americans. Furthermore, independence might not only serve as an example for similar movements in Spanish America but also the North Americans might themselves encourage revolt, seek to conquer parts of the Spanish Empire, or both. As signs of Spanish distrust, the Mississippi River, open to United States commerce as a wartime measure after 1779, was closed when the war ended, and United States agents, appointed by the Congress to New Orleans and the West Indies, never enjoyed formal recognition and had to withdraw from their posts after 1783.

II

 With independence definitively won by the Treaty of Paris, the United States inherited a large share of the long-festering British-Spanish rivalry. Despite misgivings, Spain had believed that the American Revolution actually offered her an opportunity to weaken Great Britain and thereby to strengthen her own position in North America. These expectations proved wrong. One of the greatest threats to Spanish imperial designs in North America was the land hunger of the Anglo-Americans. Western settlements expanded from Kentucky to Georgia during the Revolution, and after 1783 the new United States proved even less willing and able than Great Britain to restrain frontiersmen and land speculators in the westward push. The navigation of the Mississippi and the right to deposit goods at New Orleans came to be the focus of the dispute. During the war Spanish arms had reconquered all of Florida and tightened their grip on Louisiana. At the conclusion of hostilities, Spain controlled both banks of the Mississippi, and closed the river to all foreign shipping. The Americans, however, through long usage had come to regard navigation of the river as a right. Larger issues were involved in the Mississippi River quarrel than simply the right to ship and deposit tobacco from the western settlements. Control over Indians, conflicting territorial claims, ownership of the Mississippi Valley, and perhaps dominance of all North America were at stake.

 From the perspective of the eastern seaboard, delay appeared to be the proper policy. Spain had difficulty attracting settlers while the United States could not restrain (even if it so desired) large groups of people from moving west. At the same time the United States Navy would confront a relatively great naval power should the United States attempt to seize New Orleans. The large United States Merchant Marine could not be adequately protected either in the Gulf of Mexico or in the Mediterranean Sea, two areas where United States commerce had great interests. In fact, in the years immediately after the Revolution, the United States Congress could probably have mustered a majority to accept Spain's closing of the river except for fear of western secession. For 12 years the dispute simmered: the United States government negotiated with Spain but declined to take military or naval action to force the issue, while Spain held grimly on to its territories bordering the United States. At the same time, frontiersmen grumbled, threatened, and conspired, but were too few and too isolated to take New Orleans by storm or to go it alone as an independent nation.

In 1795 with revolution and war engulfing Europe, Spain came to terms with the United States in order to protect her American flank. By the Treaty of San Lorenzo she not only opened the Mississippi to United States merchants and granted the right of deposit at New Orleans, but she also settled the question of the southern boundary of the United States and ended Spanish relations with the Indians within United States borders. Spain surrendered all points in the dispute with the United States with no immediate tangible gains to offset the concessions. All that she could hope for was to strengthen her territorial possessions before the next forward thrust of United States frontiersmen. For the United States the Treaty of San Lorenzo was a major triumph. Although the right of navigation and deposit were limited in details, frontier discontent and separation quickly evaporated, and boundary claims were confirmed. The navigation of the Mississippi was never again questioned by Spanish officialdom.

However satisfied for the moment were the Westerners with the Treaty of San Lorenzo, several United States political and military leaders regarded the treaty as simply the first step in an expansionist program at the expense of Spain.[1] In the waning years of the eighteenth century prominent Americans such as George Rogers Clark, Alexander Hamilton, and Aaron Burr participated in various schemes to seize Spanish territory. Rumors of plots, conspiracies, rebellion, and treason ran rampant in the United States. Plans to separate the West and attach it to Spanish territory in return for land grants; plans to revolutionize Louisiana and Florida and to use them as a base to launch a movement for independence for all Latin America; plans to expel the Spaniards from the same provinces and attach them to the

---

[1] Arthur P. Whitaker, *The Spanish American Frontier: 1783–1795. The Westward Movement and the Spanish Retreat in the Mississippi Valley* (Lincoln: University of Nebraska Press, 1969), p. 201, sees the Treaty of San Lorenzo as the beginning of the disintegration of the Spanish Empire as well as the first stage in the territorial expansion of the United States.

United States or Great Britain: all of these involved at one time or another United States citizens, British agents, Spanish officials, frontiersmen, and colonists. None of these projects ever got off the ground.

By the turn of the century, Spain had come to regard Louisiana as a liability. Besides civil and military officials there were few Spaniards in all of Florida and Louisiana. Americans, British, and blacks (as slaves) predominated among the some 6000 polyglot Floridians,[2] and the 20,000 inhabitants of Louisiana were almost equally divided between African slaves and French settlers. Spain could not recruit its own people, and the petty tyranny of officials and the numerous restrictions in Spanish-controlled areas contrasted sharply and often unfavorably with the free if not chaotic conditions in nearby United States settlements. In monetary terms, Louisiana cost the Spanish crown $500,000 per year, a considerable sum for an impoverished and wartorn country of that period. By contrast United States frontier settlers numbered about 75,000. Although these settlers paid few, if any, taxes to the federal government, still the land cost nothing to acquire. Largely self-sufficient in food and basic necessities, the settlers could trade for the items they required, and furnished their own military protection through their local militias. Temporarily quiet in 1800, they would eventually flow over not only into Louisiana and Florida but into Texas and lands westward to the Pacific.

Although Spain had approached France as early as 1795 about the purchase of Louisiana, no agreement could be reached until Napoleon Bonaparte came to power. Ambitious to revive France's overseas empire, Napoleon in a preliminary agreement with Spain promised to establish a kingdom for the displaced House of Parma in return for the cession of Louisiana to France (October 1, 1800). Although Napoleon failed to uphold his part of the bargain, the Spanish court agreed to deliver Louisiana without the settlement of the Parma question. Spain did stipulate that

---

[2] For a discussion of some problems on Florida see Samuel Proctor, "Research Opportunities in the Spanish Borderlands: East Florida, 1763–1821" and J. Leitch Wright, Jr., "Research Opportunities in the Spanish Borderlands: West Florida, 1781–1821," *Latin American Research Review*, Vol. VII (Summer 1972), No. 2, pp. 8–34.

Napoleon not cede Louisiana to a third party without first giving Spain an opportunity to recover it. Napoleon accepted the terms in July 1802, and Charles IV of Spain in October ordered his colonial officials to deliver Louisiana to the agents of Napoleon.

In the last years of Spanish Louisiana, official control over the population became very lax at the very time that the authority of both the federal and state governments of the United States was becoming more effective. By 1802 American immigrants had begun to move again into Spanish territory to escape all kinds of authority including taxation. Spanish efforts to restrict entry were unavailing. New Orleans with a resident population of about 8000 also had a floating population of some 3000 Americans in the course of a year consisting of boatmen, merchants, and their assistants. To these transients, to parties interested in the New Orleans trade, and to United States government officials the transfer of the province to France was deeply troubling. Not only could United States commerce be damaged, but the eventual United States acquisition of Florida and Louisiana might be long delayed if not prevented. Belatedly the Federalists became supporters of Western interests, and some of them called for war. Congress, however, appropriated $2 million to purchase New Orleans and the Floridas, and President Jefferson dispatched a commission headed by James Monroe to Europe with extraordinary authority. In the meantime, facing the imminent renewal of war in Europe and the disasters that attended French arms in Santo Domingo, Napoleon ordered the sale of Louisiana before Monroe arrived in Europe. Negotiations moved rapidly once the commissioners arrived in Paris, and in May 1803 they signed an agreement to purchase all of Louisiana. On November 30 Spanish officials delivered Louisiana to a French agent and a volunteer company of Americans assisted him in keeping order. The United States took possession December 20.

European turmoil once again redounded to the benefit of the new republic. Again Spain was forced to retreat, this time not by the Americans but by her supposed ally France (or better said Napoleon). Spanish policy had tried to capitalize on sectional rivalries within the United States, and for a time Spain's policy proved successful. By the turn of the century, however, the situation was completely reversed. While leading factions in the

United States were reconciling differences and nationalizing interests, their European competitors were consuming resources in continuing conflict. The United States was becoming more unified, while Europe continued its quarrels; Spain suffered the greatest damage. Whatever his constitutional scruples about presidential power Jefferson seized his opportunity, and purchased the whole Louisiana territory, more than doubling the territory of his country.

Spanish leaders recognized that the acquisition of Louisiana merely whetted American appetites for more territory. They attempted to ward off further losses through diplomatic negotiations and by the establishment of military colonies in Texas and Florida. In 1803 Spain still possessed considerable naval strength and expected to support her outposts with sea power. Nonetheless her position in Florida was extremely weak. For example, British companies doing business in the area recognized the local shift in power. Rather than continue their efforts to incite the Indians against the United States, they began to conciliate the Americans. In Europe the Spanish military decline continued. In 1804 France forced Spain into war against Great Britain, and at Trafalgar Spanish sea power was all but obliterated. In 1808 the Bourbon royal house was replaced by a brother of Napoleon, and the empire verged on collapse.

During these years United States-Spanish relations remained tense. Both sides avoided open conflict, the one fearing the loss of all its colonies to a joint British-American venture, the other fearing an eventual Napoleonic domination in Europe and in overseas colonial territories. Although many Americans still distrusted Great Britain, others saw the reentry of Spain into war as a golden opportunity for attacks on Spanish America. Some Americans joined an expedition led by Francisco de Miranda to revolutionize Venezuela, while others conspired more pragmatically to attack Florida, Texas, and Mexico. Although the United States government approved none of these schemes, important public figures and much of the public were enthusiastic supporters. Andrew Jackson and Westerners in general either hated or despised Spaniards.

Most notorious of these projects was the Burr conspiracy. In the spring and summer of 1805 Aaron Burr, the vice-president during Thomas Jefferson's first administration, traveled through the West mustering support for a campaign to destroy the Spanish Empire in America. He met with Henry Clay in Kentucky, Andrew Jackson in Tennessee, and General James Wilkinson at Fort Massac, finally arriving in New Orleans in late June. By September rumors were circulating in the West that Burr was going to separate that region from the Union, and was bribing potential followers with promises of Spanish plunder. His political and military preparations continued into 1806, and in July of that year he wrote Wilkinson that he planned to move down to Natchez with 500 to 1000 men. He again visited Jackson who, like many Westerners, expected war with Spain at any moment over boundary disputes arising from vague delimitations in the Louisiana purchase treaty. Contrary to expectations the Spanish commander withdrew beyond the Sabine River into Texas, thus evacuating the territory claimed by the United States. Burr's opportunity consequently vanished, Wilkinson turned informer and made an agreement with the Spaniards, and Jefferson moved rapidly to stop Burr's activities. Wilkinson, who had been raising troops in New Orleans, arrested many of Burr's followers, and himself finally surrendered at Natchez.[3]

Thomas Jefferson was only marginally interested in the independence of Latin America. His primary concerns were internal issues, United States relations with Great Britain and France, and the border disputes with Spain over Florida and Texas. In foreign affairs his policy was to maintain peace, but with respect to Cuba, Florida, and Mexico he stood ready to oppose the transfer of American colonial possessions from Spain to a third party. In October 1808 his cabinet unanimously agreed to inform influential Cubans and Mexicans unofficially that the United States would be satisfied to see those areas remain under Spanish control but "extremely unwilling" to see them fall to the British or French. Furthermore, they were to be informed that if they chose independence, the United States would be friendly, but that it

---

[3] An interesting account of the Burr conspiracy can be found in John Rydjord, *Foreign Interest in the Independence of New Spain. An Introduction to the War for Independence* (Durham: Duke University Press, 1935), pp. 209–222.

could not commit itself to support independence movements in Latin America. At the same time Jefferson wrote to Governor Claiborne of Louisiana in somewhat stronger terms that United States interests and those of Cuba and Mexico were the same in "that the object of both must be to exclude all European [i.e., French and British] influence from the hemisphere."[4]

III

When Napoleon deposed the Bourbon king of Spain, Ferdinand VII, and placed his own brother Joseph on the throne of Spain, a constitutional crisis broke over the Spanish dominions. Many jurists claimed that, according to Iberian law, when the legitimate king was removed, authority reverted to the various component kingdoms that comprised the Crown of Castile. Incipient independence movements arose in Spanish America proclaiming loyalty to Ferdinand; civil war broke out in the peninsula itself. In Mexico the governing elites divided into several factions; some advocated a thinly disguised independence; others adhered firmly to the Spanish junta that was attempting to resist the Bonapartes in Spain. Few if any could be found to support Joseph, whom most considered an imposter. At the same time a truly revolutionary movement was brewing in the small town of Dolores to the north of Mexico City. Led by the parish priest Miguel Hidalgo and supported by some local military officials (all native born in New Spain), the group advocated not only independence from the mother country but social and economic changes beneficial to the lower class, particularly the Indians. Taking the banner of Our Lady of Guadalupe as his standard, proclaiming death to the Gachupines (peninsular-born Spaniards) and loyalty to Ferdinand VII, Hidalgo launched his revolt on the night of September 15-16, 1810.

Catching the governing class by surprise with his daring and with the enthusiastic support of thousands of Indians and campesinos, Hidalgo won a series of astonishing victories. Instead of driving his horde directly toward Mexico City, however, he turned away from the capital for reasons that are not entirely clear. With the breathing spell this gave to the established forces,

---

[4] Quoted in Arthur P. Whitaker, *The United States and the Independence of Latin America 1800–1830* (New York: Norton, 1964), p. 43.

troops were gathered, and in a decisive encounter at the bridge of Calderón in January 1811, Hidalgo's mass army suffered a severe defeat and great casualties. He could not sustain a setback of this magnitude, and many of his followers began to disperse. Retreating northward, Hidalgo was relentlessly pursued and finally captured. He was eventually tried, defrocked, and executed. The rebellion that he began, however, was never completely suppressed by loyalist forces in New Spain. Other priests and laymen took up arms and, although many paid with their lives, new leaders always appeared to carry on. Independence was finally achieved in 1821 when the small bands of rebels fighting in the hills to the south of Mexico City were finally joined by the loyalist army sent out to destroy them. Ironically, Mexico finally achieved its freedom from Spain not under the leadership of the reformist heirs of Father Hidalgo but instead under the conservative military successors of the leaders who destroyed him. In 1820 following the vicissitudes of the Napoleonic era, an anticlerical liberal movement in Spain forced a constitution on the restored Ferdinand VII. The attempts to impose liberal legislation in New Spain aroused the ire of the old elites (lay, clerical, and military) who subsequently withdrew their loyalty from the mother country. Mexico achieved political independence, but its social and economic structures remained little changed for many years.

These events, momentous and often destructive for the people of Mexico, were viewed at best with mild interest by the people and government of the United States. President Madison toyed for a brief time with the idea of cooperating with France to revolutionize all of Latin America, but the War Hawks, the embargo, and finally the War of 1812 diverted his interests to more immediate and pressing issues. Some eastern commercial interests opted for intervention, but most merchants and shipowners strongly opposed intervention not only because it would disrupt valuable trade with Cuba and the Iberian peninsula, but also because it would expose United States shipping to British and other privateers. During most of the decade United States interests were more narrowly focused on territorial gains on the periphery in Canada and Florida instead of on the broader commercial and political gains encompassing the whole continent.

During most of the struggle for independence in Latin America, the United States government observed a nominally strict and impartial neutrality but, in fact, the highest officers of the government repeatedly expressed their sympathy for the insurgents. On the other hand there was no disposition to open hostilities with Spain; watchful waiting instead of aggressiveness characterized United States policy during these years. Despite a widespread desire for territorial aggrandizement there was no unified sentiment for war on Spain, and many observant leaders feared the possibility of a concerted attack from Europe, after Napoleon's fall in 1815, to restore not only European dynasties but disrupted empires. It was feared that any United States involvement in Latin American revolutions might well bring an attack on the United States itself should the Concert of Europe attempt to restore the status quo ante in the Americas.

IV

Mexican revolutionary leaders were hopeful that aid more tangible than expressions of sympathy would be forthcoming from the United States, which they regarded as a champion of freedom and independence. In December 1810 Hidalgo's government dispatched Pascasio Ortiz de Letona to the "supreme congress" of the United States as Ambassador and Plenipotentiary with full power to sign trade treaties and offensive and defensive alliances. His instructions were liberally sprinkled with the words "independence," "freedom," and "three hundred years of tyranny" because as Allende, one of Hidalgo's lieutenants, later explained "the United States have sworn to aid all people who attempt [to win] their independence."[5] Ortiz, a young Guatemalan botanist living in Guadalajara, never made it to the United States. He was captured on the road to Veracruz and poisoned himself. After Hidalgo's defeat at Calderón, his lieutenants stripped him of his command and named Allende as generalisimo. With his followers losing heart, Allende determined to make one more effort to solicit help from the United States. He commissioned Ignacio de Aldama as Minister Plenipotentiary and named Friar Juan de Salazar as his aide. He charged them to obtain whatever diplomatic support they could, to pur-

---

[5] Quoted in Hamill, op. cit., p. 211.

chase munitions, and to enlist 30,000 mercenaries. For this task Aldama and Salazar were provided with 100 bars of silver and other funds. They traveled northward into Texas as that appeared to be the safest route, since the northern territories had fallen under rebel control. Allende, with his fortunes deteriorating in central Mexico, followed his emissaries and contemplated going himself to Washington; however, he was captured along with Hidalgo and most of the other leaders. Aldama and Salazar reached San Antonio, the capital of Spanish Texas, but on March 1, 1811 a counterrevolt occurred, and both were taken prisoner.

With the end of the Hidalgo rebellion, new leaders arose to carry on the struggle. For the next four years the most prominent of these was José María Morelos y Pavón, another Catholic priest. In the early summer of 1811 Morelos sent David Faro, a survivor of a filibustering expedition from the United States, and Mariano Tabares of Acapulco to the United States to negotiate for assistance. This mission also failed to reach its goal not because of Spanish military resistance but because another rebel leader dissuaded them. Morelos later wrote that he was so desperate for aid in 1811 that he was ready to cede Texas to the United States in return for substantial support. Before his own capture and death in 1815, Morelos made two more efforts to solicit help public or private from the United States. In 1814 he sent Peter Bean (a United States citizen and his gunpowder expert) to the United States to initiate a military campaign against Spanish authorities in Texas. Bean was also to purchase arms. He made his way successfully to Veracruz and from there sailed to New Orleans, arriving in September in the company of José Pedroza and Juan Anaya, who were representatives of different rebel factions. Stymied for the moment by the British blockade of New Orleans, they renewed their efforts after Jackson's victory in January. Their plans came to naught, however, and Bean returned to Morelos. While in New Orleans Bean had met José Alvarez de Toledo, a former deputy to the Spanish Cortes from Santo Domingo, a champion of independence, and organizer of filibustering expeditions. Alvarez advised that the Morelos government dispatch an agent to the United States. Morelos accepted the advice, and commissioned José Manuel Herrera as Minister

Plenipotentiary to the United States with full powers to negotiate. After some difficulties Herrera arrived in New Orleans in
early November. He became involved in various filibustering
enterprises, and although he planned eventually to proceed to
Washington, he gave up the idea in December when he received
news of Morelos' capture.

For outside contacts the Mexican insurgents were forced to
rely on adventurers and professional revolutionaries who frequently victimized them. They paid exorbitantly for weapons
and financed expeditions that had no chance of success. On the
other hand, many filibusterers were well-meaning but ineffectual. Alvarez was apparently well motivated. He tried to raise
a revolt in Texas in 1813 but failed. Later he tried to foment
revolution in northern Mexico; he failed again. In October 1815
Alvarez did succeed in landing a cargo of military supplies on
the Mexican coast, but otherwise he could not carry out his
grandiose schemes. Discouraged, he sought the King's pardon
in 1816. Simón Tadeo Ortiz de Ayala of Guadalajara was a
world traveler. A student in Europe, briefly a prisoner in France,
a friend of Alvarez, a resident of New Orleans, Ortiz had contacts not only with rebels in the field like Morelos, but also with
underground insurgent sympathizers in Mexico City, the Guada-
lupes. Convinced that the United States was ready and able to
supply aid if communications could be established between the
rebels and the United States government, he urged the rebel
groups to dispatch official representatives. Ortiz believed that
the United States would supply not only arms but troops, and
would sign alliances as soon as the Spanish American nations
won their independence. Recognizing the difficulties facing the
United States with the War of 1812, Morelos sent Ortiz in 1813
to New Granada to buy weapons, seek financial aid, and form
an alliance with the rebels there. Ortiz was captured but eventually made his way back to Mexico in 1822 after independence
had been won.[6] Actually the United States government could
give no aid during the War of 1812, and with the war's end in

---

[6] For additional details on these attempted contacts see Wilbert H. Tim-
mons, *Morelos. Priest, Soldier, Statesman of Mexico* (El Paso: Texas Western College Press, 1963), pp. 142–151.

1815, it was reluctant to get involved in another conflict. At the same time, however, the United States refused to take vigorous action against rebel agents and would-be filibusterers who sought a firm base from which to assist the revolutionary movement in Latin America. The Spanish minister, Luis de Onís, protested in vain. Perhaps the most serious expedition launched from the United States against Mexico was led by Francisco Xavier Mina in late 1816. Mina had fought Napoleon's troops in Spain in guerrilla actions, but with the restoration of the autocratic Ferdinand VII, he fled Spain and eventually came to the United States. In the latter country he quickly began organizing an expedition to attack royalist forces in New Spain. Setting out with his small fleet on September 1, 1816, he made his way by slow and circuitous stages to the Santander River in northern Mexico, and in late April 1817 he captured the village of Soto la Marina. For the next six months he fought a series of engagements with royalist forces over a wide range of territory in the northern and central parts of the country. In the end he was captured and shot.[7] His ill-fated venture contributed little to the eventual achievement of independence for Mexico, but it further intensified Spanish fears of United States designs on the empire.

V

In the meantime, because of the vagueness in the definition of boundaries in the Louisiana treaty, the United States claimed that West Florida and Texas were included in the purchase of Louisiana. Spain denied the claims, and the United States Congress passed the Mobile Act in 1804 asserting jurisdiction over part of West Florida. The United States government made no attempt to enforce the act, but tensions continued between the two countries. In 1810 the United States seized a portion of West Florida, and during the War of 1812 annexed the Mobile District. Between 1815 and 1818 war seemed imminent on several occasions, and in 1818 unavoidable when Jackson in fighting the Indians drove his troops across the border into Indian

---

[7] Harris Gaylord Warren, "Xavier Mina's Invasion of Mexico," *The Hispanic American Historical Review*, Vol. XXIII (February 1943), No. 1, pp. 52–76.

sanctuaries in Florida. The Spanish court, however, decided that Florida was indefensible and late in the year instructed Luis de Onís, Spanish Minister in Washington, to concede most of the points demanded by the United States. Negotiations moved rapidly forward, and a treaty was signed on February 22, 1819. Its terms confirmed the United States in possession of those parts of Florida already seized and granted to it all of East Florida. More importantly perhaps, the United States gained its first clear claim to Pacific coast territory when Spain surrendered its territorial claims on the Pacific north of the 42nd parallel in return for United States renunciation to its own claim to Texas. Finally, the United States assumed $5 million owed to United States citizens with damage claims against Spain. Spain ratified the treaty February 22, 1821.

Obviously, Jackson's Florida sally contributed to the Spanish capitulation. Perhaps of greater significance was the fact that in 1818 Spain was preparing to launch a major effort to recapture her rebellious American possessions, and knew that she could expect little help from her European neighbors. The Spanish court probably believed that the surrender of Florida, which could not be defended at any rate, might well restrain United States aggressive moves against other parts of Spanish America, particularly Texas and other north-Mexican provinces. Such reasoning also explains the long delay of two years in Spanish ratification of the treaty. Certainly most Spanish American leaders (including those in Mexico) viewed the treaty in this light. Many regarded it as the deliberate sacrifice of Latin American independence by the United States in the furtherance of its own immediate interests. Some believed that the treaty contained a secret clause in which the United States agreed not to aid or recognize Latin American independence movements. (The treaty contained no such clause.) Others, both in Europe and Spanish America, believed that, regardless of United States intentions, the treaty gave Spain a free hand to subjugate her colonies. Whatever the ultimate truth, the United States continued to stand aloof from Spanish America's attempts to gain independence. This fact and the interpretation given the treaty antagonized many of the new leaders of Latin America. Specifically, it clouded United States relations with Mexico, which gained its independence in late 1821. Ironically, the treaty also provoked some sharp criticism in the United States, for a sellout not of Latin American independence but of United States claims to Texas. Demands began to be heard for "the reannexation of Texas."

VI

As independence became an accomplished fact in various parts of Spanish America by 1820, the United States had to decide how to respond to the new political realities. With respect to Mexico the problem was particularly acute. On the one hand the United States could welcome a new ally in its own struggle against European colonialism and imperialism and hopefully expect the birth of another republic at a time when that form of government was regarded by the great powers of Europe not only as a maverick form but as a dangerous source of radicalism and rebellion. On the other hand, if Mexico were accepted as a friendly power, what would happen to the United States urge for territorial expansion, especially to the demand for the reannexation of Texas? And what attitudes should the leaders of newly independent Mexico take toward its aggressive and restless northern neighbor? Despite a political act of revolution, many of the new leaders were not radicals, but rather upperclass landowners and men of property whose enthusiasm for liberalism was at best superficial, and who felt stronger ties with the aristocrats of Britain and France than with shippers, land speculators, frontiersmen, and merchants of the United States. How were they to contain those roving backwoodsmen and their land hunger? How were they to defend the vast tracts of sparsely settled northern Mexico?

In 1821 the two peoples and their governments faced each other with mutual misgivings and ignorance. United States contacts with Latin America and specifically with Mexico had been extremely limited. In the eighteenth century direct knowledge of the area in the United States had been restrictd to Louisiana, Florida, and Cuba. Until 1815 at least, Latin America was unknown in the United States except to a handful of scholars and seamen. It was "a *terra incognita,* a Dark Continent." No American had written any kind of a comprehensive or current account of Latin America or of any major region. The government itself had little reliable information. Even James Monroe, John Quincy Adams, and Henry Clay, who involved themselves deeply in diplomatic relations, had no special training or knowledge. None had ever visited the area, and only Monroe had a good command of the Spanish language. For their part Spanish Americans were woefully ignorant of the United States. Mexicans knew of Franklin for his work on electricity and, in a general way, Spanish Americans knew of the United States struggle for independence and something of the political theory that emerged. They had, however, virtually no information on the practical side of United States politics: its party system, federalism, or system of political checks and balances.

Most contacts between the United States and Latin America prior to the latter's independence came through commerce. During the opening decade of the nineteenth century United States commerce had extended to every major region of the continent. These commercial relations led to the first United States government agencies (quasi-consular posts) in the Spanish colonies. Later they provided personnel for quasi-diplomatic contacts with revolutionary governments. In Mexico such contacts never developed, however, because United States trade with New Spain grew slowly at best. Not only did United States products compete with Mexican foodstuffs in other parts of Spanish America, but the British who had established themselves early, dominated Mexican trade, both illicit and legal. United States business agents from 1806 to 1807 received a percentage of a silver shipment that they helped to ship from Mexico to Spain, and engaged in some overland and coastal smuggling prior to 1821. This, however, constituted a mere driblet of Mexican commerce.

After 1815 United States interest in Latin America began to increase substantially. Letters and reports from United States citizens in the area, information in foreign books, magazines, and newspapers, and propaganda in the United States flooded the country in the last round of the struggle for Latin America's independence. Almost every aspect of life was described by writers of many nations: naval officers, businessmen, diplomats, scientists, and travelers. Ironically the least-discussed area was Mexico, and until the publication of *Notes on Mexico* in 1824 by

Joel Roberts Poinsett, first U.S. Minister to Mexico, the people of the United States knew less about Mexico than any other important part of Latin America. United States interests in Mexico, at both private and governmental levels, had concentrated on revolutionizing it, or colonizing it, or conquering its border provinces.

If Mexicans and Americans knew little of each other, they inherited from their forebears hostile feelings ranging from mild suspicion to loathing and hatred. The Spaniards had early recognized the vast territorial ambitions of the new republic and feared for the peripheral provinces of their American empire. Count D'Aranda, who had signed the Treaty of Paris in 1783, warned the King that the Americans coveted Florida and sought to dominate the Gulf of Mexico. Manuel de Godoy, the great Prime Minister later called Americans the "natural enemies" of Spain and accused them of designs on Mexico. The predictions were soon borne out with filibustering expeditions, claims on Texas, and conspiracies to seize large portions of Spanish territory. During the struggle for independence in New Spain, the loyalist creoles and conservatives not only feared the political and territorial threat from the north, but also the cultural domination of Anglo-Saxon Protestantism. With its doctrines of freedom of speech and religion, the United States epitomized the decay of religion and morals, and the destruction of Spanish Catholic civilization. Rebels and radicals proved more ambivalent. They too recognized United States territorial threats, but they sympathized with its political ideals and hoped for assistance in their struggles. Many used bases in the United States to recruit fighters for their cause or a haven from which to launch an attack. José Antonio Rojas in New Orleans, for example, in a pamphlet attack on the Spanish regime contrasted the political suppression and the poverty of New Spain with the liberty and the prosperity of the United States. On the other hand the radical Fray Melchor de Talamantes pointed out the dangers from the north in the aftermath of the Burr conspiracy.

British Americans had no great love for Spaniards or Spanish Americans. A long tradition of belief in the cruelty, bigotry, tyranny, and trickery of Spaniards had been harbored in Great Britain and her American colonies. Some Americans, imbued with the liberalism of the eighteenth century believed that all men were basically and naturally good and that the institution of freedom would reveal their innate virtue. Still others believed that the New World contained a special and unique virtue and that it could become manifest once European domination were ended. Most Americans, however, subscribed to the Black Legend. "By 1803 Spanish duplicity was a byword throughout the whole country, regardless of party, creed, occupation, or loyalty."[8] The United States frontiersmen particularly loathed Spanish officials.

Most American leaders also believed that Spaniards were beyond redemption and Spanish Americans barely salvageable. Thomas Jefferson expected as a natural development the expansion of the United States into the sparsely populated areas of Latin America, and perhaps the control of the remainder. He remarked once that he feared that Spain was too feeble to maintain control "till our population can be sufficiently advanced to gain it from them piece by piece." When approached in France in 1787 by a Mexican agent with a plan for liberating the country, he informed the Congress that the mind of the Mexican people had to be emancipated first. Although somewhat more discreet in his language when president in later years, Jefferson did not hesitate to seize Louisiana and claim parts of Florida and Texas. He also wrote in 1803 that creoles (Spanish Americans) were not prepared to govern themselves in view of the despotic government under which they had lived. John Adams was more blunt. Speaking of Miranda's attempt to liberate Venezuela, he said that it could make just as much sense to talk of establishing democracies among the birds, beasts, and fishes. Federalists such as Alexander Hamilton and Gouverneur Morris constantly attacked Spaniards and urged territorial expansion at Spain's expense.

In sum, there was little firm ground on which to build a substantial foundation for amicable and cooperative relations between Americans and Mexicans in 1821. They feared, distrusted,

---

[8] Arthur P. Whitaker, *The Mississippi Question 1795–1803. A Study in Trade, Politics, and Diplomacy* (New York: Appleton-Century, 1934), p. 258.

and even hated each other for reasons based on differences in religion, culture, tradition, and history. Beyond these emotional responses, there also existed a very real clash of material interests. Beyond their commercial competition, there was the enormous pent-up energy of the northerners for territorial expansion, land grabbing, exploration, and economic growth. On the Mexican side there was a keen determination not only to maintain independence but to retain the vast unpeopled territories on which the Yankees were converging. Appeals to common ideals of anticolonialism, Western-Hemisphere identity, and even republicanism were ineffectual. Finally, among Mexican leaders in 1821 (conservatives for the most part) there was much greater affinity for Great Britain than for the United States in terms of commerce, sea power, and geographical distance. Great Britain was unlikely to make territorial demands, its navy could protect the new state from reconquest, and British commercial and cultural ties were well established with the Mexican elite. For many Americans Great Britain appeared to offer more benefits and far fewer liabilities than the United States. To confront the territorial ambitions of its northern neighbor, Mexicans were beginning to think of a "balance of power," however incipient and unformulated the concept.

CHAPTER II

The First Contacts

THE UNITED STATES APPROACHED the question of recognizing the new Spanish-American countries with great caution, and always with one eye on European developments. The myth of the power and malevolence of the Holy Alliance to restore colonial rule in America persisted in American thought for some years. True, the refusal of England to cooperate with the continental powers in suppressing reformist movements by force, especially constitutional monarchies, offered some comfort to United States leaders, but not complete reassurance. They did not yet have the courage to go it alone. In January 1819 John Quincy Adams, U.S. Secretary of State, suggested to the British government joint action in recognizing the independence of several Spanish-American governments. When the British rejected this plan of cooperation, Adams retreated from the ideas of immediate recognition and involvement with Great Britain, although both continued to have some support in important United States political circles.

The question of the timing of recognition of Latin American governments and the nature of United States relations with Europe divided American public opinion in both private and government circles. The influential *Edinburgh Review* in May 1820 proposed British-United States cooperation to meet the threat of the Holy Alliance, while Henry Clay and his supporters advocated some degree of United States-Latin American cooperation. Moreover, early in 1821 Clay introduced, and succeeded in having adopted, a Congressional resolution expressing the "deep interest" of the United States in the success of the Spanish American struggle for independence. The resolution also spoke of seeking early recognition. Although mild and rather cautious, this action constituted the first official move toward recognition by any organ of the United States government. On the other hand, Edward Everett, the editor of the prestigious *North American Review*, wrote in April 1821 that the notion of a "community" of the Americas was fallacious and a partnership of the continent wrongheaded. Everett condemned any projects for continental solidarity as Yankee imperialism, but he also expressed the New England Puritan's distrust of Latin Americans and Roman Catholics. His article displayed widely felt misgivings about the political and social virtues of Latin people, and reflected two popular basic assumptions broadly accepted in the United States: (1) the United States ought to cultivate its own garden; and (2) the United States ought to be wary of any entanglements with the alien peoples of Brazil and Spanish America. The isolationist sentiment ultimately triumphed in government circles, and manifested itself in the July 4, 1821 speech of John Quincy Adams. Supremely confident of the ultimate triumph of liberty over despotism, Adams warned of the dangers of the Holy Alliance but cautioned about entanglements with England. His primary thrusts were anticolonialism, nonintervention, and isolationism.[1] On the other hand, the United States government offered modest and unofficial financial support to various Latin American representatives residing in Washington and proceeded, however cautiously, with recognizing certain Latin American governments.

By the end of 1821 the United States knew that Mexico had won its independence from Spain, and Mexico for its part quickly sought recognition. United States leaders had mixed emotions. Some had watched the uprisings of Hidalgo and Morelos with interest and sympathy. The winning of independence, however, came as a surprise, and not an entirely agreeable one, when it became known that a native monarchy was established. Some Westerners were fearful that an independent Mexico might prove more efficient in defending disputed territorial claims on the Louisiana frontier than the departed and distant Spaniards.

---

[1] See Whitaker, *The United States and the Independence of Latin America*, pp. 334–337 and 358–359.

General Iturbide (soon to be Agustín I), the leader of the conservative forces that achieved independence, expressed his admiration for Henry Clay and his appreciation for Clay's championship of Mexico in Congress. Whatever misgivings he had, President Monroe on March 8, 1822 in a message to Congress declared that five Spanish American countries were entitled to recognition and requested an appropriation to establish suitable diplomatic missions. Mexico was among the five. Apparently, the President contemplated sending the first minister to Mexico, although Mexico was the newest and least-known state. On the other hand, such an action could be defended on the pragmatic grounds that, for the United States, a contiguous country with a long ill-defined border posed problems that only official and formal communications could handle. Also, such a mission would be least alarming to the great powers of Europe. Despite the protests of the Spanish Minister in Washington, Congress passed the requested appropriation bill on May 4. The press for the most part warmly supported the move not only because the administration had a reputation for prudence, but also because it was clearly recognized that there could be no reconciliation between Spain and her former colonies. Some observers expressed the hope that recognition would lead to expanded trade and commerce between the United States and the new countries. Monroe himself had talked of commercial possibilities, but he was also aware of the current resentment in Latin America over his long delay and the question of the Florida Treaty. He hoped to counter some of this hostility and to increase United States political influence in the area at the expense of Europe.

Despite the rapid response of the Congress to Monroe's message, recognition developed slowly, and the full exchange of missions glacially. Congress had first advised that the administration wait for the new states to send representatives to Washington before dispatching its own people. In 1822 only Manuel Torres, representative of Gran Colombia, remained of the several representatives that had resided in the United States at one time or another. Consequently Colombia was the first to be recognized. Then in the late summer of 1822 Monroe sent Joel Roberts Poinsett, a congressman from South Carolina, on a fact-finding mission to Mexico. In the meantime a representative of the Mexican Empire arrived, and without waiting for Poinsett's report, Monroe extended formal recognition on December 12, 1822. Poinsett himself disapproved of the action mostly because of his dislike of monarchy.

Iturbide's representative to Washington was equally distrustful of the government to which he had been accredited. His government had instructed him to ascertain the official United States position concerning the monarchy as well as United States territorial ambitions toward Mexico. He reported widespread hostility toward monarchy and recommended that the government regard the United States as inimical because of popular aspirations for Texas.[2]

Despite recognition two more years passed before the United States accredited a representative to Mexico. Monroe offered the post first to Andrew Jackson early in 1823, but Jackson declined on the grounds that Mexico was a monarchy. A year later Monroe approached Ninian Edwards, Senator from Illinois, but he resigned after his appointment on grounds unrelated to Mexican affairs. Finally, Monroe offered the position to Poinsett, but the presidential campaign and inauguration delayed the formal process. Not until June 1, 1825 did Poinsett present his credentials in Mexico as official representative of the United States.[3] By that time Iturbide had been overthrown and a republic established.

The first United States minister to Mexico embodied a series of contradictions. A Southerner, from that most "Southern" state, South Carolina, he remained a free trader and ardent nationalist until his death in 1851. An able politician at home, in some respects a statesman, he proved politically inept on several occasions in diplomatic missions abroad. Well-educated, widely traveled, conversant in world affairs, he believed that the system of government operating in the United States was virtually perfect and hoped to extend it to all the countries of

---

[2] José Rogelio Alvarez, "Los Primeros Contactos Diplomáticos de México," *Historia Mexicana* Vol. III (July–August 1953), No. 1, pp. 87–101.

[3] George Lockhart Rives, *The United States and Mexico, 1821–1848*, 2 vols. (New York: Scribner, 1913; reprinted, New York: Kraus Reprint Co., 1969), Vol. I, p. 46.

Spanish America. His zealous evangelism was to make his name forever anathema to Mexican nationalists, not so much for the principles that he espoused but for his interference in internal Mexican politics and his unabashed bluntness in pressing for the interests of his country. Setting off on his first Mexican mission of 1822, he brought with him a strong prejudice against monarchy; in all his reports it is difficult to find a favorable comment about Iturbide. He was convinced that most Mexicans favored a republic, and advised Monroe against recognition, because he did not believe that the empire would last more than a few months. Although the United States government at this time believed that recognition should be simply the acknowledgment of accomplished fact, Poinsett insisted that recognition should be an instrument of policy. He argued that Monroe had not only made the United States a party to a factional conflict in Mexico, but also that it had backed the wrong party.

Poinsett's second arrival as Minister to Mexico was met with mixed emotions by Mexican leaders. Not only were they suspicious of United States motives for the general delay in recognizing Latin American states, they were specifically offended by the further delay in the sending of a United States representative to Mexico. There was also a division of sentiment within the Mexican leadership over the Monroe Doctrine that had been proclaimed in 1823. Many Mexicans were uncertain about the meaning of the Doctrine. On the one hand, it seemed to portend United States support of Latin America in protecting newly won independence. On the other, the United States government rebuffed various suggestions, some from Latin America itself, for the establishment of defensive alliances. Moreover, Monroe took no further positive steps toward supporting his principles of republicanism (he recognized monarchies in Brazil and Mexico) and inter-American cooperation.

Conservatives in Mexico tended generally to be cooler and more hostile toward the United States than did liberals. Lucas Alamán thoroughly distrusted the Monroe Doctrine. President Guadalupe Victoria, a Liberal, appeared relatively friendly toward the United States. Although his government advocated an American customs union without the United States, he personally included the United States whenever he spoke of the

American nations. At his insistence (together with that of Vice-President Francisco de Paula Santander of Colombia) the United States was invited to the Congress of Panama in the hope of translating the Monroe Doctrine into a defensive alliance.[4] Poinsett finally disabused him of this notion. When he recognized that Mexico could not expect material help from his northern neighbor if Spain attempted a reconquest, he began to look to Great Britain to support Mexico's independence. Only in cultural exchange and commercial relations did there appear to be some mutuality of interests during Poinsett's term in Mexico. Even Alamán, in correspondence with the editor of the *North American Review,* indicated a warm interest in cultural interchange among all countries of the Americas, and both Mexican and United States citizens seemed eager to maintain the flourishing trade between their countries that had blossomed since the middle of the previous decade. That trade, from the United States perspective, remained the most important in all of Latin America until the late 1830s.

If conditions in Mexico were not auspicious for the success of the U.S. Minister, Poinsett's instructions were something less than helpful. Secretary of State Henry Clay fed Poinsett's own biases by urging him to advocate "democracy," meaning, in fact, to extol the virtues of the United States system of government. Clay also instructed him to represent United States business interests in complying with complicated Mexican commercial regulations and to negotiate trade agreements on the basis of most-favored-nation principles. Worst of all, Clay requested that he inquire cautiously about moving the boundary beyond the Sabine and south of the Red and Arkansas rivers, that is, to inquire about Mexico's willingness to surrender all or most of Texas. Clay further informed Poinsett that he might point out to President Victoria that these suggested boundary changes would relieve Mexico of the burden of administering territories so far removed from the capital, transfer the troublesome

---

[4] Randolph Cambell, "Henry Clay and the Poinsett Pledge Controversy of 1826," *The Americas,* Vol. XXVIII (April 1972), No. 4, p. 431; C. Harvey Gardiner, "The Role of Guadalupe Victoria in Mexican Foreign Relations," *Revista de Historia de América* (December 1948), No. 26, pp. 386–388.

Comanche Indians to the United States, and avoid the possibilities of border clashes with United States citizens who were presently moving westward. Clay also told him to inform the Mexican government that the United States would not interfere with Spain in Cuba, that it opposed either European or Spanish-American intervention in the island, and that if the island changed hands it should be attached to the United States. At the time Mexico and Gran Colombia were discussing concerted action to free Cuba from Spain.[5]

Poinsett served four and a half years as United States Minister to Mexico. Much of that time he devoted his time to intrigues with Mexican political factions and to a rivalry for prestige and influence with Henry George Ward, the British chargé d'affaires. Ward who arrived before Poinsett, had well-established political ties with the more conservative elements headed by Lucas Alamán, and sought to convince Mexican leaders that Great Britain had more to offer Mexico than did the United States in commercial and security benefits. Poinsett conceived it as his duty to tie Mexico to the United States. He identified himself with the liberal faction in Mexican politics and helped it to establish York Rite Masonic lodges as a focus for political opposition to the Scottish Rite lodges that served the conservatives. Poinsett believed that large groups of legislators in the Mexican Congress and most people in the country favored the United States. He saw Ward as the evil genuis counseling the old-line aristocrats, monarchists, and other Europeanophiles surrounding and controlling President Guadalupe Victoria and directing Mexican foreign policy. At first Poinsett's politicking seemed to succeed as Alamán and other conservatives were removed from the cabinet and replaced by friendly liberals. Ironically, at the height of his supposed success, public outcry against Poinsett's meddling in Mexican politics forced the government to request his recall in 1829. In a tactful letter to President Andrew Jackson, Vicente Guerrero, newly seated as President of Mexico explained the difficulty of governing under the accusation of subservience to a foreign

---

[5] J. Fred Rippy, *Joel R. Poinsett, Versatile American* (Durham: Duke University Press, 1935), pp. 106–107.

power.[6] By the time Poinsett departed Mexico in 1830 the Guerrero administration had been overthrown by a conservative revolt.

Poinsett enjoyed only scant success in his diplomatic mission. He found his hosts infuriated with the position of the Adams administration on Texas, and his conveyance of his instructions on Cuba further annoyed them. Mexican fears of United States territorial encroachments, moreover, were fed further by the warnings of the British chargé, H. G. Ward, and by the report of General Manuel de Mier y Terán on conditions in Texas. Because of Mexican sensitivities he advised his government not to press the issue of territorial adjustments. Clay at first agreed, but in March 1827, he instructed Poinsett to offer $1,000,000.00 for a shift of the boundary from the Sabine to the Rio Grande River. Poinsett never submitted the offer. Poinsett was also frustrated in his efforts to conclude a commercial treaty. He negotiated a trade pact in mid-1826 but the Mexican Congress refused to ratify it in part because it contained a provision for the return of runaway slaves to the United States.[7] Mexican nationalists also feared certain clauses concerning the control of Indians along the border and the whole question of free trade versus protectionism. Poinsett renegotiated the treaty in early 1828. Realizing the futility of effecting boundary changes, he reconfirmed in the treaty of 1828 the frontier as established by the Transcontinental Treaty of 1819.[8] Nonetheless, it too failed to be passed.

Andrew Jackson inherited both problems (the Texas question

---

[6] *Ibid.*, pp. 109–129. See also the account of the Poinsett mission as outlined in William R. Manning, *Early Diplomatic Relations Between the United States and Mexico* (Baltimore: The Johns Hopkins Press, 1916; reprinted, New York: Greenwood Press, 1968) and Dorothy M. Parton, *The Diplomatic Career of Joel Roberts Poinsett* (Washington, D.C.: The Catholic University of America Press, 1934).

[7] Carlos Bosch García, "Discusiones previas al primer tratado de comercio entre México y Estados Unidos: 1822–1838," *El Trimestre Económico*, Vol. XIII (July–September 1946), No. 2, pp. 329–345, says that the weakness of the Mexican merchant marine vis-à-vis that of the United States troubled the Mexican negotiators.

[8] Samuel F. Bemis, *The Latin American Policy of the United States. A Historical Interpretation* (New York: Harcourt, Brace, 1943), p. 75.

and the commercial treaty) from his predecessor, John Quincy Adams. Late in the summer of 1829, Jackson's old friend Colonel Anthony Butler presented the new administration with two papers on Texas: one on the economy and geography of the region and the other on the means to persuade Mexico to sell it to the United States. As a result of these documents Jackson ordered Secretary of State Martin Van Buren to direct Poinsett to reopen the question of boundary modifications, and to offer a maximum of $5,000,000 if the Mexican government would accept the watershed between the Nueces and Rio Grande rivers, and proportionately less for less territory. At the same time a newspaper debate opened on the desirability of acquiring Texas, a debate in which the overwhelming sentiment was positive. Negative responses came generally from the abolitionist movement.

Shortly before Poinsett's recall, Jackson appointed Butler as Chargé in Mexico. A native of South Carolina, but a longtime resident of Kentucky, Butler earned his colonelcy in the War of 1812. He served under Jackson at New Orleans and thereby formed a long and close friendship. Later Butler speculated in Texas lands, turning up in Washington in 1829 to persuade his old friend to assist United States citizens settling in that Mexican border province. Butler's arguments proved successful, and he eventually succeeded to Poinsett's position as Minister to Mexico.

Jackson erred badly in appointing Butler as Minister to Mexico. Within a few days of his arrival in mid-December 1829, Mexico City newspapers attacked Butler and his government over his instructions to purchase Texas. Apparently he also deserved all of the many accusations levied against him. Vain, insolent, immoral (personally and politically), profligate, ignorant, and scurrilous, Butler was also called a liar, scamp, bully, swashbuckler, and swindler. Despite constant rebuffs from the Mexican government Butler repeatedly insisted in his dispatches that an agreement on the acquisition of Texas was about to be signed. Jackson, always loyal to old troopers, may have been partially persuaded. At any rate he retained Butler in his post until late 1835 despite the demands of several Secretaries of State for his removal. On several occasions he advised

Jackson to seize portions of Texas by force, and late in 1833 he recommended that he be supplied with several hundred thousand dollars to respond to a bribery suggestion from high Mexican government officials. Early in 1835 the Jackson administration determined to abandon all attempts to purchase Texas and with Butler's recall late in the year all official moves in that direction ceased.[9]

Butler did enjoy one victory. He succeeded in concluding the negotiations for a boundary treaty and a treaty of commerce, friendship, and navigation, in both of which Poinsett had failed. The trade treaty omitted the offending article on fugitive slaves, but the Mexican Congress still delayed ratification until Butler threatened to close down the legation. Ratifications were finally exchanged April 5, 1832.[10]

The 1830s marked a turning point in United States relations with Latin America, in general and with Mexico in particular. The previous decade had opened with high hopes for the promotion of United States interests in the area, but by the close of the decade it had become obvious that several United States interests mutually clashed. Some hard choices had to be made. On the one hand there had been general satisfaction over the independence movement not only because its success meant the removal or at least a great weakening of an old rival, Spain, but also because it meant the likelihood of the creation of several republican governments with common interests in confronting Old World monarchies. Some Americans foresaw close bonds between like-minded states born from the ideas and ideology of European revolutionary movements of the eighteenth century. By the early 1830s, however, many Americans were seriously questioning these first expectations. Independence and republicanism proved no panaceas. Dictators like Antonio López de Santa Anna seemed to be at best slight improvements over the Bourbon kings or Iturbide I. Ignorance, fanaticism, and military despotism still prevailed over political freedom, civil rights, and

---

[9] *Rives, op. cit.*, Vol. I, pp. 234–261.
[10] *Ibid.*, pp. 235–261; Frederick C. Turner, *op. cit.*, pp. 36–37; and James Morton Callahan, *American Foreign Policy in Mexican Relations* (New York: Cooper Square, 1967), p. 76.

general toleration. Even European influences had not been driven from the Americas. Spain had virtually disappeared, but Great Britain had stepped into the breach.

Americans also found their economic hopes unfulfilled. Agricultural and food products such as corn and flour found only modest markets, and manufacturers, after a spurt of export growth in the 1820s, suffered in competition with European wares. United States shippers continued to have an important but declining interest in Latin American trade. Trade and commerce that had extended all the way to Cape Horn and into the Pacific began to contract in the 1830s and became largely restricted to Mexico, Cuba, and Brazil. Moreover, the merchants were beginning to lose out politically at home to the new industrialists who were promoting the home market and pressuring for protective tariffs. Finally the growing controversy over Texas led to a precipitous decline in trade with Mexico, the leading commercial partner of the United States in the Western Hemisphere (Table 1).[11]

Table 1   United States Trade with Mexico 1826-1845

Year	Mexican Imports	Mexican Exports
1826	$6,281,050	$3,916,198
1830	4,837,458	5,235,241
1835	9,029,221	9,490,446
1840	2,515,341	4,175,001
1845	1,152,331	1,702,936

This combination of developments accelerated a general decline of United States political and economic interest in Latin America, an interest that did not revive for almost 50 years. When the British and French intervened in the Plata area in the 1830s and 1840s, few Americans protested the violation of the Monroe Doctrine. United States leaders were directing their attention toward internal economic growth, the increasingly dangerous slavery question, and the drive for territorial expan-

---

[11] The chart on United States-Mexican trade is taken from Norman A. Graebner, "United States Gulf Commerce with Mexico, 1822–1848," *Inter-American Economic Affairs*, Vol. V (Summer 1951), No. 1, p. 49.

sion, now about to be called Manifest Destiny. United States political interests came to be focused primarily on Mexico, not to establish close and harmonious relations but, instead, to divest her of large parts of her territory. As a consequence, for the next two decades United States-Mexican relations generally revolved around the Texas question and other United States territorial ambitions.

United States policies and attitudes of course adversely affected Latin Americans' response to the northern republic. First, United States threats to Mexico's territorial integrity and the open ambitions over Cuba damaged good relations and struck fear not only in Mexico but in many other parts of the hemisphere as well. Second, many of the leaders of the new states belonged to the old oligarchy, an untitled aristocracy, that saw little in common with United States egalitarian rhetoric. They felt more comfortable with English gentlemen than with the more rough-hewn United States political types and pragmatically put greater trust in the British fleet to protect them from reconquest by the Holy Alliance. Third, the continuance and the growth of slavery in the United States not only alienated potential liberal allies, but intensified suspicions that United States proclamations of equality, brotherhood, and common ideals simply provided a cover for a drive toward United States hegemony throughout the hemisphere. Fourth, most Latin Americans resented the efforts of United States representatives to impose United States political forms, style, and substance upon them. Although most of the new states adopted republican forms of government (including Mexico after a brief experiment with monarchy), their politics actually differed radically from that of the United States. Finally, the United States delay in recognizing the new states and the failure of the United States to commit itself to defensive alliances with them convinced many Latin Americans that they indeed shared few interests in common with their Anglo-American neighbors.

How did Mexico and the United States compare as they headed on a collision course? In population and territory the United States and Mexico were similar in 1821, the year of Mexico's independence. After emerging in 1783 as an independent state with almost 890,000 square miles, the United States slightly more than doubled its territory to 1,788,000 square miles with the Louisiana Purchase of 1803 and the Trans-continental Treaty of 1819. Mexico emerged in 1821 as an independent state with 1,710,000 square miles, not counting the disputed Oregon territory. While the United States, however, was strengthening its hold over its possession, and its adventuresome frontiersmen and ambitious politicians were seeking new acquisitions, Mexican leaders were facing an increasingly difficult task of simply holding on to what they claimed. When Texans declared their independence in 1836, the exact boundaries between Mexico and Texas remained undertermined, but Mexico lost complete control over at least 250,000 square miles of territory. In addition, effective control remained tenuous over other vast northern sections, including New Mexico and California, because of constant political instability in the core area.

In population also, the two countries appeared to be generally similar at the time of Mexico's independence, although the United States advantage was more pronounced. More ominous, however, from the Mexican viewpoint were the population growth trends and internal migrations in each country. Whereas in 1790 Mexico had a population of about 5,000,000 compared to 4,000,000 for the United States, by 1810 this advantage had been reversed. Mexico now had about 6,100,000 people, and the United States 7,200,000. During the decade of the Mexican struggle for independence, Mexico's population apparently remained stagnant while that of the United States continued its rapid growth. In 1830 the United States population of almost 13 million was double that of Mexico, which was about 6 million, and by 1845 on the eve of war the United States population was almost triple the Mexican: 20.1 million compared to 7.5 million.[12] Foreign immigration contributed somewhat to the United States population increase, but not substantially during

---

[12] The United States figures are based on decennial census and intercensal estimates; the Mexican figures are based on irregular census, partial census, and estimates. The long-term trend of Mexican population growth makes the above figures seem reasonable estimates. See U.S. Bureau of the Census, *Historical Statistics of the United States, Colonial Times to 1857* (Washington, D.C.: Government Printing Office, 1960) and a listing of the early Mexican census and estimates in Dirección General de Estadística, *VII Censo General de Población—1960* (México: Talleres Gráficos de la Nación, 1962), p. xxii.

this period. In the 1820s it averaged about 15,000 per year, in the 1830s about 55,000, and in the early 1840s about 85,000. Immigration into Mexico appears negligible, but the vast discrepancy in population growth rates must be attributed to natural causes instead of to immigration.

More important than the gross population figures are the distribution of that population and its internal shifts during the first half of the nineteenth century. In the Spanish census of 1793 the Californias were composed of about 12,500 and New Mexico about 31,000 people. In 1810 Texas was estimated at 5000, and while over the next 30 years all of these areas gained population, some of it included the migration of United States frontiersmen into Mexican territory. This was particularly true of Texas where the Mexican population actually declined between 1810 and 1820, and after 1825 never against constituted a majority. By 1839 the Californias had increased to 33,500 and New Mexico to 57,000, but these increases do not indicate any great mass movement of people. Moreover in the latter year the whole northern frontier including, in addition to the above listed territories, Coahuila, Tamaulipas, Nuevo León, Sonora, and Chihuahua, contained only 636,000 inhabitants and, when the North Americans are subtracted, only slightly over 600,000 people held these immense reaches against a potential wave of an alien people on the move within their own frontiers. In contrast, the frontier regions of the United States were growing rapidly in population. The single state of Missouri grew from less then 20,000 in 1820 to almost 400,000 in 1840, and the territory north of the Ohio River and west of the Alleghenies comprising the present states of Ohio, Indiana, Illinois, Michigan, and Wisconsin grew from 51,000 to almost 3,000,000 between 1800 and 1840. Similarly on the southern frontier the growth was just as impressive. The states of Kentucky, Tennessee, Alabama, and Mississippi grew from about 110,000 in 1790 to almost 1,200,000 by 1820, and then more than doubled to over 2,500,000 by 1840. At the same time the population of Arkansas and Louisiana increased from about 75,000 in 1810 to over 350,000 in 1840. It was only a question of time before this mass movement burst through its national boundaries to occupy the vacant lands to the west.

Mexico's population disadvantage in her confrontation with the United States becomes yet more severe when certain qualitative differences are considered. Both states contained large numbers of people who were counted in total population figures, but who did not constitute effective or full members of the national community. In the United States Negro slaves made up most of this group, but some Indians were also included in the nonwhite category in the decennial census. Between 1800 and 1840 the nonwhite sector comprised between 20 and 24 percent of the total population with the proportion slowly dropping during these years. Accurate figures are lacking for Mexico, and the various estimates disagree, but one estimate of 1810 and another 50 years later in 1861 place the Indian population near 60 percent.[13] Allowing for some overestimation, but considering the remoteness of some parts of the population and the prevalence of subsistence agriculture and tribal and local community loyalties, it can be estimated safely that at least 50 percent of the total population could not be mobilized for national political, economic, or military efforts. Although this was more than double the proportion of the United States population in a similar category, the blacks in the United States could at least be mobilized for economic purposes and, in fact, their labor contributed substantially to the agricultural growth of the country.

Similar differences apply to education and literacy. Although we do not have comparable data for the pre-1845 period, we do have some gross information for later years. In the United States census of 1860, for example, 50.6 percent of all children between 5 and 19 years of age were enrolled in schools. However, only 1.9 percent of nonwhites were so enrolled, while 59.6 percent of white children were in school. In the Mexican statistical report for 1861, less than 15 percent of all students were enrolled, and it may be presumed that the vast majority of these were Western-oriented. The differences are also apparent in literacy estimates. For much of the nineteenth century literacy

---

[13] Fernando Navarro y Noriega, *Memoria sobre la población del reino de Nueva España* (México: Oficina de d. Juan Bautista de Arizpe, 1820) and José María Pérez Hernández, *Estadística de la República Mexicana* (Guadalajara: Tip. del Gobierno, 1862).

is estimated at 10 to 15 percent for Mexico, while in the United States the census of 1840 reported a literacy rate of 78 percent for persons over 20 years of age. While the nonwhite population was only 12 percent literate the white population was 91 percent literate. Given, therefore, this social composition of the peoples of the two states, the United States enjoyed enormous advantages over its neighbor, far more than a simple comparison of territorial extent and population figures indicate.

Finally, in economic strength the United States far surpassed Mexico in the years between 1821 and 1845. Following its independence in 1783 the United States quickly put its own house in order economically and politically. With the adoption of the Constitution, a long period of stable government was inaugurated that contributed to economic growth. Although the War of 1812 caused a decline in the shipping industry, that same war proved a boon to domestic manufactures, and shipping recovered quickly once the war ended. The invention of the cotton gin accelerated cotton production and exports, and the federal assumption and payment of the revolutionary war debts gave the young country a high credit rating and made it an attractive area for foreign investments. All of these factors were operative by 1821 when Mexico gained her independence.

Mexico unfortunately emerged from her wars of independence politically divided and economically devastated. During the next 25 years the country enjoyed only four years of relative stability, and during those years (1824–1828) the country's economy proved its resilience through increases in agricultural productivity, the attraction of foreign capital to reopen its mines, and the placing of foreign loans at terms moderately favorable for the times. But its promise was never to be fulfilled. The disorders that plagued the country in its first years of independence returned in 1828 and recurred throughout these years. A second flight of capital occurred with the expulsion of the Spaniards in 1827, and civil war broke out in 1828. Although budgeted expenditures for the military averaged 50 percent of revenues annually (approximately the same rate as for the United States) extraordinary expenditures and disorder in the national treasury led to defaults on the foreign debts and increased domestic borrowings on a short-term basis at usurious rates. Since Mexico collected over 60 percent of her income from internal tax sources (contrasted with the United States that collected 90 percent of federal income from custom revenues), the internal conflicts proved extraordinarily disruptive. Over these years average annual revenue totaled about $20 million annually. Mexican foreign trade remained stagnant at about $25 million annually[14] while United States foreign trade grew rapidly from $156 million in 1824 to a high of $319 million in 1836. In fact, United States exports of tobacco and cotton alone in the late 1830s and early 1840s amounted to triple the value of Mexico's mining production at its peak. Figures on general productivity are at best gross estimates and probably not strictly comparable. The statistics that are available, however, seem to indicate that United States productivity was more than three times that of Mexico. In the use of machinery, in particular, the United States was rapidly assuming the lead. In textile manufacturing, for example, one of Mexico's oldest and most developed industries, the United States had far surpassed her neighbor by the 1840s with something over 1,750,000 spindles to Mexico's 115,000. The same discrepancies can be noted in virtually every line of economic endeavor, for example, banking, transportation, construction, technology, communications, and inventions. For example, modern banking and railroading did not come to Mexico until after 1875, while both of these enterprises were growing and developing in the United States by the 1830s. Throughout these years the economic gap between them continued to grow.

Contributing to Mexico's failure to keep pace with United States economic and population growth was the fragmented nature of its social and political elites. For many reasons Mexico emerged from her colonial period to independent status with a society, discounting its Indian communities, that had little sense of unity of purpose or direction. The wars of independence, instead of bringing the society together, shattered it, and the

---

[14] Some estimates report that about one-third of Mexico's foreign trade consisted of smuggling. For a review of Mexican economic and financial conditions in the early nineteenth century, see Robert C. Wyllie, *México. Noticia sobre su hacienda pública bajo el gobierno español y después de la independencia* . . . (Mexico: Impr. de I. Cumplido, 1845).

alliance of loyalists and patriots in 1820 only assured the continuity of the conflict under other guises. In the United States the "patriots" won a clear victory, and many of the Tories left the country after 1783. The few that remained could demonstrate their opposition only by drawing their blinds and shutters on the Fourth of July—and that display of pique lasted only a few years. In Mexico, on the contrary, the irreconcilable conflict between liberal and conservative political leaders opened the way for military dictatorship. Upon close examination many of these so-called military uprisings were not so much professional armed forces arrayed against civilian groups as they were one military-civilian faction arrayed against one or more similar military-civilian factions. In the light of irreconcilable political, philosophical, and personal differences Mexico was never able to construct in these years a viable political system that could gain the support of all major groups. No administration was "legitimate" to any appreciable political groups except the immediate victors. In the competition that quickly developed between these two neighbors, one was politically unified, economically developing, and territorially expanding; the other was politically fragmented, economically disordered, and territorially defensive. It may not have been clearly perceived at the time, but present evidence indicates that the scales were tipped decisively in the favor of the United States, and only a major reorientation in Mexican society could have preserved the state intact.

CHAPTER III

The Texas Question
and the Mexican-American War

By the transcontinental treaty of 1819 the United States in exchange for Florida renounced its dubious claims to the Spanish province of Texas. Some prominent Americans such as Henry Clay refused from the start to accept the treaty as definitive, and they severely criticized the Monroe administration for deeding away the territory. Others such as John Quincy Adams, who negotiated the treaty, and Andrew Jackson, who initially supported it, later regreted this action that surrendered United States claims to Texas. Both Adams and Jackson attempted to purchase the territory during their presidencies but abandoned the effort in the face of Mexican resistance and the growing sectional conflict in the United States. In the end the acquisition of Texas by the United States resulted as much from the mass movement of people as it did from decisions made in Washington and Mexico City.

Until the late 1820s the western two-thirds of present-day United States, including Texas, remained virtually unknown and undiscussed by the American public. A few officials in Washington showed interest and some Westerners like Jackson or Senator Thomas H. Benton of Missouri grumbled about the Treaty of 1819, but they comprised only a small fragment even of the politically active population. Very few people had any clear ideas about those lands. For a long time the central portion of what is today the United States was known as the Great American Desert, and overland travel to Mexico through Texas or New Mexico was so difficult and dangerous that virtually all communication between the two counties was by water. The boundaries of Texas remained in large part indefinite, although

51

few people seriously questioned the Sabine River as its eastern boundary with Louisiana. The inhabitants of Texas widely understood the general limits to be those charted on a royal map of 1805 and an administrative order of 1811. By these documents the boundary, beginning at the mouth of the Nueces River, ran northwesterly along the river to its junction with Moros Creek. From that point it extended in an arc to the Medina River and then roughly eastward to the Red River and south to the Sabine along approximately 94°31′ longitude.

At the beginning of the nineteenth century the population numbered about 5000 inhabitants (not counting tribal and warlike Indians) scattered in three main settlements and in several presidios and mission outposts. By far the largest town was San Antonio de Béxar with 2500 people; then came Nacogdoches with something under 800 permanent inhabitants and an unknown number of transients who were constantly crossing back and forth across the border. The smallest of the three towns was La Bahía del Espíritu Santo (Goliad) with 600 inhabitants including some 200 mission Indians. Only with difficulty did Spain administer this vast tract of land, and without much success did she try to attract settlers to confirm her possession. During the wars for independence Texas was ravaged by filibustering expeditions from the United States and by savage although small-scale civil conflicts. By 1821 the territory had been severely damaged and the population reduced to about 4000. The new Mexican government exercised only feeble authority, local caciques (political bosses) held sway, and United States frontiersmen were beginning to move into the territory. In 1824 the province of Texas was joined to Coahuila to form the state of Coahuila and Texas in the new federal system. It was the poorest and least populated state of the republic.[1]

In November 1820 there arrived in Béxar a native of Connecticut named Moses Austin who for some years had been

---

[1] Félix D. Almaráz, *Tragic Cavalier: Governor Manuel Salcedo of Texas* (Austin: University of Texas Press, 1971), pp. 4–11; see also Vito Alessio Robles, *Coahuila y Texas desde la consumación de la independencia hasta el Tratado de Paz Guadalupe Hidalgo*, 2 vols. (México, 1945–1946), Vol. I, pp. 31 and 168–169.

drifting south and west, settling at one time in Louisiana when it was still ruled by Spain. After some negotiations and through the auspices of an old acquaintance from his Louisiana venture, Don Felipe Henrique Neri, Baron de Bastrop, he succeeded in obtaining from the governor provisional permission to settle 300 American families in Texas. The grant was confirmed by the Spanish viceroy in New Spain, but before he could lead an expedition into Texas, Moses Austin died in St. Louis, Missouri in June 1821. His project, however, was pursued by his oldest son, Stephen, who was in New Orleans at the time of his father's death. Meeting representatives of the governor at Natchitoches, Stephen Austin led an exploring party to San Antonio where he confirmed the grant to his father. The Spanish terms were exceedingly generous: unlimited grants of land anywhere in the province for 300 families in return for an oath to defend the king and government and a profession of the Catholic faith. Austin selected a site on the Colorado River and returned to New Orleans to recruit and equip the new colonists.

By the time Austin returned to Texas in December with his first colonists the political situation in New Spain had changed radically. The Spaniards had been expelled, and representatives of an independent Mexican government informed him that he had to reconfirm his grant with the Mexican Congress. Austin arrived in Mexico City in April 1822, but because of the disturbed nature of the Mexican political scene, the government did not consider the problem of frontier colonization until January 1823. By the so-called Imperial Colonization Act the government of Iturbide provided for the distribution of public lands, both for grazing and crops, within set limits. Slaves could be imported but not sold within the country, and the children of slaves were born free. Contractors who sponsored settler families would receive bonus grants. Tax benefits were included for a limited period of time, and citizenship was granted at the end of three years to foreigners who could support themselves. All colonists were required to profess Catholicism. Under this law Austin applied for a grant for himself and his followers. One of the last acts of Emperor Agustín I was to sign the decree approving Austin's request. On March 19 Iturbide abdicated, but the new government confirmed Austin's grant. He set off for Texas, with his mission successfully accomplished, on April 28, 1823, one day less than a year from the date he first entered Mexico City.

The Austin application for land grants and the favorable responses by successive Spanish and Mexican governments laid the groundwork for the United States-Mexican conflict over Texas. The imperial colonization act of Iturbide and its confirmation by the succeeding republican government provided complex and complicated stipulations for would-be colonists, but no adequate administrative or judicial machinery was ever established to oversee compliance or interpret and settle disputes. Two issues in particular arose to create animosity between the colonists and the Mexican government: religion and slavery. Austin never seems to have explained clearly to his original settlers their obligation to adopt Catholicism. Most of them apparently understand only that Catholicism was the official religion of the country and others were tolerated. With respect to slavery, many of the settlers moved into Texas with their human chattels and simply expected that their legal status was roughly similar to that in the United States. Most of the immigrants became Mexican citizens and a few became nominal Catholics, but for the most part they retained the English language, the Protestant religion, and in general their United States customs, including slavery.[2]

Texans soon came to regard their land as an outpost of the United States instead of an integral part of Mexico. Mexican migration into the province remained negligible while Americans poured in. By the 1830s the population was predominantly from the United States, and economic activity more closely linked to the north than to the south. Americans controlled local government, and the province while formally a part of Mexico was administered largely as a separate unit. The Mexican government could not enforce its antislavery laws nor collect its tariffs. Demands for annexation to the United States were beginning to be heard. As conflicts developed between the settlers and Mexican officials, the Mexican government tried to restrict im-

---

[2] See Eugene C. Barker, *The Life of Stephen F. Austin, Founder of Texas, 1793–1836. A Chapter in the Westward Movement of the Anglo-American People* (Austin: The Texas State Historical Association, 1949).

migration and to regain control of the territory. All such efforts failed because of the enormous communications problems coupled with a scarcity of resources and of Mexican settlers in the area. Mexico's difficulties were further compounded by domestic political struggles in the heart of the country. At the very time that the Texas problem was becoming critical, a series of coups and military conflicts were wracking the central valley. In the midst of this turmoil Santa Anna once again seized the government, overthrew the Constitution of 1824, and abolished the federal system. The last act bore serious implications for the colonists in Texas who, since they comprised the majority of the population, controlled their local municipalities and districts as long as federalism held sway.[3] With the institution of a centralized political system, this advantage disappeared, and local laws and customs became subject to veto from Mexico City. Since these frontiersmen disliked all central authority and regarded Mexicans as an inferior race, any attempt to control them from the national level must lead to conflict.[4]

In their protest over the abolition of federalism the American settlers had considerable support from local Mexican officials, notably in the state of Coahuila y Texas. Citizen meetings were held in various parts of the state to determine the mode of resistance to national government interference. Through most of 1835 the peace party predominated, but since the central government authorities were determined to enforce Mexican laws in the area, resistance stiffened and several armed skirmishes took place in the late summer. Finally on October 9, a small group of colo-

---

[3] Rives, op. cit., Vol. I, pp. 153–182, estimates that the population of Texas in 1825 numbered between 7000 and 7500 and was about evenly divided between Mexicans and Americans settlers. By 1827 it had increased to 10,000 and then doubled to 20,000 by 1830. The increased population was almost totally comprised of colonists and settlers from the north while the Mexican population remained virtually stationary.

[4] For a brief resumé of local and state politics and government in the Mexican state of Coahuila y Texas, see Eugene C. Barker, Mexico and Texas, 1821–1835 (New York: Russell and Russell, 1965), pp. 24–25. See also Samuel Harman Lowrie, Culture Conflict in Texas, 1821–1835 (New York: Columbia University Press, 1932) for an emphasis on differences between Mexicans and Americans in terms of folkways, culture, customs, and mores.

nists attacked and overwhelmed the small Mexican garrison of 30 men at Goliad. The war for Texan independence had begun.

At a meeting of delegates from all parts of Texas early in November, the majority voted against a declaration of independence. Most of the delegates seemed to believe that independence was inevitable, but some felt that the time was not propitious. Whatever their motivations the majority party took a position in support of the federal Constitution of 1824 that provided for state and local self-government. A few people hoped to enlist the assistance of liberals in other parts of Mexico. Within several months, however, it became obvious that no support would be forthcoming from other parts of Mexico. Santa Anna had completely cowed the Liberal Party but, more importantly, few Mexicans of any political stripe sympathized with the Texas rebels.[5]

On March 1, 1836 in convention at the village of San Felipe, the Texans declared their independence from Mexico. Within the next few weeks they adopted a constitution, organized a provisional government, established an army, and provided for the holding of elections, including a referendum on the constitution. In the midst of these political preparations, armed conflict continued. Several minor skirmishes and fire fights between small forces inflicted relatively high casualties on both sides but proved indecisive politically. Then a series of military disasters overtook the Texan army. At the Alamo in San Antonio, Mexican forces wiped out the garrison, and destroyed several other small parties in the field. During March about 500 Texans were captured. Some were eventually released to the United States, but more than 350 were executed on March 27 on orders of Santa Anna.

These Mexican successes, however, proved to be Pyrrhic victories, because they further aroused Texan determination to resist and more importantly outraged opinion in the United

---

[5] Federalists in the northern states of Tamaulipas, Nuevo León, and Coahuila proclaimed the independence of the Republic of the Rio Grande in January 1840. They sought support from Texas but were crushed within three months; see David M. Vigness, "Relations of the Republic of Texas and the Republic of the Rio Grande," *Southwestern Historical Quarterly* Vol. LVII (January 1954), No. 3, pp. 312–321.

States. With volunteers arriving to swell the Texan army, the opposing forces met again at San Jacinto on April 21, and this time the outcome proved decisive. Mexican forces were completely routed, Santa Anna was captured, and Texan independence was never seriously threatened thereafter.

When the fighting began, Texan leaders appealed to the government of the United States for help. The Jackson administration refused official support. Jackson declined to recognize a state of belligerency (i.e., to "declare neutrality") and instructed United States officials to prohibit the outfitting of armed expeditions in the United States (i.e., to enforce current neutrality laws). The laws did not, however, forbid the enlistment of United States citizens in the Texan armed forces nor the export of war materials. On several occasions federal law officers confiscated war materials and arrested violators of the neutrality laws, but when the cases came to court, juries in the southwestern states refused to convict.

The neutrality laws and their violations caused severe strains and tensions in United States-Mexican relations. The Mexican representatives in Washington did not seem to understand the limitations of the laws nor the rules governing the operation of the United States federal system. They remained convinced that the United States government and people were singlemindedly pursuing a policy to annex Texas. This erroneous interpretation, combined with a misunderstanding of the United States political-legal system, restricted the effectiveness of Mexican diplomacy in taking advantage of differences of opinion within leading United States political circles.

The Texas question sharply divided public opinion in the United States. It cannot be denied that the Jackson administration and Jackson personally favored the annexation of Texas. It is also true that annexation had a large popular following, especially in the South. But in the growing North and East sentiment was at best mixed. The antislavery movement had revived, and by the mid-1830s had grown so strong that it was impeding the expansionist movement, particularly in a territory where slavery was likely to follow. Antislavery elements interpreted the move to annex Texas as an attempt to increase the power of the "slaveocracy." Once-ardent annexationists such as John

Quincy Adams now opposed annexation and Henry Clay even temporized on recognition of Texas independence. Because of these sectional differences and the bitter political conflicts that they were capable of generating, the United States government adopted a cautious policy on the Texas question in the late 1830s. At the very end of his administration in March 1837, Jackson finally recognized Texas independence, but only after Texas had clearly demonstrated its ability to defend its independence and Mexico appeared incapable of mounting a major offensive. Throughout the next administration despite continued Texas requests for annexation, President Martin Van Buren refused to advocate it for fear of raising the sectional conflict. The question remained dormant until 1840.

In the meantime the Texans attempted to reach a political settlement through Santa Anna, whom they had captured after the battle of San Jacinto. Fearing for his life, he signed two treaties with his Texan captors, one public and one secret. In the public treaty Santa Anna agreed to a cessation of hostilities, an exchange of prisoners, and the evacuation of Mexican troops beyond the Rio Grande. For its part the Texas government promised fair treatment of prisoners and the return of Santa Anna to Mexico. In the secret treaty Santa Anna promised that he would arrange for the recognition of Texas independence and a settlement of boundaries in which Texas would not extend beyond the Rio Grande. Mexican officials, anticipating pressure on Santa Anna, had declared that the government would not consider valid any agreements made between Santa Anna and his captors as long as he was a prisoner. Despite some difficulties Santa Anna eventually gained his release and traveled to Washington to see President Jackson. Apparently Santa Anna offered to sell Texas to the United States, but Jackson replied that the Texans had to be consulted and matters arranged through normal diplomatic channels between Mexico and the United States. Jackson also suggested that Mexico might cede Texas and Northern California to the United States in a definitive settlement. The meeting between the two presidents produced no further agreements, and Santa Anna returned to Mexico.[6]

---

[6] Rives, *op. cit.*, Vol. I, pp. 357–361.

When the United States rejected the Texan request for annexation, the new state had to face the problems of independence and self-government. Texas leaders quickly established a political regime modeled upon that of their original homeland. In foreign policy they attempted to gain the recognition of other states, particularly Mexico. France and Great Britain proved crucial to this effort not only because of their prestige as international powers of first rank, but also because of their potential influence with Mexico for a final peace settlement. France recognized Texas in 1839, but Great Britain held out until 1840 in an attempt to pressure Texas to abolish slavery. When that failed, the British finally recognized the new state in an effort to block annexation to the United States. Following recognition Great Britain signed three agreements with Texas: a treaty on commerce and navigation; a treaty to suppress the African slave trade; and a convention on the public debt. The latter provided that Britain would mediate with Mexico for recognition of Texas independence and that if successful Britain would assume one million pounds of Mexico's foreign debt. The slave trade treaty ran into opposition in the Texas congress, and ratifications were delayed until 1842.

Texas southern and western boundaries remained a problem both of internal politics and of international negotiation. The Texas government officially claimed the Rio Grande, although the commonly acknowledged frontier of the old Spanish province was the Nueces River. The area between the two was sparsely settled, with most of the population residing on the north bank of the Rio Grande. Some Texans, moreover, had grandiose schemes for further enlarging their territory westward at Mexico's expense. In 1836 Jackson had advised a Texas agent in Washington to claim territory to the Pacific Ocean in order to arouse support from powerful United States shipping interests in the north and east for annexation. With much of northern Mexico frequently in turmoil and Mexican authority weak, the prospect of enlarging Texas did not appear unrealistic. In 1836 the first Texas Congress claimed the boundary of the Rio Grande from its mouth to its source and then due north to 42° latitude. In 1842 the Texas Congress claimed parts of Tamaulipas, Coahuila, Durango, and Sinaloa as well as all of Chihuahua, New

Mexico, Sonora, and Upper and Lower California. President Sam Houston vetoed the bill as visionary.[7]

After several years of relative quiet in United States-Mexican relations, some dramatic changes in United States domestic politics created new antagonisms. In the elections of 1840 the Whig Party succeeded in electing to the presidency William Henry Harrison, an old warrior with antislavery sentiments. Upon assuming office he appointed Daniel Webster, who shared his sentiments, as Secretary of State. It appeared that the policy of the preceding administration toward Texas would continue. Unexpectedly, however, Harrison died only a few weeks after his inauguration, and his Vice President, John Tyler of Virginia, a former Democrat, succeeded to the office. Tyler, a partisan of territorial expansion, soon found himself politically isolated when the Whigs read him out of the party for vetoing Clay's National Bank Bill, and when the Democrats repudiated him as a deserter of their party. In an attempt to win popular support, Tyler raised the question of Texas annexation. Webster stayed on as Secretary of State because of his own interest in settling territorial disputes with Great Britain primarily in Maine but also in Oregon. Tyler shrewdly tied these problems to the Texas question. After his successful settlement of the Maine boundary, Webster proposed to split the Oregon territory with Great Britain, to negotiate a peaceful settlement, and to buy a section of northern California from Mexico, the proceeds of the sale to be used to settle United States and British claims. Webster hoped to appease expansionist desires by such a tripartite agreement. Tyler, however, determined to push forward for the annexation of Texas and Webster resigned over the disagreement. Tyler then proceeded with his plans for both Oregon and Texas and let the California issue fade away. He appointed Abel Upshur, a friend of John Calhoun and an annexationist, as his new Secretary of State.

Mexico, of course, still regarded Texas as a province in revolt against lawful authority. When additional colonists entered

---

[7] Glenn W. Price, *Origins of the War with Mexico: The Polk-Stockton Intrigue* (Austin: University of Texas Press, 1967), pp. 156–158.

Texas from the United States in 1843, Mexico warned the United States that land grants made by the Texas government would not be recognized if Mexican arms should prevail. Furthermore, the Mexican secretary of foreign relations, José María Bocanegra, declared that his government considered any act to incorporate Texas into the United States as an act of war against Mexico.[8]

The new secretary of state was not to be dissuaded by an official from a country he regarded as impotent as well as inferior. While Upshur negotiated a treaty of annexation with the Texas government, Jackson from retirement urged Houston to work for its acceptance among the Texas populace. Discussions had proceeded to a satisfactory conclusion when Upshur was accidentally killed. Tyler thereupon appointed Calhoun as secretary of state, but lost the opportunity to obtain Senate ratification of the treaty when Calhoun publicly declared that one of its purposes was to prevent the abolition of slavery. The Senate killed the project, but annexation sentiment still flourished in the country.

For the election of 1844 the Whigs nominated Henry Clay who had led the recent attack on annexation. The Democrats nominated James Polk of Tennessee, a friend of Jackson and another ardent annexationist. Polk campaigned so successfully on a platform calling for the "reannexation" of Texas and the "reoccupation" of Oregon that toward the end of the campaign Clay found that he himself had to support annexation in the face of growing popular support for territorial expansion. Polk won handily, and his victory was interpreted by the populace as well as by the administration as a victory for Manifest Destiny. Tyler, the lame duck president, attempted to secure his own niche in history and justify his own position by advocating annexation by an act of Congress rather than through the treaty process.

British and French agents, in the face of these developments, made one last move to keep Texas an independent state. By a joint representation they persuaded the Texas government to

---

[8] Carlos Bosch García, *Historia de las relaciones entre México y los Estados Unidos, 1819–1848* (México: Escuela Nacional de Ciencias Políticas y Sociales, Universidad Nacional Autónoma de México, 1961), pp. 66–68.

sign a protocol preliminary to a peace settlement. The terms of the protocol provided that Mexico would recognize Texas independence and that Texas would agree not to subject itself to any third country. In the meantime just a few days before the expiration of Tyler's term, the United States Congress had passed a joint resolution to annex Texas. After a long delay the Mexican Congress and President finally accepted the Anglo-French protocol on May 20, but it was too late by then to stop the merger. The Texas Congress in joint session on June 18 voted unanimously for annexation and the Texas Senate voted unanimously to reject the proposed agreement with Mexico. Overwhelming public support for annexation forced Texas politicians to accept the United States offer whatever efforts were made by the British and French, whatever reluctance still existed among some Texas leaders, and whatever threats or concessions that Mexico continued to make.

United States expansionist arms and Mexican compulsion to defend its rights, honor, and dignity made war virtually inevitable. Nonetheless, when word of the annexation resolution reached Mexico, the Mexican government did nothing more than to break off diplomatic relations. The boundary dispute proved to be the catalyst to armed conflict. Nearly all Texans insisted on the Rio Grande as their southern boundary, and in response to an inquiry by Houston, Polk replied that the United States would protect all of Texas' territorial rights. With the exception of Corpus Christi and a few other settlements just south of the Nueces, Texas' actual authority stopped at that river. Mexico effectively controlled the settlements along both banks of the Rio Grande. In effect, the boundary ran somewhere through the uninhabited area between both rivers. Despite this de facto situation that had persisted for several years, Commodore Robert Stockton, a personal agent sent by President Polk to report on conditions in Texas, reported that Mexicans were crossing the Rio Grande and taking possession of territory on the left bank in order to claim sole possession when annexation would be accomplished. Stockton's attitude reflected a growing sense of belligerency both in Texas and in the United States. By the end of May it appeared that Texans might well launch an attack on Mexican settlements north of the Rio Grande. President Anson

Jones of Texas desired a peaceful settlement and managed to control the hotheads in his administration. The United States government, however, took an equivocal position. Polk and Secretary of State Buchanan, in letters to Chargé Andrew Donelson, stated that the United States would refrain from all hostile acts toward Mexico except in self-defense. However, in dispatches less than two weeks later from the State and Navy Departments, Donelson was instructed to urge Texans to attack Mexican forces in the disputed area. Buchanan said that Texans should drive out Mexican intruders north of the Rio Grande, while Secretary of the Navy George Bancroft instructed Stockton to help defend Texas from aggression and to encourage Texans to repel the invasion of their territory, that is, lands north of the Rio Grande.

During the summer of 1845 unofficial word reached Washington that the Mexican government might well be disposed to receive a commissioner from the United States to negotiate the dispute over Texas. Following some weeks of inquiry and continued contacts the Mexican government verified the report. Polk then named John Slidell of Louisiana, at that time a member of the House of Representatives, not as a commissioner but as Minister Plenipotentiary. Slidell's terms to the Mexican government included a new frontier along the Rio Grande to El Paso and then due west to the Pacific. In return for the grant he was to offer $25 million. His several fallback positions were to offer $20 million for the northern part of California, and $5 million for New Mexico. Polk expected the acquisition of Texas with the Rio Grande as its boundary. On all of these propositions the United States would assume certain claims against Mexico by United States citizens.

Slidell's appointment as Minister Plenipotentiary instead of Commissioner ad hoc created a crisis in the Mexican government. When he arrived in Mexico on December 6, the administration of President José Joaquín de Herrera refused to receive him. The government argued that his title, a violation of the original understanding, would be interpreted by the Mexican public as a prior acceptance of annexation. Despite President Herrera's efforts to protect his regime from charges of treason by his political opposition, the government fell to a military revolt. General Mariano Paredes, who led the uprising, named himself president at the very end of the year. After consultation with Washington, Slidell approached the new government to open discussions. The Paredes administration like that of Herrera before it refused to treat with an official United States diplomatic representative, but again like its predecessor intimated that it would meet with a commissioner ad hoc solely on the Texas question. Polk dismissed the offer as insincere.

In the meantime, upon learning that the Herrera government refused to receive Slidell, Polk ordered General Taylor at Corpus Christi to proceed to the Rio Grande, to occupy all the north bank, and to repel any attempt by the Mexicans to cross over. Taylor received the orders on February 3 and began his march south on March 8. Upon his approach many Mexicans burned their buildings and fled across the river. On April 13 the United States Navy blockaded the mouth of the Rio Grande, and on April 23 President Paredes called upon the Mexican armed forces to repel the United States forces from the Rio Grande area. His action was not technically a declaration of war against the United States, but its effects were the same. Two days later a minor skirmish occurred between the opposing forces on the north side of the river. Polk described it as the shedding of American blood on American soil. On May 11, 1846, he sent a war message to Congress, and Congress promptly declared war.

Wide territorial expansion, to the Pacific instead of the simple annexation of Texas, underlay public agitation, newspaper propaganda, the presidential campaign of 1844, United States negotiations with Texas and Mexico and, finally, the declaration of war. As early as 1840 the California question began to emerge as an important element in Manifest Destiny when New Englanders began to show interest in the commercial potentialities of the west coast area. For some time the Oregon negotiations overshadowed interest in California; in fact, California seemingly was important only to some politicians in Washington and to the commercial elite in the northeast. Although Jackson and Tyler both tried to purchase the territory, California did not figure importantly in the election of 1844, and newspapers made little reference to it prior to Polk's inauguration. Polk, however, clearly had his eye on the Pacific, and although there is little evidence today that the British had any intention of seizing the territory,[9] Polk did fear British designs. What he apparently hoped for was a Texas-type operation whereby local Californians would declare independence and then seek annexation. Some turmoil had already occurred in the early 1840s, and Mexico had to send troops to quell an uprising in 1842. A more serious revolt broke out in 1845. The Californians defeated forces from Mexico, and various adventurers began to talk of a Republic of California. Most of these settlers coming to California in the early 1840s were American pioneers who were arriving steadily by land and sea. In 1845 they probably outnumbered Mexican inhabitants. When war came in May 1846, United States forces quickly and easily occupied New Mexico and California against only light resistance.

Shortly after hostilities had begun, the United States government was approached by a certain Colonel Alejandro J. Atocha, an agent of Santa Anna who at the moment was in exile in Cuba. Atocha persuaded Polk that if the United States would assist Santa Anna in returning to Mexico, the latter would agree to terms. In July the president's agent in Havana informed Santa Anna that Polk's terms for ending hostilities were the annexation of Texas with the Rio Grande boundary and a part of California including the Bay of San Francisco. According to the United States agent, Santa Anna agreed, and on August 8 he left Havana for Veracruz. In the meantime a liberal revolution unseated the Paredes government, and despite serious misgivings Santa Anna was appointed president and Valentín Gómez Farías vice-president. Whatever his agreements with Polk, Santa Anna organized military preparations to resist the United States invasion while Gómez Farías and his liberal followers sought to finance the war with the resources of the Catholic Church. This uneasy political alliance produced internal conflict within Mexico and seriously undermined the war effort.

---

[9] Norman A. Graebner, "American Interest in California, 1845," *Pacific Historical Review*, Vol. XXII (February 1953), No. 1, p. 15. British bondholders did attempt to have the Mexican government mortgage the province to them as payment of the debts, but when Mexico refused the British did not press the issue.

The war itself lasted just under two years. Taylor's troops advancing into northern Mexico captured Monterrey, and at the very end a force from El Paso took Chihuahua. Naval forces also occupied various towns and cities on both coasts. None of these operations proved decisive, however. The main effort was a stroke at the heart of the country from Veracruz to Mexico City. A United States army of about 10,000 men was assembled under General Winfield Scott, transported on naval vessels, and landed near Veracruz on March 9, 1847 with no resistance. The city was attacked and finally occupied on March 29. United States forces advanced into the central plateau, capturing Mexico City in September; by the time all fighting ceased in March 1848, they occupied about half of Mexico.

After Veracruz fell Polk immediately ordered a Minister Plenipotentiary to military headquarters in Mexico to negotiate peace terms. For this office he selected Nicholas P. Trist, Chief Clerk of the state department. Trist had the proper abilities, experience, and good political connections. He had married a granddaughter of Jefferson and had served for a time as Jackson's private secretary. He not only was well educated but spoke Spanish, having served as Consul in Havana. Trist arrived in Veracruz early in May and communicated his orders to General Scott. Conflict immediately developed between these two zealous, sensitive, and often intemperate individuals. After some bickering, they finally settled their differences and presented a united front to the enemy. Trist, however, had little to do for some months, since the Mexicans were unwilling to negotiate. As United States forces approached Mexico City, the Mexican leadership made overtures to the Americans and agreed to a temporary armistice in late August. The terms of the opposing sides, however, remained irreconcilable, whereupon the armistice expired and the war resumed. When the news of the failure of these negotiations reached Washington, the government ordered Trist home on the grounds that the United States would make no new offers until Mexico sued for peace. With the slowness of communication, the military and political situation in Mexico had changed dramatically by the time these orders reached Trist in mid-November. The Americans had captured Mexico City, Santa Anna had fallen from power, and a new Mexican government had reopened peace negotiations. When Trist's recall orders arrived, the Mexican commissioners, supported by General Scott urged him to remain to complete his work. After some hesitation, Trist agreed to stay on. The negotiators eventually agreed upon the terms and signed the treaty of peace at Guadalupe Hidalgo on the outskirts of Mexico City February 2, 1848. Despite some misgivings and anger with Trist for disobedience, Polk submitted the treaty to the Senate with recommendations only for some minor changes. The Senate supported the president, ratifying the treaty on March 10, 1848. The Mexican Senate ratified May 25. By its terms the United States obtained the Rio Grande boundary to El Paso and the line from there west to the Pacific. In return the United States paid a cash indemnity of $15 million and assumed claims of United States citizens against Mexico up to February 2, 1848, payments that would not exceed $3,250,000.

The war had cost the United States about $100 million and about 13,000 lives, but for Mexico the costs were staggering. Mexico lost over half her national territory, perhaps 50,000 lives, and large amounts of real estate, foodstuff, and livestock.[10] The war also increased the level of factional bitterness in Mexico, heightened doubts about the national purpose and sense of direction, and increased the danger of further territorial fragmentation. Mexico had to endure another 25 years of turmoil, civil war, and foreign intervention before a degree of national unity was achieved, not under a democratic, but under an authoritarian, technocratic, and positivist regime.[11] Worse still for Mexican national sensitivities, the disparities between the two countries became sharply delineated and permanently set. Not only had the one greatly shrunk in territory to about 760,000 square miles while the other expanded to over 3,000,000 square

---

[10] For some estimates on costs see Justin H. Smith, *The War with Mexico* 2 vols. (Gloucester, Mass.: Peter Smith, 1963), Vol. II, pp. 253–267 and 318–319.

[11] See Turner, *op. cit.*, p. 39 for a discussion of the effects of the war on Mexican nationalism and Horace V. Harrison, "Los federalistas mexicanos de 1839–40 y sus tanteos diplomáticos en Texas," *Historia Mexicana* Vol. VI (January-March 1957), No. 3, pp. 321–349, for discussion of the dangers of internal fragmentation of Mexico.

miles, but the one advantage that Mexico appeared to have over the United States prior to the war, that is, a standing army several times larger and presumably more powerful, had completely evaporated.[12]

The war proved to be a turning point in United States-Mexican affairs. Although economic relationships remained fundamentally the same for many years (i.e., limited trade, few investments, and no loans) the political-military situation had shifted drastically. After 1848 no one could seriously question United States predominance, while Mexican hopes of great-power status withered and died. Furthermore, the dramatic evidence of United States superiority in economic strength and technological development eventually convinced a later Mexican leadership that if the country was to survive at all, Mexico would have to emulate the northern colossus by means of economic modernization. In other words the war did not lead immediately to United States economic penetration of Mexico, but its outcome prepared the way.

A second question has been raised about who bears the major responsibility for the war. Blame for the outbreak has been variously placed on President Polk and his expansionist friends as well as on "uncompromising" and "unrealistic" Mexican leaders like Presidents Herrera and Paredes. Admittedly, Polk was ambitious, greedy for territory, and contemptuous of Mexico and Mexicans. His agents in Texas and Mexico and most of his closest advisers and collaborators in Washington shared these views. But the administration was seemingly bent not directly on fighting, but on bullying and bribing tactics, a policy that no Mexican government could accept and survive.[13] Polk wanted the fruits of war, and was willing to risk war, but he tried throughout to persuade Mexico to sell him what he wanted. As late as March 1846 he was considering making an offer of from $500,000 to $1,000,000 to President Paredes. For their part

---

[12] Smith, *op. cit.*, estimates the Mexican army at about 32,000 men in 1845 (Vol. I, p. 157) and gives United States forces as 7224 with 3554 on the Texas frontier (Vol. II, p. 511, footnote 15).

[13] Charles Sellers, *James K. Polk: Continentalist, 1843–1846* (Princeton: Princeton University Press, 1966), pp. 399–400.

Herrera and Paredes found themselves severely limited in their negotiating maneuverability, whatever their personal views, by the fragmentation of Mexican politics, by the consuming ambitions of rival leaders, and by the high level of emotion among the populace over the conflict. Could the mild and compromising Herrera have negotiated with a commissioner ad hoc in December 1845, or would the more aggressive and bombastic Paredes have revolted anyway? Could Paredes have negotiated in March 1846, or would the revolution that unseated him in August have occurred earlier had he tried? Could any regime, administration, or leader have surrendered Texas, and then survived to make it stick? It seems highly unlikely.

Finally, what accounted for the series of catastrophes that overtook Mexico in the 1830s and 1840s? Superficially Mexican deficiency in military preparedness bears the responsibility but, more basically, political, cultural, and social fragmentation lies at the root of the disasters.

Most Mexicans lamented the loss of Texas and the invasion from the United States, but relatively few were willing to risk their lives or their fortunes to defend the territorial integrity of the state. Their primary interests were the defense of political and ideological interests in the core of the country. All national energy seemed to converge on the center, as the control of most resources became concentrated in Mexico City. It became more important for all power contenders to protect their interest and position at the center than it was to divert forces to maintain the periphery. Not only were there no colonists and no capital to develop Texas or California, there were few troops available to fight a handful of United States settlers in Texas who revolted in 1836. Even when the more serious conflict with the United States developed in 1846, the internal quarrels did not cease. Vice-President Gómez Farías provoked dissension by an attempt to finance the war through confiscation of Church properties. Several battalions of the National Guard, known as *Polkos*, which had been organized late in 1846 ostensibly to meet the threatened invasion, rebelled against the central government. Although supported and financed in part by Church sources, the revolt had broader support. It forced the ouster of the President and the Vice-President, and paved the way for the return of

Santa Anna to power. The upheaval occurred in the weeks prior to and during the United States attack on Veracruz and in fact ended less than a week before United States forces captured the San Juan de Ulúa fortress in the Veracruz harbor.[14] Obviously the defeated political forces hated and distrusted Santa Anna. Although he was the most prestigious military leader in Mexico, some of his subordinate commanders refused to obey his direct orders in battle. The Mexican army in the field did not win a single engagement of major proportions, and appeared helpless to stop the march from Veracruz to Mexico City. Moreover a moderate-sized but first-rate United States navy with some 30 vessels at sea faced no opposition at all from the few small coastal ships that comprised the Mexican navy. Unopposed United States landings at Veracruz and elsewhere added to the humiliation and loss of morale of Mexico's armed forces.

The Americans, by contrast, with a basic consensus on political issues, were free to turn their energies in other directions. Their enormous migrations west and south over the North American continent, their ventures overseas, and their experimentation with new economic activities and new technology led to a veritable outburst of new wealth. There was no convergence on Washington; in fact, the center was greatly distrusted and, in the American myth, virtue was to be found in the periphery on the frontier, not in the national capital. Young men were encour-

---

[14] For a discussion of the controversies surrounding the *Polko* rebellion (February 27 to March 23, 1847) see José Bravo Ugarte, "La misión confidencial de Moses Y. Beach en 1847, y el clero mexicano," *Abside*, Vol. XII (October-December 1948), No. 4, pp. 476–496, and Michael P. Costeloe, "The Mexican Church and the Rebellion of the Polkos," *The Hispanic American Historical Review* Vol. XLVI (May 1966), No. 2, pp. 170–178. At the same time Yucatán had become a virtually independent state and declared its neutrality in the war. Torn by elite fictions and faced with an Indian uprising, its leaders sought aid and eventually intervention from the United States in the spring of 1848. The United States Congress balked, however, and Yucatán had to make its peace with Mexico City. See Mary W. Williams, "Secessionist Diplomacy of Yucatán" *The Hispanic American Historical Review* Vol. IX (May 1929), No. 2, pp. 132–143, and Louis de Armond, "Justo Sierra O'Reilly and Yucatán—United States Relations, 1847–1848," *The Hispanic American Historical Review*, Vol. XXXI (August 1951), No. 3, pp. 420–436.

aged to seek their fortune not in the center of government, but on the sea, in business enterprise, or on the frontier. When the war came, United States volunteers rallied to the call to arms, and although their romantic dreams dissipated rapidly on the battlefield, they acquitted themselves well. Relatively well disciplined, politically unified, and technologically superior, the United States armed forces demonstrated a capability far superior to the estimates of Mexican observers. At the moment of military confrontation in 1846, the outcome in a sense had already been decided.

CHAPTER IV

The Easing of Tensions, 1850–1910:
Domestic Strife and Economic Development

FOR A PERIOD OF 60 YEARS relative peace and tranquility marked United States-Mexican relations. To be sure there were moments of tension, and for some years after 1848 many Mexicans harbored not only intense bitterness but deep suspicion that the United States coveted still more territory. These fears were not without foundation, but as both countries turned toward ever-increasing domestic conflicts, their mutual relations played a decreasing role in their overall affairs. Both became embroiled in frightful and costly civil wars, and Mexico for several years experienced foreign invasion and conquest. For a moment the United States government and the Juárez regime perceived a mutual interest in driving Europeans from American territory. With the danger removed in 1867, hostility increased once more over border problems, raiding Indians, and general lawlessness on the frontier. Pressures and threats from the United States renewed Mexican fears of another loss of territory, while President Sebastián Lerdo de Tejada (1872-1876) resisted American requests for railroad concessions despite growing Mexican interest (including his own) in improving Mexican transport facilities. When General Porfirio Díaz became dictator, he restored order and invited foreign capital to develop the country. Successive United States administrations responded favorably to these overtures, particularly since the United States had embarked on its own program of modernization and economic development. For most political and business leaders in the United States economic opportunities replaced territorial expansion in Mexican relations. Secretary of State Seward particularly promoted a policy of peaceful economic penetration. Capital in the United States was seeking foreign outlets, and Mexico became an increasingly attractive area for investment. Despite the concern of United States libertarians with the lack of democracy in Mexico, the tyrannical nature of the Díaz regime, and the harsh treatment meted out to the poor and the Indians, the government of the United States and most of its citizens regarded Mexico as progressive and modernizing. Only in the last decade of the dictatorship (1900–1910) did serious criticism of the Díaz regime arise in the United States.

I

Mexico emerged from the war over Texas politically rent as well as economically prostrate. Moreover, many Mexicans believed that the United States was only biding its time until it could seize more territory, perhaps all of Mexico. As the war drew to a close, a moderate faction seized control of what was left of a central government and overruled extremists on the right and on the left who advocated fighting on with guerrilla tactics. Former President Herrera, again appointed to office in 1848, concluded peace with the United States and at the end of his legal term in 1850 passed on the mantle of the chief executive to his constitutional successor. This was the first peaceful transfer of the presidency since independence.

The calm at the national level lasted three more years, but regionally the country remained disorganized and fragmented. Outside Mexico City, the national government exercised only limited authority. Customs house officials, upon whom the government depended for a substantial portion of the income, pocketed much of the receipts. Border governors ruled as autonomous satraps, and tribal Indian and bandit groups raided almost at will.[1] Liberals and conservatives continued to battle politically and intellectually, if not militarily. When liberal groups won control of several state governments notably Oaxaca and Michoacán, the conservatives became thoroughly alarmed. Fearing further United States encroachments on one side and a

---

[1] For details on border problems, see Clarence C. Clendenen, *Blood on the Border. The United States Army and the Mexican Irregulars* (London: Macmillan, 1969), pp. 16–18.

liberal takeover on the other, some conservatives began to argue that the traditional values and institutions of Mexico could be preserved only by an alliance with a European power or the establishment of a monarchy with a European prince. Some Mexican diplomats began to discuss with Spanish officials in Madrid the availability of likely regal candidates.

American political leaders and newspapers contributed to Mexican internal anxieties. Some publicly lamented that the Polk administration had not incorporated all of Mexico. Others criticized Mexicans as treacherous, undependable, harshly cruel, and most ominously incapable of self-government. Still others accused Mexican officials of at least tacit consent to the numerous Indian raids made from Mexican territory into the United States. It is not surprising in view of such bombast that all political factions in Mexico believed that the United States was preparing for another land-grabbing operation.

Before a European prince could be invited to Mexico, the conservatives had to set up a transitional government. In 1852 Lucas Alamán, the ablest conservative of his generation, began to plan for another military dictatorship to serve as a bridge for the reestablishment of the monarchy. A conservative rebellion broke out in midyear in Guadalajara and from there spread to other regions of the country. President Mariano Arista failed to rally support and resigned in January 1853. The victorious rebels then invited Santa Anna to return from his exile in Venezuela to assume dictatorial powers for one year. Alamán as Foreign Minister headed the cabinet. In line with his hopes for European support he sounded out the French minister about a guarantee against United States territorial encoachments, but the outbreak of the Crimean War ended these conversations. Alamán also attempted to control local caciques and to undertake various economic development projects.

With the death of Alamán in June, the last administration of Santa Anna decayed rapidly. Besides systematically looting the treasury, Santa Anna began to set up the trappings of royalty around his own regime. Refraining from crowning himself as did Iturbide, he reestablished Iturbide's Order of Guadalupe and took to himself the title of Most Serene Highness. As he exhausted his resources, however, Santa Anna found himself abandoned by his former supporters. Taxes proved insufficient to maintain his court and retinue, and the clergy refused to lend him money. Early in 1854 a revolt erupted in the mountains of Guerrero and slowly spread to neighboring Michoacán. For a time Santa Anna staved off final defeat through the income available to him from the sale to the United States of a small piece of territory in the Gila River valley, known as La Mesilla. Despite some victories, Santa Anna was never able to crush the rebellion entirely, and the longer the conflict lasted, the more uncertain became his position. In early 1855 the revolution gathered momentum and in August Santa Anna finally abdicated and fled the country.

An uneasy coalition of moderates and liberals succeeded the fallen dictator in Mexico City, but the conservatives still held strength in several states and regions. Some of the liberals like Benito Juárez and Miguel Lerdo pushed through by executive decree radical changes in the status of the Catholic Church, the armed forces, and the judicial system. These moves alarmed not only the moderates supporting the regime, but permitted the conservatives to rally their forces for a counterattack upon the reformers. The first serious uprising occurred in Puebla, a very Catholic and conservative provincial capital. Although government forces crused the rebellion there and exiled the local bishop, other revolts broke out in the fall of that year. Fighting quickly spread to a half-dozen states or more. Again the government responded vigorously, and by March 1857 order was restored.

A new constitution, completed in February 1857, stirred up further antagonisms. Not only did it provide for a return to federalism, and guarantees of civil and political rights, but it curbed the special privileges of groups like the clergy and the military. The Catholic bishops almost unanimously condemned the document and forbade Catholics to take the oath of allegiance to it. A large section of the military rejected it too, and regional commotions and disturbances plagued the countryside. Finally in December, General Félix Zuloaga, commanding troops just outside Mexico City, pronounced against the Constitution, captured Mexico City, and seized most of the cabinet. Benito Juárez escaped, and in an emergency convention at Querétaro his supporters proclaimed him president. Rapidly, conservative forces advanced northward, and the liberal government had to flee. After a harrowing journey to the west coast, thence to Panama, Havana, and New Orleans, Juárez eventually made his way to Veracruz, a staunchly loyal liberal city. A three-year civil war raged with great losses in lives and property. The liberals established their headquarters in Veracruz, the country's main port and, hence, a source of considerable revenue, while the conservatives based themselves in Mexico City, the political, economic, and cultural center of the country.

Although in general the liberal and conservative factions split on ideological and political issues, much of the division also occurred as a result of local and even personal considerations. Some local officials and leaders preferred the dominance of Mexico to that of provincial chieftains while Indian groups particularly could be rallied to the cause of the Church, as well as against the depradations of local liberal bosses who coveted their lands. Pillage and rapine occurred on both sides, as did acts of generosity under trying conditions. The point is that the ferocity of the war made political compromise of an earlier time impossible, and the conflict took on the characteristics of a fight to the death. One side or the other would emerge victorious, and the winner would take all. After many months of indeterminate fighting, the liberal armies began a decisive offensive during 1860. On January 1, 1861 they captured Mexico City, and Juárez arrived from Veracruz 10 days later.

These victories brought no peace. Conservative guerrilla forces still roamed the mountainous countryside north of Mexico City, and raided to the very gates of the city. The treasury was empty, but troops and politicians demanded their pay. Much of the country's productive capacity had been ruined. At the same time foreign claims mounted as debts were not paid and foreign interests damaged. British citizens, for example, had been relieved of about 1.75 million pesos by military forces of both sides. Since French and Spanish interests had also suffered, the three governments signed a convention in 1861 for the joint occupation of Veracruz to force the Juárez regime to come to terms over debts and claims. A Spanish force arrived in December, with British and French contingents joining in January. The three allies soon began to quarrel among themselves over goals and procedures. The British and Spanish wanted only to seize the Veracruz customs house to apply the receipts to the payment of the debts, while the French had more far-reaching political ambitions.

Monarchy died hard in Mexico, although it had little if any real chance of long-term survival. Various conservative exiles from the time of Iturbide had been quietly working over the years for the reestablishment of the Mexican throne. They were joined in the 1850s and 1860s by some recent followers of Alamán and Santa Anna and by several high churchmen expelled from their dioceses. During these years a nephew of Napoleon Bonaparte had seized power in France and crowned himself Emperor Napoleon III. With ambitions of emulating and perhaps surpassing his great predecessor, Napoleon III listened sympathetically to the requests for aid from the Mexican conservatives. He used the 1861 convention with the British and Spanish as an initial cover for a scheme to create a satellite state in Mexico. When the plans of the French were clarified, Napoleon's allies withdrew from Mexico, but French forces began moving into the interior. Despite a setback at Puebla in May 1862, they occupied most of the country within a year. An assembly of conservative leaders then met and offered the Mexican crown to Maximilian, Archduke of Austria. In April 1864 he accepted and in June arrived in Mexico City. Initially his plans prospered, and the resisters were reduced to a few guerrilla bands in the northern deserts and in the southern mountains. These centers of resistance could not be destroyed, however, and after the United States Civil War ended in April 1865, the Juarista forces were soon furnished with munitions and other supplies. By mid-1865 the tide began to turn, and growing hostility to the war in France itself forced Napoleon to withdraw his forces. In March 1867 the last French troops embarked from Veracruz, Maximilian made a last stand in May at Querétaro, where he was captured, and in June Mexico City fell. Juárez ordered Maximilian executed.

In 1867 the country was utterly exhausted after more than 10 years of civil war and foreign invasion. Besides property damage and general economic disruption, the country suffered an estimated 300,000 deaths as a consequence of the fighting.

Juárez, reelected president in 1867, attempted to pull the country together and to initiate the process of reconstruction and reconciliation. His task was made doubly difficult by the wrangling that broke out within the victorious liberal forces. Dismissed soldiers grumbled about being deprived of the spoils of victory, dissatisfied politicians plotted to gain office, and the more fanatical wing of the party complained of Juárez' attempts to reconcile the beaten conservatives to the new government. Despite his enormous prestige Juárez had to face several revolts, some quite serious, against his rule until his death in 1872. His heir and successor, Sebastián Lerdo de Tejada, retained power four more years, but when he sought reelection in 1876, he was brought down by a widespread revolt headed by Porfirio Díaz, one of the more successful generals in the war against the French.

During these years of stress, civil war, foreign intervention, and reconstruction in Mexico, the United States suffered its own internal upheaval. Although the issue of slavery constituted the most dramatic source of conflict, other issues involving sectional power struggles, states' rights, and the maintenance of the union were also involved. Although many of the founding fathers expected that slavery would eventually become extinct, the invention of the cotton gin and its wide applicability in the United States South soon demonstrated that economic interests would prevail over ideological purity. The whole sectional-slavery controversy intruded into the drive for Manifest Destiny, and northern fears over southern expansion had been allayed only temporarily by Polk's acquisition of Oregon as well as of Texas. In August 1846, however, David Wilmot, a representative from Pennsylvania, tacked a provision to an appropriation bill providing that slavery be prohibited in territories acquired from Mexico. Every northern state legislature but one passed resolutions supporting the Wilmot proviso while southern Democrats furiously opposed it. Wilmot's amendment did not pass, but the principle advocated became a major issue in United States politics.

Civil war was the ultimate outcome of the controversy, as various peace projects proved fragile and ephemeral. The slavery issue could not ultimately be solved by political compromise.

When Abraham Lincoln, perceived as an enemy by the South, was elected president in 1860, the move for southern secession, suppressed for 10 years, could no longer be contained. Lincoln ordered the raising of troops to restore federal authority. The fighting lasted almost exactly four years, most of it taking place within the boundaries of the rebellious states. Property damage was extensive in certain areas particularly in Georgia and Virginia, but the United States as a whole did not suffer damage in any way comparable to that of Mexico's during these years. The productive capacity of the North not only remained untouched but increased substantially because of what amounted to government subsidies for materials to conduct the war. Human losses, however, were staggering, amounting to almost 1,000,000 people dead as a direct result of the conflict. Battle casualties accounted for about 200,000 deaths, while disease and accidents among the troops claimed another 425,000 lives. The remaining losses were civilians. At the end of the war in the spring of 1865, the Confederate states were occupied by Union troops as conquered provinces for nine years. In the north, however, an unprecedented industrial and financial development got underway. This was to make the United States a major world power and to reduce Mexico to economic dependency by the turn of the century.

II

Although interest in Mexico dropped appreciably in the United States after the Treaty of Guadalupe Hidalgo, many Americans continued to advocate further expansion at Mexico's expense. United States opinion on the matter was divided. Some Americans resisted entirely any move for further territorial acquisitions, some advocated the purchase of parts of Mexico, some wanted merely transit or communications concessions, and some argued for forceful conquest of all or parts of Mexico. A few extremists like William Walker led filibustering expeditions into Mexico in the 1850s. None of these expeditions seriously threatened Mexican territorial integrity, and none of them dangerously embroiled the United States and Mexico in disputes, although one expedition suffered some 60 executions after it surrendered. Mexican leaders, on the other hand, could never be sure of the United States government's intentions. After the enormous losses suffered in 1848, every Mexican official took seriously indeed the danger that filibustering raids, newspaper demands for more territory, and supposedly peaceful offers to buy land or concessions might lead to a new invasion and further losses.

The extension of the United States from the Atlantic to the Pacific and especially the discovery of gold in California in 1848 emphasized the need for communications links from coast to coast. United States leaders considered various solutions to shorten the all-water route around South America: roads, railroads, or canals at Panama, Nicaragua, or the Isthmus of Tehuantepec in Mexico. Because of British preeminence in the Caribbean, the Mexican route appeared the most practical. Negotiations were begun shortly after the signing of the peace treaty in 1848 but progressed slowly. They were complicated by the fact that a United States operation had bought out a concession held by British citizens to construct a road across the Isthmus. Eventually in June 1850 the United States and Mexico signed a treaty by which the Mexican government promised protection to such entrepreneurs and granted the United States the right to protect the project with military and naval forces during and after completion. The United States for its part disavowed any claims of sovereignty in the area. Twice the treaty was presented to the Mexican Congress and twice it failed to be ratified because of widespread popular disapproval and fear of the United States.[2]

Ironically where efforts to obtain concessions failed, efforts to obtain additional territory succeeded. With the failure of the Tehuantepec negotiations, the United States government turned its attention to a railroad linkage across the continent. Most observers believed that a line westward across the Mississippi could not be built because of the mountain barrier. It was argued that only a southern route through the Gila River valley was feasible. The territory, however, was undeniably Mexican. In

---

[2] James Fred Rippy, "Diplomacy of the United States and Mexico Regarding the Isthmus of Tehuantepec, 1848–1860," *Mississippi Valley Historical Review* Vol. VI (March 1920), No. 4, pp. 508–511.

the spring of 1853 the Pierce administration sent James Gadsden, a prominent railroad man, as Minister to Mexico with instructions to purchase the necessary territory to construct the railroad. With President Santa Anna strapped for money, as we have seen, the Mexican government welcomed the offer and signed a treaty at the end of the year. Despite opposition from antislavery forces the Senate ratified the treaty (after some modification) in July 1854. The United States received territory forming part of the southern boundaries of the states of Arizona and New Mexico for $10,000,000. Gadsden had succeeded in including a small bit of territory bordering the Gulf of California, but the United States Senate moved the boundary to the north. Upon further instructions Gadsden later tried to obtain additional territory in return for claims, but the Mexicans adamantly resisted. As the prospects of success grew less, Gadsden became highly annoyed, and greatly alienated his hosts. He requested money from Washington to bribe the proper officials, and eventually advocated the establishment of a United States protectorate over all of Mexico.[3]

The success of the Gadsden Treaty seemingly revived interest in the Tehuantepec project and whetted American appetites for further border "adjustments." Moreover, persistent pressure on Mexico continued no matter what the nature of the government either in Mexico or the United States. Although United States political leaders consistently stated a preference for Liberals over Conservatives in Mexican politics and strongly opposed plans for the reestablishment of monarchy, they showed in practice little or no supportive behavior to liberal regimes when they came to power. Most United States citizens welcomed the overthrow of Santa Anna by liberal forces in 1855, but the Buchanan administration readily recognized the conservative-clerical Zuloaga regime when it seized power in December 1857. Shortly thereafter President Buchanan in his State of the Union message recommended to Congress the partial occupation of Mexico, especially the northern states of Sonora and Chihuahua. In February John Forsyth, the United States Minister, reported

---

[3] Frederick S. Dunn, *The Diplomatic Protection of Americans in Mexico* (New York: Columbia University Press, 1933), pp. 74–77.

that prospects seemed promising on the possibility of obtaining, for a price, transit rights across the Isthmus of Tehuantepec and changes in the Mexican-United States border. He noted that the clergy, already heavily burdened by government loans were anxious that the regime find other sources of income. Working through the Archbishop of Mexico, Forsyth arranged to meet General Félix Zuloaga, the provisional president. Although Zuloaga seemed willing to grant some concessions, negotiations foundered over growing opposition within the government. Moreover, when the regime levied a special war tax that included taxation of foreigners living in Mexico, the United States severed relations.

Having failed to obtain concessions from the Conservatives, the Buchanan administration turned to the Liberals. At the end of 1858 Secretary of State Lewis Cass sent an executive agent, William Churchwell, to Veracruz to sound out the Juárez regime on concessions similar to those pursued with Zuloaga. Finding the Liberals receptive, Churchwell recommended recognition. Cass then appointed Robert McLane as minister to Mexico in March 1859 with instructions that if he found Juárez exercising general authority and seemed likely to maintain it, he was to extend formal recognition. Juárez, in return for recognition and cash, was prepared to go to great lengths to meet United States demands. Shortly after arriving in Veracruz, McLane did grant recognition and began negotiations for a treaty.

The discussions took as their point of departure the issues originally drawn up by executive agent Churchwell. These included the cession of Lower California, transit rights across the Isthmus of Tehuantepec as well as from the Gulf of California to some point in the United States, adjustment of claims, trade agreements, purchase price, and the protection and defense of the transit areas. The Mexican Minister to the United States José María Mata wrote to Foreign Minister, Melchor Ocampo, in February 1859 that he believed that $20 million was a fair price for Lower California. At first Miguel Lerdo, another member of Juárez inner circle, opposed selling the territory except at an "exorbitant" price, that is, $30,000,000, but by the summer had begun to change his mind, proposing a sale price of $15,000,000. Still hesitant over selling Lower California, Lerdo journeyed to the United States in July and August seeking loans to replace the need of the sale. Unable to contract a loan, he did make an agreement with a United States banker to raise 10,000 men to fight for the Liberal cause. The Juárez Cabinet rejected the contract and, in fact, Ocampo called Lerdo a traitor. In the meantime McLane had reported to Washington that while Juárez appeared ready to cede Lower California, the next Mexican Congress would probably balk at ratification.

Despite serious disagreements among the Liberal leadership the Juárez government signed a treaty (the McLane-Ocampo Treaty) in December 1859. By its terms the United States agreed to pay Mexico $4,000,000 half of which was to be remitted to the Mexican government and the other half to United States citizens to settle outstanding claims against Mexico. In return Mexico ceded perpetual transit rights across the Isthmus of Tehuantepec and across northern Mexico from the Gulf of California to points in Arizona and Texas with free ports at the end of these routes. In addition the United States also obtained the right to employ military forces in these areas to protect persons and property in transit. In an ominous additional convention the United States also got the right to support the Juárez government militarily to carry out the terms of the treaty. McLane reported to his superiors that he had difficulty persuading the Juárez government to accept the convention, but that it capitulated when he pointed out that the United States would act eventually, without reference to any government, to defend its treaty rights and its citizens.[4]

The treaty was never implemented. When President Buchanan presented the treaty to the Senate, it was obvious that sentiment ran strongly against it. On May 21, 1860 it was decisively rejected by a vote of 27 to 18. Because all Senate discussions were held in executive session, it is not known precisely why a treaty so favorable to the United States was rejected. From the evidence available, it appears that the slavery issue, that is, the fear of Northerners over the extension of slave territory into northern Mexico, proved decisive. Despite this rebuff and despite continu-

---

[4] The political struggles within Mexico are well described in Walter V. Scholes, *Mexican Politics During the Juárez Regime, 1855–1872* (Columbia: University of Missouri Press, 1969), pp. 31–36.

ing dissension among the Liberals, some members of the Juárez government continued to work for ratification even after the Conservatives failed in their second drive to capture Veracruz.[5] In early October 1860 a majority in the Cabinet favored extending the time limit for ratification, but by that time Juárez himself opposed pursuing the matter, and his opinion prevailed.

Although the Liberals decisively defeated the Conservatives at the end of 1860, they were not to enjoy their victory for long. Foreign creditors, as we have seen, clamored for payment, and when the Mexican Congress in July suspended payment on all obligations for two years, the foreign powers threatened intervention. The United States was almost as anxious as Mexico to stave off the threat, but all efforts failed. Mexico was too weak to resist, and the United States was too embroiled in civil conflict to lend effective support. A Mexican government effort to float private loans in the United States had no success, and a treaty negotiated in 1861 by the United States minister in Mexico, Thomas Corwin, failed to get Senate ratification. The treaty provided that the United States pay the interest on the Mexican foreign debt for five years in return for a lien on public lands and mineral rights in four northwestern Mexican states. The lands would have become United States property at the end of six years of default in reimbursement. At the very end of the year England and Spain invited the United States to join the planned intervention, but Secretary of State William Seward refused to participate. Instead he circulated a memorandum to the powers that the United States would not sanction a change of government in Mexico through foreign intervention. Juárez had hoped for a stronger statement, but the Lincoln administration refused to go further with a civil war on its hands.

The United States response to the French intervention varied

---

[5] Early in 1860 the Conservative government bought two ships and supplies in Havana in order to block Veracruz and to supply the Conservative forces. The Liberal government notified United States authorities that the ships should be considered piratical. On the night of March 6 a United States naval squadron captured the vessels and sent them to New Orleans. There the United States District Court declared the action illegal, but the Conservatives' plan to launch an attack by land and sea had been disrupted. General Miguel Miramón, in charge of the offensive, abandoned the campaign.

directly with the fortunes of northern arms in the Civil War. In the early stages of the conflict with the South victorious Secretary of State Seward confined his remarks to modest but firm objections. After Gettysburg, with an ultimate Northern victory in sight, public opinion began to express itself indignantly against Napoleon III. In April 1864 Congress passed a unanimous resolution condemning the invasion. Until the war ended, however, the United States would render no direct assistance to Juárez except moral support and refused to recognize the Maximilian regime. Throughout the conflict, the Juárez government instructed its Minister in Washington, Matías Romero, to negotiate for loans, military supplies, and troops but warned him not to compromise Mexico's territorial integrity. Romero became increasingly frustrated with official policy, but gained the sympathy and support of a number of influential people. As a result, the Liberals received substantial but unofficial arms aid from the United States.[6]

Secretary of State Seward in all his negotiations and dispatches over the intervention refrained from using the term, Monroe Doctrine, although clearly its principles were at stake. His policy of "cautious moderation" was designed to avoid antagonizing Europeans, Latin Americans, and especially Mexicans who disliked the arrogance of the Monroe Doctrine but who could understand in this particular situation how the United States might believe itself threatened. Official reticence, however, did not inhibit the citizenry. Congressmen, newspapermen, and many leading citizens constantly referred to the creation of the empire as a violation of the Monroe Doctrine. In fact the French intervention breathed new life into a doctrine of United States foreign policy that seemed to have been forgotten during the three decades prior to 1860.

Although the Confederacy sympathized with the conservative faction and even with the imperial forces in Mexico, the govern-

---

[6] Robert Ryal Miller, "Matías Romero: Mexican Minister to the United States During the Juárez-Maximilian Era," *The Hispanic American Historical Review*, Vol. XLV (May 1965), No. 2, p. 245; for the development of the Monroe Doctrine in official and private United States circles during these years see Dexter Perkins, *The Monroe Doctrine, 1826–1867* (Baltimore: The Johns Hopkins Press, 1933), pp. 420–461.

ment of Jefferson Davis approached the Mexicans with the same caution as did Lincoln's administration. Much of what there was of contact between the South and Mexico was carried on with Santiago Vidaurri, a regional caudillo in northern Mexico based primarily in Nuevo León. Vidaurri shifted between the Liberals and Conservatives on several occasions in the decade between 1854 and 1864, but ideology apparently was not the primary consideration; instead it was his assessment of his own power position. At one time he contemplated seceding from Mexico to establish a Republic of the Sierra Madre comprising much of northern Mexico. By 1861 he had abandoned this plan and proposed to unite the states of Nuevo León and Coahuila to the Confederacy. In June a Confederate agent, Juan A. Quintero contacted Vidaurri to sound him out. In August Quintero presented Vidaurri's request for annexation to Jefferson Davis, but the Confederate president politely but firmly rejected it. He suggested instead a close association on limited matters, especially trade. Vidaurri responded favorably by reducing the tariff on cotton and permitting Mexican merchants to negotiate contracts with Confederate agents. This trade reached its peak from 1862 to 1863 and represented the South's largest commercial outlet after the Union closed Texas ports in mid-1862. Cotton was shipped out of Matamoros and Tampico, and the South in return received lead, powder, saltpeter, bread, cloth, and shoes. When the French invaded Mexico Vidaurri tried to remain neutral. Juárez declared him a traitor when he arrived in Monterrey in March 1864. Vidaurri fled to Texas but returned to Mexico within a few months and joined Maximilian. He was executed in 1867.[7]

With the war successfully concluded, the United States took a progressively firmer stand toward the French. First, the administration deployed General Philip Sheridan's 52,000 troops along the Mexican border, and although he was counseled to observe strict neutrality, he interpreted orders liberally. Sheridan reviewed his troops as though preparing for a campaign, openly sent messengers to Juárez about routes into Mexico, and inquired about the availability of forage and the manner of purchasing

---

[7] R. Curtis Tyler, "Santiago Vidaurri and the Confederacy," *The Americas*, Vol. XXVI (July 1969), No. 1, pp. 66–76.

supplies in that country. Sheridan also declared weapons and ammunition surplus, and "destroyed" them by depositing them at various points along the border after informing the republican forces. Then in February 1866 Seward demanded to know when French military operations in Mexico would cease. Two months later the French government announced publicly that troops would be withdrawn over a period of 19 months. When it was learned, however, that 4000 Austrian volunteers might join Maximilian, Seward instructed. the United States minister in Vienna to protest. It is debatable what respective weight United States threats, rising popular opposition in France, and the menace of Prussia had on the final French decision to withdraw from Mexico. In any case, Napoleon III withdrew his troops and support from Maximilian in the spring of 1867, and no amount of pleading from the Mexican conservatives or from the wife of the emperor could dissuade him from abandoning the enterprise. When Maximilian fell to the Juaristas and was condemned to death, Seward joined with pleas from all over the world to save the Austrian Archduke—to no avail.

With their internal conflicts concluded, the two countries turned to settling one of the major issues outstanding between them, that is, the claims of United States citizens for damages since the last agreement of 1848. In the spring of 1867 Seward proposed to Minister Matías Romero a treaty not only to settle claims but also to exempt United States citizens from military service and forced loans. A year later the Juárez government responded favorably, instructing Romero to negotiate such an agreement. After a little more than two weeks a treaty was drawn up, and three days later on July 4, 1868 it was signed. The United States Senate promptly ratified it, and before the end of the year so too had the Mexican Congress. Presidents Juárez and Grant then signed it. The treaty did not itself settle claims but provided for a commission to review and pass judgment on them. The commission was duly appointed and began its labors; by 1876 all claims were finally adjudicated, and payments then began.

A second major problem, lawlessness on the border, proved more troublesome. Along the Rio Grande from Piedras Negras to Matamoros there lived an unsettled Mexican population in a band of territory 65 to 125 miles wide. Many of these people were adventurers and fighters who lived by their wits. On the Mexican side the central government's power remained weak as it had from the beginning of the republic. The situation on the United States side was just as bad if not worse. In addition to the Mexican minority, the descendants of old Texan colonists, there was a heterogeneous group from the United States and foreign lands. Many were criminals, and the Civil War had added to the turbulence. During the reconstruction period some order began to emerge, but political squabbling as well as lawlessness continued to disrupt the area. In this society smuggling flourished as a major occupation. In 1851 Mexico had created a free zone in Tamaulipas to encourage settlement in the north to protect the country from further losses of territory. In the zone foreign goods could be imported duty free. Because of lack of law enforcement agencies a thriving contraband trade developed both in the Mexican interior and into Texas. Veracruz merchants as well as United States officials complained, forcing Mexican authorities to choose between abandoning a scheme to protect the north through settlement or retaining it and perhaps losing the territory anyway. From the Texas side the problem eventually solved itself as United States industry began to provide quality products at competitive prices, making smuggling unprofitable.

Bandits and Indians, some in collaboration with local officials, posed the most serious problems. Cattle rustling had long been a major issue. In 1872 the United States Congress had authorized the president to name a commission to investigate crimes and robberies along the Rio Grande. The Mexican government appointed a similar committee although it studied Indian raids primarily. The Americans, perceiving that the central government exercised almost no control over local caciques, reached the conclusion that the Mexican government was unable and unwilling to cooperate in controlling the frontier. Some Americans believed that the best remedy was to provoke war, conquer the territory, and establish a new frontier. The chief of the Texas Rangers in the 1870s, Captain L. H. McNelly, advocated this course of action, not hesitating himself to cross the border in hot pursuit. The Mexicans reached somewhat different conclusions. They believed that Mexico suffered more than the United States from Indian raids and that the venality of United States officials, their uncooperative attitude in fighting Indians, and the presence of malefactors on both sides constituted the roots of the troubles in Texas. Undoubtedly in the mid-1870s the old rancors, antagonisms, greed, racial prejudice, and bitterness of past years contributed to a lack of cooperation, but the inability of the Mexican central government to impose a policy made the problems doubly difficult to handle. In addition the Mexicans seemed to be totally uninterested in the Indian problems except as a cause of friction with the United States. Warlike Indians within Mexico were treated in much the same way that they were in the United States: conquered, scattered, forcefully settled, or exterminated.

Although the cooperation of the two countries had softened some of the bitterness felt by Mexicans over the losses of 1848, much suspicion remained. The United States was not always served well by its representatives abroad, and continued pressure for concessions and territory did not help to allay distrust. One United States Minister in the late 1860s had been an imperial sympathizer and another was an intolerable chauvinist. The latter, General W. S. Rosecrans, concluded just shortly after his arrival that some sort of United States political control over all of Mexico was inevitable because the government was weak, corrupt, and opposed to the introduction of United States commerce, industry, and enterprise. Fortunately for harmonious relations his views met with no sympathy in Washington. The Grant Administration had no territorial ambitions in Mexico. Seward himself made a goodwill visit to Mexico in 1869. He was "hospitably" received but, not surprisingly, suspicion of United States intentions remained firmly rooted in Mexican consciences.

IV

When Porfirio Díaz, hero of the war against the French, seized power in November 1876, he appeared to be but one more in a long line of ambitious but politically incompetent military leaders. His action also temporarily renewed tensions with the United States, because many United States leaders believed that Mexico was reverting to a political style of the pre-Reform era. Talk of-annexation or of a protectorate became once more current. especially since the United States was quickly putting its own house in order after the Civil War and Reconstruction periods. Mexican fears of intervention rose accordingly.[8] On the contrary, however, Díaz within a few months demonstrated a political astuteness (and ruthlessness) that far surpassed that of any of his predecessors. Not only did he mollify or suppress his political opponents with a policy of "Pan o Palo" (Bread or the Stick), but he soon embarked on a program of economic growth that produced a degree of development unprecedented in the history of Mexico. The fruits of this economic expansion were never distributed equitably among the population, but the program itself, with its accompanying invitation and encouragement to foreign capital to participate in Mexico's development, struck responsive chords in the United States where a massive industrialization program was well underway.

Díaz seemed to understand that the greatest danger of another round of United States intervention and territorial expansion at Mexico's expense would be the continuation of internal strife within his country. One of his first moves in coming to power was not only to consolidate his immediate position but to lay the groundwork for a long-term settlement. At the same time he had to appease the jingoists in the United States who were clamoring for action because of unsettled conditions along the border. Within these narrowly construed goals Díaz handled the situation in an exemplary way. In return for cooperation along the border and mildness in protesting United States pursuit of bandits and Indians across the frontier, he gained recognition for his regime; to quiet domestic enemies he distributed economic benefits and public offices to the various military and political factions. For the old conservatives and Catholics, he refrained from strict enforcement of the anticlerical legislation of the Juárez period. Over several decades the formula worked, and Mexico enjoyed 35 years of political stability and economic

---

[8] The nature of United States threats and territorial ambitions and the Mexican response in this period is well discussed in Daniel Cosío Villegas, *Historia Moderna de México. El Porfiriato: La Vida Política Exterior* (México: Editorial Hermes, 1963), Vol. VI, Part 2, pp. 271–278.

growth. The Díaz era lacked one vital ingredient, a certain humanity. The lower classes benefited only slightly and when they protested, they were brutally suppressed. When economic and political opportunities were closed off toward the end of the regime for various middle- and upper-class groups as well, the country became ripe for revolution. The dictatorship came crashing down in 1911, but during the years of the Díaz era relations between Mexico and the United States were on the whole peaceful and harmonious. Talk of annexation died down in the United States, and United States capital and businessmen poured into the country.

Díaz' first diplomatic problem on coming to power in 1876 was to gain recognition from the powers, especially from the United States. A series of disputes and conflicts of many years duration hampered that seemingly simple task with his northern neighbor. The most serious was the border problem consisting of three interrelated difficulties: the incursions of raiding Indians on both sides of the border, cattle stealing and other crimes by lawless elements in that area, and smuggling into Texas from the Mexican Free Zone in Tamaulipas. In addition there was the frequent annoyance of "forced loans" exacted from United States citizens in Mexico whenever the government ran into financial problems. Such loans resembled the special war tax as levied during the French intervention, but were collected after 1867 as "loans" especially when uprisings occurred. And finally there was the friction between the two countries over the Mexican prohibition of foreigners acquiring certain types of real estate. During Díaz' first administration (1876–1880) most of these problems began to dissolve if not disappear.

Shortly after Díaz took Mexico City in his uprising, John W. Foster, the United States Minister, called a meeting of the diplomatic corps and advised that the powers continue to recognize the Lerdo government. They might at the same time, he said, maintain personal and unofficial relations with the authorities in the capital. This recommendation was approved unanimously by the corps, and supported by the United States Department of State. Foster himself maintained such "unofficial" communications with Ignacio Vallarta, Díaz' secretary of foreign affairs. In addition to the festering problems noted above, the Díaz government also faced the obligation of making the first payment on the claims settlement just recently signed. The first payment, due January 31, 1877, found the Mexican Treasury almost empty as a result of the recent disturbances. Díaz, fearing the reaction in the United States if payments were not made, sought both Mexican and foreign loans from wealthy families in the country. Ignacio Mariscal, Mexican Minister to the United States, reported that the payment ranked above all other considerations in immediate relations with the United States. He advised Díaz that he might delay the payment for a short while, but that he risked serious dangers in holding back long after March 1. Díaz, himself disposed to honor the obligation on time, took the advice of the Mexican Minister,[9] and had Mariscal make the first payment in January in the name of the Mexican Republic with no suggestion of the United States recognizing the new government. The promptness of the payment created a favorable reaction in the United States. Unofficial sources stated that if Mexico remained at peace and if Díaz were elected according to legal formulas, United States recognition would follow;[10] Foster concurred with this assessment.

Stability of the frontier, not the "legitimacy" issue, was paramount in the recognition of the Díaz government. The Grant administration was inclined to recognize the new regime but the War Department urged caution. The army wanted to pursue Indians, bandits, and cattle rustlers into Mexico and advised the administration that an agreement with Mexico ought to be arranged for this purpose. The State Department concurred, and instructed Foster to advise Mexican officials that it appeared to

---

[9] Mariscal was a Lerdo appointee retained by Díaz in his post. His making the payment in Washington nicely avoided the question of recognition.
[10] Introduction of the "legitimacy" principle into United States recognition policy, while not unique in United States diplomatic practice, was highly unusual in Mexico where the United States had normally recognized the authorities controlling Mexico City. Of course this formula was broken in the late 1850s with the recognition of Juárez during both the civil war and the French intervention. Perhaps it was the notion that Juárez and his immediate successor Lerdo enjoyed some sort of popular legitimacy that Díaz too had to demonstrate. Whatever was behind the idea it was certainly abandoned once Díaz gained initial recognition.

the United States that the Mexican government was unwilling or unable to combat frontier banditry. He also advised that if the situation did not improve, United States forces might have to pursue raiders across the border without Mexican approval, although the United States would prefer to have official Mexican consent. Foster, in fact, informed Vallarta that the main issue impeding recognition involved the northern frontier: smuggling, cattle rustling, and the escape of criminals across the border, especially a certain General Juan N. Cortina, a partisan of Díaz, wanted in Texas for murder and robbery among other crimes. During February Foster added complaints about marauding Indians and the Free zone. These diplomatic pressures were reinforced by widespread newspaper demands that Mexico do something about the frontier problems. Some people argued that Mexico could never obtain political stability and economic progress under its own management but only under the protection of the United States. Not surprisingly Mexican officials became alarmed.

Basically because of these border difficulties, the United States delayed de jure recognition of the Díaz government for about 17 months. In February 1877, however, Minister Foster informed Vallarta that the United States now recognized the regime de facto, meaning in practical terms that the United States would not permit hostile groups to organize in its territory. When Rutherford B. Hayes succeeded to the presidency in March, he followed his predecessor's delaying tactics, with Foster advising that it would be best to wait until after the elections before recognizing. Following the elections and Díaz' inauguration on May 5, the State Department informed Foster that the United States would accept the elections without much scrutiny, but that it would not recognize Díaz until it became convinced that the people approved the election and that Díaz would institute a stable government and respect international law and contractual obligations. In the meantime the other powers began to extend recognition. When Italy complied at the end of July, all the states with which Mexico had had relations before the change of government had recognized it except the United States.

On the border the situation remained tense through much of 1877. General William T. Sherman, the commander of the United

States Army, on June 1, 1877, ordered General Edward Ord of the Military District of Texas to pursue marauders across the Rio Grande, to punish them, and to retake stolen property. Ord was at all times to seek the cooperation of local Mexican officials in pursuit of bandits but to use his own discretion in the particular circumstances that he faced. The Díaz administration proposed as a response to border crossing a treaty whereby the military forces of the two countries cooperate in providing law and order, but that each operate solely within its own territory. The Mexicans totally rejected the idea of mutual border crossings to pursue, apprehend, or punish lawbreakers. After two months of fruitless talks in Washington, Mata resigned. Although the treaty effort failed, Díaz ordered General Jerónimo Treviño to disperse his forces to prevent bandits from crossing the river and to cooperate with United States forces whenever possible. Treviño, however, was ordered not to authorize United States troop crossings of the Rio Grande. Surprisingly Sherman's orders of June 1 provoked only moderate protest in Mexico. The Porfiristas still feared an invasion in force and did not wish to aggravate an already dangerous situation. Instead of villifying the United States, the official press attacked Lerdo for creating the original problem.[11] When United States troops actually crossed the border in pursuit, however, popular passions ran high against both Lerdo and the United States. Late in 1877 the tension began to ease somewhat, especially in the United States. Ord testified before Congress that the Mexican government was working in good faith to restore order. He reported that the 4000 Mexican troops plus the addition of 2000 more on the way would be sufficient to control bandits and Indians.

The border remained a source of discord for about two more years, but in April 1878 the United States finally granted Díaz de jure recognition. The response in Mexico was one of general approval and relief. Some opponents of the regime, especially the Catholics and the Lerdistas, expressed their criticism particularly about the United States statement of conditions necessary for recognition. On March 15 Díaz and his cabinet approved a

---

[11] Lerdo was in Washington trying to persuade the Hayes administration to support him.

proposal to request from the Senate permission for reciprocal troop crossings of the Rio Grande. By the terms of the proposal the two presidents would agree on specific areas for crossings, and pursuing forces would return to their own country when they subdued the bandits or Indians, when they lost the trail, or when they met forces of the other country. Although the Mexican Congress granted the authorization to proceed, public debate became shrill and the political opposition to Díaz increased. A Lerdista rebellion broke out, disagreements surfaced within the government, United States border crossings continued, and some United States jingoists still talked about punishing Mexico or seizing more territory. General Sherman insisted that Mexico be held responsible for continued border turmoil and advocated seizing San Juan de Ulúa fortress, bombarding Veracruz, occupying the border states, and levying taxes. The Secretary of War, however, rebuked Sherman and ordered that United States troops were not to attack Mexicans except in self-defense and were to avoid all hostile acts or conflict with Mexican troops. Although Minister Foster was subjected to an embarrassing outburst of anti-United States sentiment in September, he continued to work for a peaceful solution.

Through the remainder of his first term Díaz continued to play a cautious role on border negotiations. He refused to knuckle under to United States demands, although he recognized the need for a final settlement on the frontier. By late 1878 he made it clear that Sherman's order of June 1, 1877 had to be publicly revoked. There the situation remained all through 1879, but in March 1880 with the border notably quiet, Foster reported to Díaz that the order had been officially revoked. Díaz' first term was ending, however, and he was determined to leave the signing of the treaty to his handpicked successor and old comrade, General Manuel González. Final arrangements were further delayed until the new administration had consolidated its power. By 1882 González had secured his domestic position and had won international recognition. With the border area becoming more and more stable and with a new administration in Washington, the treaty providing for reciprocal crossing of borders in pursuit of bandits and Indians was signed. By that time the problem had largely disappeared as both countries were better able to police their own territories. The treaty was renewed for two-year periods several times.[12]

The frontier clashes between Mexico and the United States in effect solved themselves, but the solution could only come as both governments made their authority felt in the area. Professional military forces on both sides greatly decreased the incidences of rustling and raiding, while growing populations, improved communications, and economic improvement all brought more stable social conditions. Just three months before leaving office at the end of his first term in 1880, Díaz successfully overcame nationalist sentiment in Congress and secured authority to contract with two United States railroad enterprises to build lines connecting central Mexico with Ciudad Juárez and Nuevo Laredo, both on the border. The frontier had been stabilized.

V

During the 30-year period from 1880 to 1910, Mexican-United States relations revolved not around political disputes or military threats as in previous decades, but around economic issues. Trade, direct investments, and bondholding replaced Indian raids, recognition policy, and border banditry as subjects of negotiations. During these years both countries concentrated their energies on reconstruction following destructive internal strife. The United States, however, already far advanced beyond Mexico in productive capacity and technological development, not only widened the gap but reduced its neighbor virtually to an economic satellite. United States direct investments and trade grew steadily throughout the Díaz era, and toward the end American bankers entered the Mexican bond market. Because of broken diplomatic relations between Mexico and most European countries, the United States had virtually no competition when it began to move into the Mexican market. By the mid-1880s its economic stake in Mexico surpassed both the French and the British, which had been dominant in the country. Although relations were eventually restored between Mexico and

---

[12] A fascinating account of these negotiations is Daniel Cosío Villegas *The United States Versus Porfirio Díaz*, translated by Nettie Lee Benson (Lincoln: University of Nebraska Press, 1963).

Western Europe, and European trade and investments resumed, the United States retained its overall primacy. Only in public services did the British substantially surpass the Americans and moderately in bondholding, real estate, and petroleum. The French predominated in bondholding as well as in banking, manufacturing, and internal commerce. The Americans captured the bulk of Mexico's foreign trade (Table 2).[13]

The Díaz administration pursued a series of interrelated foreign economic goals: to increase its commercial ties to the United States, to retain its important connections with the major European markets, and to attract United States and European investments. Under Díaz' leading economic and financial adviser of the early years, Matías Romero, the government negotiated a series of commercial treaties with leading commercial states in the 1880s, and with some less important markets in the next two decades. Among its leading trading partners, Mexico failed to conclude such a treaty only with the United States. A treaty signed in 1883 failed to pass in the United States Congress because of protectionist fears, and the McKinley Tariff Act of 1890 removed any further possibilities of a reciprocal commercial agreement. Despite the lack of a treaty, however, the United States constantly increased its trade with Mexico, while the European countries lost ground.

In terms of its goals the Díaz economic policies were strikingly successful. Between 1877 and 1911 not only did trade multiply by a factor of seven but exports overall grew faster than imports, with the result that during most of the period Mexico enjoyed a favorable balance of trade. Moreover, the country diversified its exports. Therefore, while it still depended heavily on primary products, such humble items as henequen, rubber, coffee, copper, and lead cut into the dominant trading position of the more glamorous and traditional precious metals. Nonetheless at the end of the regime gold and silver still accounted for about half

---

[13] See the accompanying table that is taken from Harry K. Wright, *Foreign Enterprise in Mexico: Laws and Policies* (Chapel Hill: University of North Carolina Press, 1971), p. 54; also see Alfred Tischendorf, *Great Britain and Mexico in the Era of Porfirio Díaz* (Durham: Duke University Press, 1961).

Table 2 Foreign Investment in Mexico in 1911

	Millions of U.S. dollars					Percentage of Direct Investment	Percentage of Direct Investment
	Total	U.S.A.	Great Britain	France	Other		
Total	1700.4	646.2	494.7	454.3	105.1	100	
Indirect (public debt)	249.0	29.7	41.4	164.1	13.9	15	
Direct	1451.4	616.5	453.4	290.3	91.2	85	100
Railroads	565.3	267.3	200.7	58.1	39.1		38.9
Mining	408.6	249.5	58.4	89.8	10.9		28.2
Public services	118.9	6.7	105.8	5.0	1.3		8.2
Real estate	97.2	40.7	45.5	8.0	3.0		6.7
Banks	82.9	17.2	8.8	50.0	7.0		5.7
Manufacturing	65.5	10.6	5.4	36.0	13.5		4.5
Commerce	61.1	4.5	.1	40.0	16.4		4.2
Petroleum	52.0	20.0	28.6	3.4	—		3.6

Original Source. Luis Nicolau D'Olwer, "Las inversiones extranjeras," in *Historia moderna de México*, edited by Daniel Cosío Villegas, vol. 7, *El Porfiriato: La vida económica* (México, D. F.: Editorial Hermes, 1965), tables 65 and 66, pp. 1154–1155. Amounts were converted from pesos to U.S. dollars by Wright at the prevailing exchange rate of 1 peso= .50 dollar. Because individual entries have been rounded off, they may not add up to the totals.

of Mexico's exports. The nature of imports also changed. While consumer goods represented 75 percent of imports in the mid-1870s, they represented only 43 percent in 1911, the remainder constituting intermediate or capital goods. Despite this generally favorable trade relationship, the value of primary products tended to decline while that of manufactured goods increased. In the last decade of the regime, therefore, Mexico's favorable balance of trade slowly but persistently declined.

The United States, an important trading partner of Mexico since the latter's independence, became predominant in this period, particularly in the absorption of Mexican exports. The rapid expansion of the United States in population and industry, the construction of a Mexican railroad system connecting major centers of Mexican production with the United States, the rapid expansion of United States capital into Mexican mining and agriculture all contributed to a major shift in orientation of Mexico's economy. Although the United States purchased 36 percent of Mexico's exports at the time of Juárez' death in 1872, the volume had already increased to 42 percent when Díaz came to power. In the next decade it jumped to 67 percent and by the early 1890s it reached 75 percent and maintained that level to the end. United States exports to Mexico also grew rapidly but not as spectacularly. Amounting to 26 percent of Mexican purchases in 1877, they grew to 56 percent by 1890 and then leveled off. In sum the United States provided a major market for Mexican products, but Mexico divided her purchases almost equally between the United States and Western Europe. With the United States, Mexico enjoyed a favorable balance of trade with which it paid off its unfavorable balance with Europe.[14]

Despite geographic contiguity and substantial commercial relations, relatively few Americans had visited Mexico prior to the 1880s. Poor communications throughout the north, health hazards at Veracruz, political disruptions, and banditry along the roads discouraged businessmen as well as more casual visitors.

---

[14] Fernando Rosenzweig, "El Comercio Exterior," in *Historia Moderna de México*, edited by Daniel Cosío Villegas, Vol. VII Part 2, *El Porfiriato: La Vida Económica* (México: Editorial Hermes, 1965), pp. 635–644, 658–661, 688–691, and 710–723.

Díaz hoped to change all this. Even prior to the settlement of the recognition and frontier problems, he began to encourage United States visits and investments. At first the response was slow and cautious, but in the early 1880s Americans suddenly recognized Mexico as a secure and potentially rich but fallow country, only awaiting United States capital and know-how to make it bloom. One pamphleteer in 1884 called it "a second India, Cuba, Brazil, Italy, and Troy all rolled into one."[15] On the American side a few observers counseled financial caution, and on the Mexican side a few worried about political dangers, but both groups were overwhelmed by the flood of capital that poured into Mexico.

Railroads proved to be the primary target of United States interests. Although some Americans had begun to invest in railroads modestly after 1867, that area remained under British predominance until the 1880s. In fact the British had completed the Mexico City–Veracruz line, the first significant railroad route, only in 1873. In the meantime Matías Romero, who alternated between the Mexican Ministry in Washington and the Treasury Department in Mexico City, had become convinced that United States capital held the key to Mexican economic development.[16] Then early in 1880 ex-President Ulysses S. Grant, with a party of leading political and business people, visited Mexico to inquire about investment opportunities. Upon their return Romero entered into correspondence with Grant about railroad prospects and in November he hosted Grant and a group of United States capitalists to a banquet and a discussion session. In March of the following year the New York State Legislature incorporated the Mexican Southern Railroad with Grant as president and with joint United States and Mexican financing. President Díaz of Mexico participated. The undertaking did not prosper and finally collapsed in 1884, but the format of joint capital venture and high-level Mexican political participation became a pattern for United States railroad operations in Mexico.[17]

---

[15] David M. Pletcher, *Rails, Mines, and Progress: Seven American Promoters in Mexico, 1867–1911* (Ithaca: Cornell University Press, 1958), p. 2.
[16] *Ibid.*, pp. 13–14.
[17] Osgood Hardy, "Ulysses S. Grant, President of the Mexican Southern Railroad," *Pacific Historical Review*, Vol. XXIV (May 1955), No. 2, pp. 113–116. The British finally completed the line (Puebla to Oaxaca) in 1892.

The railroad spree was relatively short-lived, although some railroad building continued during many years of the Díaz regime until Mexico acquired almost 25,000 kilometers of track. The laws of 1880 and 1881 placed virtually all railroad, telephone, and telegraph construction under national jurisdiction, and under this authorization the Díaz and González administrations granted concessions lavishly. In September 1880, as his first administration was drawing to a close, Díaz authorized the construction of two rail lines between Mexico City and the border, while Manuel González (1880–1884) opened the floodgates for further construction. In a three-year period United States interests obtained concessions to build five railroad systems of 4000 kilometers with a subsidy of 32 million pesos. In addition in March 1881 the United States and Mexico were linked, and in May the Mexican American Cable Company opened service between Brownsville and Veracruz. Other rail lines and telephone service followed.[18]

Early in the following decade some members of the Díaz administration began to show signs of concern about foreign and particularly United States predominance in Mexican economic life. Railroads, with their use of foreign personnel and the English language, appeared especially to be an imperialist enterprise blanketing the whole country. In 1893 José Ives Limantour replaced Romero as secretary of the treasury and as Díaz' principal economic adviser. Limantour not only argued against railroad subsidies but advocated outright government management. After the turn of the century he took advantage of weaknesses in the two major lines, the Mexican Central and the Mexican National, to buy control and to merge them and their smaller operations into the National Railways of Mexico, a private company with government majority ownership. The administration carried out this project without loss of foreign confidence or credit. On the one hand, the government issued bonds to pay for its railroad shares, while on the other many investors were

---

[18] Luis Nicolau D'Olwer, "Las inversiones extranjeras," in *Historia Moderna de México*, edited by Daniel Cosío Villegas, Vol. VII, Part 2, *El Porfiriato: La Vida Económica* (México, D.F.: Editorial Hermes, 1965), pp. 996 and 1012.

ready to liquidate their railroad holdings, which had never realized any great profits. Construction costs had been high, too many parallel lines had been built, and some lines had been laid through unproductive areas that failed to develop.

Next to railroads, Americans invested their money in mines. In 1867 after 10 years of warfare Mexican mining was in ruins. During the 1870s the Mexican government had no capital to revitalize these mines and the British, who had been the traditional foreign developers, maintained no diplomatic relations with the country. At the very end of the González administration, the government issued a new liberal mining code that eliminated the old Spanish principle that subsoil wealth remained the property of the state (or crown). First, under the code, and with a most favorable tax law in 1892, foreign investors acquired vast mining properties. Mining in the Díaz era differed substantially from that of an earlier time. The rich silver veins of the colonial period had largely given out, and the mines worked in the late nineteenth century produced lower grade deposits that could be operated economically only on a large scale with machinery. Second, base metals increased in importance. In the 1890s William C. Greene purchased the Cananea Copper mines for 350,000 pesos and organized the Greene Consolidated Copper Company. Lead, zinc, and iron also acquired a prominent place in United States holdings. Toward the end of the century some mining operations also turned to smelting as the McKinley Tariff of 1890 placed duties on the importation of various ores, particularly iron. Finally in the last decade of the regime United States and British investors discovered and developed petroleum deposits. An American, Edward L. Doheny, brought in the first commercial well in 1901, and a British citizen, Weetman D. Pearson (later Lord Cowdray), struck oil shortly thereafter. Bitter competition developed between the two men and the companies they founded. The Díaz government encouraged both by extending tax concessions to them equally. The regime hoped that local oil would free the country from costly coal imports. Both companies continued to bring in new fields and increase production to the end of the regime.

Nationalist sentiment vis á vis mining operations developed much later than such sentiment concerning railroads and met with much less sympathy in administration circles. Bitter debate erupted in the Mexican Congress in 1909 over current mining legislation. In response, the Minister of Development submitted a bill forbidding foreigners to acquire mines in border states without special permission and requiring all foreign mining companies to reorganize under Mexican law. When the Americans protested that this would remove the protection of their own government and frighten away other capital, most of the objectionable clauses were removed. The mining law of 1910 did, however, forbid foreigners from owning claims within 80 kilometers of the border.[19]

Of much lesser financial importance, but critical for future United States-Mexican relations was the Díaz land policy. By nominal sales of large tracts of government-owned land, by the utilization of the Reform Laws that prohibited mortmain holdings (Church and Indian-village lands), and by nonenforcement of parts of the law on immigration the regime granted huge tracts of land to foreign individuals and companies for purposes of development and colonization. In return for surveying public lands, recipients received one-third the land in grant and could purchase the remainder at very low prices. In return the recipients had to sell the land to colonists in tracts not above 2500 hectares (about 6200 acres). Indians and others on such lands who did not have clear title were ruthlessly evicted. Because most of these operations failed to attract settlers, new laws in 1894 removed all requirements for colonization and the 2500 hectare limitations. By 1910 almost one-third of Mexico had been surveyed, and nearly one-fourth of the total land area had passed to foreign ownership; about one-half that amount was United States owned.[20] As early as the 1880s some protests arose over

---

[19] Pletcher, *op. cit.*, p. 306; Wright, *op. cit.*, pp. 55–56; and Marvin D. Bernstein, *The Mexican Mining Industry, 1890–1950: A Study of the Interaction of Politics, Economics, and Technology* (Albany: The State University of New York, 1964), pp. 17–26 and 49–83.

[20] Wright, *op. cit.*, pp. 57–59; Nicolau D'Oliver, *op. cit.*, pp. 993–994 points out that the law throughout the Díaz period forbade natives of a bordering country, even though naturalized Mexicans, to settle in frontier states and territories. The law was not strictly enforced; in 1881 the government granted 22 leagues of land in Sonora to a group of Americans including some of Mexican descent from California.

the acquisition of public lands by foreigners. Nationalists, protesting that it was a conspiracy by the United States to seize more Mexican territory, saw in "peaceful penetration" a change not in objectives but only in tactics. Such complaints were easily brushed aside by the statistics of wealth and modernization, but they would be raised again after the turn of the century as the golden horde of investors began to tarnish.

At the very end of the nineteenth century United States financial interests also became involved in the Mexican bond market, an area of investment that had until then constituted a European preserve. Mexico had obtained its first foreign loans in 1824 and 1825 from the British firms of Goldschmidt and Barclay. For bonds of face value of $32 million Mexico had received in fact $18.4 million and paid a real interest rate of about 10 percent; the terms were standard for the time for countries in Mexico's circumstances. The government used the loans for administrative expenses, arms purchases, and the payment of some short-term internal debts, but nothing for economic rehabilitation or development. Despite the heavy burden, the economy began to recover sufficiently to pay off the loans. Unfortunately years of peace occurred only occasionally, and each outbreak of civil war led to suspension of payments and a further accumulation of interest. Successive consolidations of interest and principal had led to an ever-mounting debt. On the eve of the war with the United States it was more than $51 million. Payments were resumed for several years in the early 1850s, but the series of revolts, civil wars, and foreign interventions from 1854 to 1867 brought suspension once more. With the restoration of peace in 1867 the Juárez government repudiated debts contracted by Maximilian, and while it acknowledged the earlier obligations, it simply stated that it could not resume payment. The debt continued to mount. When Díaz seized power, he reached an agreement with the Bondholders Association in 1886. He then borrowed $52.5 million dollars at 8 percent interest from a German firm and used $27 million to pay off the British bondholders.[21] Two more loans were made with the German house (in 1890 and in 1893), but when Mexico sought more favorable terms on

---

[21] At this rate the Mexican government repaid the loans of 1824 and 1825 in full at a real interest rate of 3 percent annually.

a fourth loan in 1899, the German firm suspended negotiations. At this point a group of New York bankers offered simply to supplant the European lenders. In the end the loan of 1899 consisted of joint United States-European participation, the first foray of the United States in the Mexican bond market. During the last decade of the Díaz regime, the foreign debt once more increased rapidly, not through default nor for the purchase of arms. Instead, a growing nationalism became evident in the early twentieth century, and the series of new loans contracted between 1902 and 1909 went mostly to purchase control of the railroads, which were generally in foreign hands. By the end of the Díaz dictatorship the foreign debt, held by British, United States, German, and French bankers amounted to well over $200 million (U.S.) of which about $70 million was railroad indebtedness.[22]

After the turn of the century, Mexican hostility toward the United States, which had been muted during the middle phase of the dictatorship, once more reasserted itself. Popular hostility became widespread and open, while government hostility was more discreetly veiled. Much of the popular outcry against the United States was indirectly aimed at the Díaz government for its concessions to foreigners, for its alleged control by foreign interests, and for its permitting foreigners to gain control of the Mexican economy. This hostility had spread to the working class by 1906 after the Liberal Party of the Flores Magón brothers had organized the workers of the Cananea Copper Company in northern Mexico. In May 1906 the miners struck the company over wages and discriminatory practices. When the company proved unable to contain the miners, the Díaz government dispatched its own forces and gave permission for United States troops to cross the border. Mexican casualties have been estimated as high as 200 dead, and the strike and its suppression served to focus attention at all social levels on Díaz' preference to foreigners over Mexicans.

Ironically, leading figures within the Díaz administration, such

---

[22] Jan Bazant, *Historia de la Deuda Exterior de México (1823–1946)* (México: El Colegio de México, 1968), pp. 150–170 and 229–233. The peso was pegged to gold and stabilized in 1905 at .50 a United States dollar.

as Limantour, had also become concerned over foreign economic penetration as indicated by the beginning of railroad nationalization. The government had to be circumspect, however, in its own program of nationalism, since on the one hand it could not admit to grave mistakes and errors without seriously damaging itself, nor could it attack foreign abuses without alienating some of its supporters and perhaps frightening foreign capital away. Mexican official disapproval of the United States included such trivia as rescuing José Santos Zelaya, former Nicaraguan dictator, when he was overthrown in a revolution supported by the United States. It also resulted in attempts to counter United States economic domination by grants and concessions from the Mexican government to European enterprise, for example, in the budding petroleum industry.

At the same time the United States viewed Mexican concern with United States Caribbean interventions as indications of hostility, and following Japan's victory over Russia in 1905, some Americans began to speak of the dangers of a Mexican-Japanese alliance. One such imbroglio concerned Magdalena Bay in Lower California. From 1897 on the Mexican government had customarily permitted the use of the bay and surrounding area for United States fleet maneuvers and shore leave. No permanent or contractual arrangements were ever concluded. In 1907 when the United States government requested more formal arrangements including the right to maintain a coaling station, Mexican newspapers attacked the proposal as a further surrender to the Yankees. Under this pressure the Díaz regime denied the request. In some United States quarters this refusal was interpreted as the first move to grant a concession to the Japanese. The inference had no foundation.[23]

Neither government wanted these relatively minor affairs to magnify into major confrontations. In 1908 Díaz granted an interview to a United States reporter for *Pearson's Magazine* in

---

[23] For a detailed account of the Magdalena Bay negotiations in the Díaz period see Daniel Cosío Villegas, *Historia Moderna de Mexico. El Porfiriato. La Vida Política Exterior*, Vol. VI 2nd Part (México: Editorial Hermes, 1963), pp. 298–320; see also Peter Calvert, *The Mexican Revolution, 1910–1914. The Diplomacy of Anglo-American Conflict* (Cambridge: Cambridge University Press, 1968), pp. 27–29.

which he stated that he would not seek reelection to the presidency when his term ended in 1910. In light of his subsequent efforts to have himself reelected, Díaz probably made the statement for consumption in the United States to improve his image and "to mollify opinion in the northern republic" that was beginning to become critical of his regime.[24] Unfortunately for Díaz it was reprinted in Mexico and increased his domestic political problems. On the other side of the border the Roosevelt administration cooperated with Mexican agents in the harassment of would-be Mexican revolutionaries, notably the Flores Magón brothers Ricardo and Enrique and their followers. The Flores Magón group had to move repeatedly from San Antonio, St. Louis, Canada, and Los Angeles. The anarchist leader, Ricardo, was several times imprisoned in the United States and ended his days in the federal prison at Leavenworth in 1922.

When President Taft succeeded to office in March 1909, the Mexican situation appeared manageable. Mexico had some internal difficulties and some minor irritations with the United States, but these did not seem to be leading toward revolution or violent confrontation. Taft was a peaceful man basically, and he sought accommodations in goodwill gestures. Upon coming to office he suggested a meeting of presidents on the frontier, and an interview was arranged for June-July 1909. Díaz responded readily in the hope of strengthening the impression of United States support. The affair came off splendidly, and when Taft crossed into Mexico it was the first time in the history of the United States that an incumbent president was to leave his country during his term of office. A year later the United States (and other powers) joined Mexico in the centennial of the latter's independence movement. These happy and pleasant affairs proved to be but the calm before the storm of revolution and international conflict.

VI

This 60-year period witnessed a major shift in the policy of the United States government and in the attitudes of leading

---

[24] Stanley R. Ross, *Francisco I. Madero: Apostle of Mexican Democracy* (New York: Columbia University Press, 1955), pp. 41–42.

Americans toward Mexico. At the beginning annexationist sentiment remained strong and some Americans looked forward to the ultimate absorption of all Mexico. With the intensification of the sectional conflict in the United States, however, territorial expansion appeared infeasible, and the nation's statesmen began to turn to treaties and conventions to gain access to and transit rights across various regions of Mexico. These efforts at penetration also failed. Then for some years both countries largely ignored their interrelationship because of internal problems. When contact was resumed in the late 1860s annexationist sentiment in the United States was not dead, but the prevailing view of American leaders favored "peaceful economic penetration." This perspective coincided with the rise to leadership in Mexico of a generation devoted to economic modernization and development. Mexican fears of annexation obviously persisted. Some critics saw peaceful penetration as only a change in tactics, but the Díaz administration and its supporters believed that they could control the penetration and balance United States interests with those of Europe to assure their own freedom of action. As a consequence United States capital flowed into Mexico from the mid 1880s to the end of the regime, and for the first time United States citizens created a large economic stake in Mexico.

Recently the theme of dependency has preoccupied scholars concerned with political change and economic development in Latin America. The term has been defined as the state or condition of a weaker state in its relations with a stronger state characterized by a need or desire of the weaker for technology and goods that only the stronger can supply, by a grid of economic ties controlled by the stronger, and by the consequent limitation of the weaker in making vital politicoeconomic decisions affecting its well-being. Obviously there are degrees of "need," "control," and "limitation," and no one has yet precisely defined these to measure degrees of dependency or to distinguish abject dependency from interdependency. Nevertheless it appears that between 1885 and 1910 Mexico became clearly dependent on the United States in a substantial way according to all three measures. Its railroad, communications, and mining technologies came from the United States and were controlled by United States citizens. Foreign trade and foreign investments were largely United States dominated, and attempts by Mexican nationalists to alter the relationships were defeated by American warnings and veiled threats. It required a revolution and a turnover of elites to modify the dependency relationship. The dependency could be broken, but the cost was high, and the ruling Díaz elite, profiting from the arrangements, hesitated to shatter the prevailing balance of interests.

One final aspect of the new relationship needs to be noted. As United States ambitions toward Mexico changed from territorial expansion to economic penetration, the likelihood of United States armed intervention into Mexico in pursuit of its interests varied with the degree of internal stability in Mexico. When internal order broke down in Mexico in the mid-1870s interventionist sentiment in the United States rose, and limited armed incursions took place along the border in pursuit of Indians and bandits. After Díaz finally established control both in the core area and on the frontiers, United States border crossings ceased and so too did virtually all talk of further acquisition of Mexican territory. Such sentiments remained quiescent until the outbreak of revolt in 1910 when various acts of United States intervention in Mexican affairs once more began to occur. That they did should not be surprising, since civil disorders threatened to damage United States interests, and the United States government has always regarded protection of the life and property of its citizens abroad as one of its major responsibilities in international relations.

CHAPTER V

The Mexican Revolution and the United States, 1910–1920

DURING HIS LONG TENURE IN POWER Díaz had pitted one political faction against another. For many years these various rival groups played their roles more or less quietly. With the publication, however, of the Creelman interview, in which Díaz talked of retirement, the factions began to surface as political clubs and even political parties. The followers of Bernardo Reyes, cacique of Nuevo León, organized the Democratic Party while Díaz's personal adherents and his *científico* advisers formed the National Porfirista Circle. More importantly for the future, an obscure, unsuccessful politician from a wealthy northern family, Francisco Madero, began to attract a following with a book he published in 1908: *The Presidential Succession of 1910.* Initially Madero did not oppose the reelection of Díaz but only asked for the introduction of some political freedom, and as a token of the good faith of the administration, the right of the electorate freely to choose the vice-president. During 1909 he toured the country, winning adherents and slowly organizing a network of clubs supporting him. Reyes, seemingly the more dangerous challenger, was ordered to Europe on a military mission, and his followers started rallying to Madero. Some of the clubs began to adopt the name antireelectionist, and in April 1910 they called an antireelectionist convention that nominated Madero for president and Francisco Vásquez Gómez, a former Reyista, for vice-president. Díaz, at first not taking the candidacy seriously, met with Madero and even approved his stated aim of interesting the Mexican people in democratic practices. When Madero, however, began to attract thousands of enthusiastic followers at his political rallies, Díaz became alarmed and imprisoned him in

June just a few weeks before the election. In September, just after the great celebrations for the centennial of the Mexican proclamation of independence, Díaz announced his reelection to the presidency with handpicked Ramón Corral as vice-president. Early in October Madero, confined to the city of San Luis Potosí, escaped to the United States.

The revolution now began. From San Antonio, Madero issued a proclamation called the Plan of San Luis Potosí (named for the city of his imprisonment). The Plan declared that the elections were fraudulent, that Madero had named himself provisional president, and that a general uprising would take place on November 20. The first sporadic attacks on the government failed badly, and Madero who had crossed into Mexico returned to the United States. Almost at the point of giving up, Madero then began to receive reports of continued uprisings and a few victories in Chihuahua, especially those led by Pascual Orozco and his lieutenant, a bandit chief named Pancho Villa. In February 1911 Madero crossed the border once more and joined the rebels in Chihuahua. With the uprising spreading into various parts of the country, federal forces proved incapable of containing the movement. Just south of Mexico City Emiliano Zapata led peasants against the local authorities and seized some of the large sugar plantations. Guerrilla bands in at least 10 other states harried loyalist troops and officials. The vaunted Díaz army, ridden by favoritism and corruption, could not coordinate its efforts. After several defeats, notably the loss of Ciudad Juárez, across from El Paso, Texas, Díaz resigned in late May, taking into exile with him his chief adviser Limantour. According to the agreement reached between Madero and the caretakers of the old regime, Francisco de la Barra, a moderate conservative, assumed the provisional presidency until elections could be held.

I

Once again the breakdown of order in Mexico created new difficulties in Mexican-United States relations. When Madero escaped to the United States, settling in San Antonio, he was careful not to violate United States neutrality laws. He denied any intention of organizing a revolution on American soil, but he made great efforts to gain sympathy for his cause by lauding the liberty and freedom enjoyed in the United States and contrasting it with the tyranny in his own country. In fact, of course, Madero was planning armed rebellion, but no evidence of illegal activity could be cited against him. After he fled back into the United States following his first unsuccessful attempt to raise rebellious forces, however, the Department of Justice ordered his arrest. The case against him was quietly dropped, and the orders were never carried out. Among the United States populace, particularly along the border, Madero succeeded in arousing considerable sympathy, and during 1911 the border people supplied the revolutionists with material and moral aid. The Díaz government early recognized this sympathy for Madero, and to counteract it Díaz sent Joaquín Casasús as a special envoy to Texas and to Washington in an attempt to get strict enforcement of the neutrality laws. The Mexican government also sent spies and private detectives to harass revolutionary agents and to gather information. Díaz complained constantly about revolutionary recruiting, arms purchases, smuggling, and movements of persons and material across the border. As the government's military situation deteriorated, Díaz became ever more irritable.[1]

As the Mexican conflict developed, President Taft's basic political instincts first led him to support constituted authority. Second, his view of United States national interests forced him to take some measures to protect United States lives and property abroad. Third, his personal inclinations restrained him from courses of action that might lead to armed intervention in Mexico. On several occasions these three pressures became mutually incompatible, and the abrupt policy shifts within the Taft administration might be interpreted as the expected difficulties that arose from attempts to reconcile these conflicting goals. At the same time, however, the Taft administration did not give unqualified support to the Díaz dictatorship. Even Ambassador Henry Lane Wilson in a dispatch of October 31, 1910 severely

---

[1] Berta Ulloa, "Las relaciones mexicano-norteamericanas, 1910–1911" *Historia mexicana* Vol. XV (July-September 1965), No. 1, pp. 25–46, holds that revolutionary activities along the border created the most serious tensions, but that Taft never really contemplated intervention.

criticized political and economic conditions in the country.[2]

When the rebellion picked up steam in late February, United States authorities became concerned about troubles along the border. Ambassador Wilson advised the sending of troops for border patrol, and on March 8, Taft ordered the mobilization of 20,000 men for duty on the Texas frontier with no advance notice to Mexico. Although the United States government explained the action as "maneuvers," wild speculation in Mexico followed the order. Although Taft took great pains to convince Díaz that the action was friendly, the general belief in Mexico was that the United States was preparing another invasion and seizure of territory. The alarm grew when it was also learned that United States naval vessels were heading for Mexican coastal waters. In agitation the First Secretary of the Mexican Embassy asked the State Department for clarification. Taft, now fully aware of the Mexican response, ordered the ships only to load coal at Mexican ports and then steam north. He also assured Díaz that the troops were only to enforce the neutrality laws. As it became clear that no invasion was to occur, the fears in Mexico dropped. The Díaz regime, however, was damaged not only by the weakness that the United States actions implied,[3] but also by accusations in some sectors that Díaz had sought intervention to save himself.

What finally can be said of United States influence on the fall of Díaz? One scholar has stated bluntly: "No revolution against the Mexican government could have succeeded so long as the United States government maintained a policy of positive support of the existing regime. At the very least an attitude of 'neutrality' would be necessary if a revolutionary group was to be able to organize, operate, and supply its forces from American soil."[4] From the evidence it appears that the United States

---

[2] P. Edward Haley, *Revolution and Intervention: The Diplomacy of Taft and Wilson with Mexico, 1910–1917* (Cambridge, Mass.: The MIT Press, 1970), pp. 14–18.

[3] Taft did instruct General Leonard Wood, the commander of the troops in Texas, to prevent insurrectionary expeditions from crossing into Mexico, but he also notified him that if Congress so directed, his troops would enter Mexico to protect American lives and property. Calvert, *op. cit.*, p. 55.

[4] Ross, *op. cit.*, p. 136.

government offered no positive support to the revolution. In fact Taft probably made no conscious efforts to influence its outcome one way or the other. His mobilization of land and naval forces did damage Díaz, but it is doubtful that it proved crucial to the outcome. More important was the relative laxity of United States authorities in enforcing the neutrality laws. Madero did proclaim his rebellion from American territory, crossed over into Mexico with hostile forces on two occasions, and brought men and supplies across the border to support his cause. By the time United States troops were placed on patrol in March 1911, the rebellion was probably uncontainable. That nongovernmental and popular support in the United States for Madero was important to his success cannot be denied. It has been estimated that 75 percent of the population in San Antonio supported him, and among the press and general population he won great sympathy. It has been alleged that Madero also had received financial support from the Standard Oil Company that at the time was battling British oil interests that were closely tied to the Díaz regime. There is no evidence at all that Madero ever received such support. In early 1911 Gustavo Madero, brother of the rebel leader, was negotiating about financing with one C. R. Troxel, who claimed he was an agent of Standard Oil. Company officials have consistently denied the connection, but Troxel's claim has never been definitively substantiated or disproved. Troxel disappeared after May 2, without coming to any agreement with Gustavo, and when Ciudad Juárez fell on May 10, the Maderos no longer needed the loans.

One last point about United States attitudes toward Mexico during the first phase of the Revolution concerns territorial ambitions. In November 1910 the British Minister to Mexico reported to the British Foreign Ministry that the United States was likely to establish a protectorate over all of Mexico, and in the following February United States Ambassador Wilson told the British chargé that the United States would like to have Lower California not for the land itself but for strategic Magdalena Bay. During that same month United States filibusterers raided Lower California, and in all likelihood many of the adventurers from the United States who joined the revolutionary movement of the Flores Magón brothers thought of separating the peninsula from Mexico and either of setting up an independent republic or attaching it to the United States. Ricardo Flores Magón himself never contemplated, should he have succeeded in his expedition into Lower California, seceding from Mexico. He rejected the Madero movement, but thought of his own anarchist revolutionary drive as encompassing all of Mexico. From all available evidence neither the United States government nor United States business interests acted in any way to support an independence movement in Lower California, although some United States enterprises paid some "protection" money to the Liberal Junta of the Flores Magón. President Taft himself had no territorial ambitions vis-à-vis Mexico, and always believed that he was acting in diplomatically correct ways toward the revolution and the Mexican government during his four years in office. What expansionist sentiment there was among the populace, individual diplomats, or congressmen received no support whatever from the president. Whatever Mexican fears, there was little real danger of a United States invasion of Mexico and much less of a seizure of territory.[5]

II

Even though some confusion and turmoil existed after the fall of the 35-year dictatorship, Mexico remained relatively peaceful during the summer of 1911. De la Barra prepared for elections to be held in the fall, and the various political groups and factions operated in a free and open political atmosphere. With most of the population uneducated and even illiterate, the number of active and informed participants was obviously a small proportion of the total population. Madero had no real competition for the presidency, but some politicking was focused on the vice-presidency. Peaceful elections were held in October with Madero and his running mate José María Pino Suárez easily winning office. Madero never fully understood the forces that he had unleashed. His primary aim always was to bring political freedom to Mexico in order that the people might freely reform their political, social, and economic institutions in conformity

---

[5] Lowell L. Blaisdell, *The Desert Revolution: Baja California, 1911* (Madison: The University of Wisconsin Press, 1962).

with their needs and desires. He never understood the implications of the prerequisites of an open political system, expecting all political leaders to operate in an attitude of trust, goodwill, purity of purpose, and willingness to compromise interests and goals.

In December 1911 Bernardo Reyes attempted an uprising in Nuevo León, and in October 1912 Félix Díaz, a nephew of the fallen dictator, rebelled in Veracruz. Both revolts were easily suppressed and the leaders captured and imprisoned. Madero personally saved them from execution. Between these two minor disturbances, in February 1912 a far more serious uprising occurred in Chihuahua led by Pascual Orozco, one of the primary leaders of the revolution against Díaz. The Orozco revolt takes on importance for what it portended for the future. First Orozco, a revolutionary, rebelled against the acknowledged leadership because of dissatisfaction with the recognition and awards given him for his role in the original movement. Thus, the revolution began to feed upon itself and devour its own. Second, Madero was forced to call on the regular army and one of the leading generals, Victoriano Huerta, to quell the revolt, thus giving a principal supporter of the Reyes forces increasing prestige and self-confidence. And third, the very success of the regular armed forces made Madero not only more dependent on the army and Huerta, but more inclined to rely on their support for his regime. At the same time that he faced these rebellions, Madero had to confront a constant threat on his southern flank from the peasants in Morelos under Emiliano Zapata. Alternately attempting to negotiate with or to suppress Zapata, Madero had to rely on the generals for support. Some officers dealt with the peasants ruthlessly and far exceeded their orders in trying to overcome resistance. The Zapata movement harassed Madero to the end of his regime.

The final act in the drama came in February 1913. For some weeks a plot was brewing to free the two rebels, Reyes and Díaz, who were incarcerated in Mexico City, and to overthrow the government. The prime movers were several generals of the army, but Madero refused to believe the reports presented to him. The outbreak occurred on February 9, and in the first volley Reyes was killed and Díaz retreated to the Citadel in the city.

Again Madero entrusted his defense to Huerta. On this occasion, however, Huerta proved disloyal, and instead of vigorously pursuing the attack, made some desultory movements and then engaged the defenders of the Citadel in a supposed artillery duel from the vicinity of the National Palace. The contenders inflicted little damage on each other but caused devastation in large sections of the business district of the capital for 10 days—the so-called "Tragic Ten Days" of the Revolution. Whether Huerta planned to betray Madero from the beginning is uncertain. In any case, he finally ended the farce by making a compact with the rebels that called for the overthrow of the Madero government and that assured Huerta of a prominent position in the new regime. The details of the agreement were worked out in the Embassy of the United States on the night of February 18–19, a few hours after Huerta's forces overthrew and arrested Madero. A promise of safe conduct out of the country for Madero and Pino Suárez was not honored. Both were shot to death on February 23 on the way from the palace, where they had been held, to the penitentiary. At the time it was officially explained that they had attempted to escape with the assistance of an armed group who attacked the escort and that both men were killed in the exchange of gunfire. A later investigation proved that henchmen of Huerta had coldly assassinated both men, but Huerta's role and responsibility have never been definitively established. Most observers presume him to be guilty of planning the murders.[6]

The role of the United States and its agents and representatives in these dramatic events has been the subject of intense debate. Particularly controversial has been the question of the responsibility of Ambassador Henry Lane Wilson both for the overthrow of Madero and for the assassination of the president and vice-president. Without question the ambassador bears at least indirect responsibility for both events. He frequently exceeded the authority of his instructions from Washington. Presi-

---

[6] For an account of the long-standing personal and professional relationship between Huerta and Reyes, as well as Huerta's negotiations with the Reyes-Díaz conspirators, see Michael C. Meyer, *Huerta, A Political Portrait* (Lincoln: University of Nebraska Press, 1972), pp. 5–17 and 46–60.

dent Taft stuck emphatically to his doctrine of support for constituted authority, and when Madero won the elections of 1911, he was the legitimate president as far as the United States president was concerned. On repeated occasions the State Department warned Ambassador Wilson against meddling in Mexican internal affairs, but early in 1913 the Department by its weak remonstrances seemed willing to support the Ambassador if his intrigues proved successful. Motives are difficult if not impossible to determine in any precise manner, and perhaps the best one can do is to review the events as impartially as possible.[7]

Henry Lane Wilson had begun his diplomatic career as a political appointee but in time became a career diplomat. He served as Minister to Chile (1897–1905) and Belgium (1905–1910) before Taft transferred him to Mexico, reportedly to protect Guggenheim interests in mining and metallurgy around Torreón. Prior to the revolution Wilson had complained of problems with the Díaz regime and its supporters. In addition the Guggenheims had quarreled over property rights with the Madero family, one of whose members led the revolt against Díaz. Wilson also attempted to protect United States petroleum interests in their competition with Lord Cowdray's Mexican Eagle Petroleum Corporation in which high Mexican government officials held stock. On one occasion Wilson reported that he always ran into opposition from the "Científicos," the Positivist coterie around Díaz, when he tried to defend American interests. In view of Wilson's later trouble with Madero and his overweening nationalism, it is difficult to evaluate his complaints. Whatever the situation in 1910, Wilson was in poor health, a habitual drinker, moody, and blustery. His personality, values, attitudes, and limited skills did not equip him to deal with the storm at whose edge he stood in 1910.

Ambassador Wilson's first response to the Madero movement paralleled that of the Díaz government: it was not to be taken too seriously. As the revolution gained strength and Madero appeared to be emerging the victor, Wilson became alarmed at the

---

[7] For an interesting discussion of these ambivalent and even contradictory United States policies, see Howard F. Cline, *The United States and Mexico*, revised and enlarged edition (New York: Atheneum Press, 1963), p. 133.

prospect of Mexico being ruled by a "dreamer" and an idealist with a political program that Wilson believed unsuited for Mexico at its current stage of development. In a sense he adopted the position of the Positivist-Científico advisory group that had long surrounded Díaz, that is, that the Mexican people after subjection to centuries of authoritarian, clerical, and doctrinaire rule could not suddenly be projected into modern democracy. They believed that a long period of tutelage with a scientific educational system and modernizing leadership would be needed before free and open politics could operate successfully. Wilson like the Científicos was fuzzy about how long the tutelage should last, but from 1910 to 1911 he believed that Díaz' methods, if not Díaz himself, were necessary to ensure peace and protect United States interests.[8]

Ambassador Wilson often saw what he wanted to see. He believed that the interim government was not only solidly Maderist but dangerously radical and "altruistic, if not socialistic" in doctrine. He saw "rapine, violence, looting and the collapse of organized government," and specifically informed Washington that the state of Tabasco was in upheaval. He was wrong on all counts. The interim government was dominated by conservatives, political turbulence was moderate, and Tabasco was quiet as the United State consul on the scene reported. Only in one item was the ambassador correct, and that was his prediction of a long period of unrest and turmoil in Mexico that would create severe problems for the United States. His prediction came true, but perhaps in part as a self-fulfilling prophecy to which he contributed by his attitude toward Madero and Madero's government.

For a brief time after Madero's inauguration, Wilson manifested some change of attitude toward Mexico's new president. After all, Madero in his first formal communication with the U.S. Department of State had pledged to recognize all treaties

---

[8] Daniel Cosío Villegas, "Sobre Henry Lane Wilson," *Memoria del Colegio Nacional*, Vol. IV (1961), No. 4, pp. 39–55, writes that the predominant note in Wilson's communications to Washington in these months was the gross exaggeration of the dangers to United States lives and property by the revolutionists, and that Taft's responses only served to heighten latent but growing anti-United States sentiments.

and to assume the responsibility for all damages and injuries to the citizens of those nations recognizing the Revolution. Wilson continued to distrust Madero's idealism, but he came to believe that Madero might be "educated" about political realities. These relatively harmonious relations lasted only a few months. During the Orozco rebellion of early 1912 Wilson exaggerated the difficulties and problems of the Madero government. He called the diplomatic corps together to consider measures for the self-defense of lives and property of foreigners and advised United States citizens to leave the area. In late March he asked the state department for 1000 rifles and 1,000,000 rounds of ammunition to defend the American colony; a few days later he doubled the request. The state department refused. During 1912 the Ambassador's doubts about Madero turned to active dislike and enmity as Wilson came to believe that anti-United States forces had gained the upper hand in the Madero government. Personality conflicts turned into conflicts of interest when Wilson perceived that Madero refused to protect foreign property interests in the way Wilson believed he should. After all, Wilson had come to Mexico in part at least to protect Guggenheim interests in northern Mexico, interests that were in conflict and competition with those of the Madero family. By the end of 1912 it appears that Wilson believed that Madero had to be replaced in the interests of Mexican stability and United States property rights.[9]

In the meantime the Taft government, in serious domestic political troubles, was attempting to avoid involvement in the Mexican situation. Immediately after the inauguration of Madero, Taft recognized the new government. A few months later, when Madero complained that arms and munitions were crossing the border, Taft had Congress pass a resolution authorizing the president to regulate the arms traffic to any American country embroiled in domestic strife. During the Orozco rebellion Taft mobilized 100,000 troops on the border, and offered reassurrances to the Madero government that no intervention was contemplated when rumors began to circulate to that effect. In

---

[9] Calvert, *op. cit.*, pp. 85–87 and 109–111; Ross, *op. cit.* pp. 176, 237, and 261.

fact, Taft embargoed arms to the rebels but permitted them to be exported to the recognized government. He also offered Madero the use of United States railroad facilities to transport troops through Texas to quell the revolt. The United States government also warned all Americans in Mexico to take no part in political activities and provided evacuation facilities for anyone who wanted to leave especially from the area of fighting. On two occasions, however, the Taft administration took a hard-nosed attitude toward Mexico over the protection of United States lives and property. In April and again in September 1912 some Democratic Party leaders in the United States began to attack the administration for inability to protect United States interests and for indifference to the loss of United States lives. Fighting for reelection in the face of revolt within his own party and against Woodrow Wilson, a strong Democratic candidate, President Taft issued strongly worded statements to both government and rebel forces demanding better treatment of United States citizens. Secretary of State Knox threatened the Mexican minister in Washington with the possibility of repealing the order that prohibited arms shipments to the enemies of the Madero government. The minister sympathized with the complaints, apparently understanding the nature of United States politics in an election year. Opposition attacks on the administration never reached serious proportions and died out once the Orozco revolt was suppressed. The two opposition presidential candidates said little about Mexico in their campaigns: Theodore Roosevelt made a few vague references, and Woodrow Wilson said virtually nothing.

At the opening of the new year, most of Mexico was at peace, and Madero's government had the support and even the enthusiasm of all except for some politicians and army officers, a few political extremists, and United States Ambassador Henry Lane Wilson. Taft and the state department were understandably mystified when Wilson began to send in alarmist reports describing the government's position as "hopeless." In late January the secretary of state, in assessing the situation for the president, asserted that he could not see any reason for pessimism regarding the stability of Madero's government. Wilson was probably privy to certain information in military circles because the Reyes-Díaz revolt of February 9 did not particularly surprise him. It did catch Taft and the state department by surprise, and for three days the United State government remained inactive. Ambassador Wilson continued to interpret events in his own distorted fashion. With little evidence he reported to the department on February 10 that practically all the state and local authorities, including the police and rurales, supported the rebels, and on the following day he reported that public opinion Mexican as well as foreign overwhelmingly favored the rebels. The ambassador recommended that Washington take a hard line with Madero about protecting foreign interests to assist him (the ambassador) in obtaining a cease-fire. Secretary Knox refused to threaten Madero for fear that such action might lead to intervention. Wilson for his part took vigorous measures to rescue foreigners caught in the area of combat, but ignored state department recommendations to move his quarters out of the line of fire. In defiance of explicit instructions he threatened United States intervention unless foreign lives and property received adequate protection. On February 12 Wilson and the German and Spanish Ministers visited Madero and insisted on a cessation of hostilities and made the same demands of Félix Díaz, whom they together with the British Minister visited in the Citadel. Madero not only agreed to a cease-fire, but on Friday February 14 he wired President Taft requesting him not to intervene and promising to reimburse United States citizens for damages. Despite the conciliatory attitude of Madero, the Spanish minister (speaking for his American, British, and German colleagues) tried to persuade Madero to resign on the morning of February 15. Wilson, with the German minister, that afternoon tried to arrange an armistice with Huerta, but without result. In the meantime Taft had ordered several battleships to Veracruz, but rejected Wilson's request for "menacing" instructions and control over this naval power. Taft reassured Madero that no intervention was planned. On February 16 Wilson finally arranged a temporary armistice to evacuate foreigners from the danger zone, and Knox commended him so warmly that Wilson apparently interpreted the response to imply approval of his total policy of mediation. Huerta in the meantime had been holding discussions with representatives of the rebel forces and with opponents of Madero in the Senate. The following day Huerta informed the ambassador that plans were maturing to force Madero from power, and Wilson reported that he made neither inquiries nor suggestions but only requested that no lives be taken except by due process of law. Remember that technically Huerta was still commander of the government's forces.

The political side of this tragedy was completed on February 18. Huerta betrayed Madero's trust, ordered the arrest of the president and the vice-president, and assumed command of the government. Huerta officially notified the ambassador of his action and requested Wilson to use his good offices to mediate between the government and the rebels. Thereupon the ambassador invited Huerta and Díaz to the embassy for consultation that evening. After several hours of negotiating, the details of the settlement were worked out, the basic agreement having been reached the previous day. According to its terms Huerta was to become provisional president with the cabinet made up mostly of Félix Díaz supporters and headed by de la Barra of the Catholic bloc. Congress would be convened, and Díaz was to stand as a candidate in the next presidential election. Nothing in the pact, however, set a date for the election nor precluded Huerta from running. Wilson reported to Washington that three other agreements were reached but not put in writing. These were that the press would be free of censorship, that Díaz and Huerta would cooperate to restore order, and that Madero's ministers would be released. Significantly nothing was said about the disposition of Madero and Pino Suárez. Two days after the signing of the pact Ambassador Wilson assembled the diplomatic corps to discuss recognition of the new regime. That same day he reported to the State Department that a wicked despotism had fallen and that the new government was firmly in control; at the same time he requested instructions for recognition. Wilson strongly favored extending official recognition and on February 21, as dean of the diplomatic corps, read a statement of congratulations to Huerta. Taft remained cautious, however, and in the closing days of his administration reluctant to take any steps that would commit his successor to a given line of action. He rejected both the advice of his ambassador to recognize the Huerta government and the clamoring of United States liberals who urged intervention to overthrow the tyranny.[10]

The personal aspect of the tragedy had yet to be played out. On the day of the coup Gustavo Madero, the president's brother and principal adviser, was taken by his political enemies with Huerta's connivance, tortured, and finally killed. Huerta explained to Wilson that soldiers had killed him without orders, and Wilson accepted the story. Wilson also took Huerta's word that he had taken every precaution to guard Madero and Pino Suárez. Secretary Knox informed the ambassador that the murder of Gustavo had created a bad impression in the United States and that he was pleased to learn that the captured president and vice president were under protection. The Cuban Minister Manuel Márquez Sterling and the other members of the Madero family, however, were fearful for the safety of the prisoners. On February 19 Madero and Pino Suárez finally resigned their offices supposedly with promises of safe conduct from Huerta. On that same day the Cuban minister wrote Wilson requesting his assistance to protect them. Wilson again visited Huerta on February 20 with the German minister, and at the request of Madero's wife asked for the safety of the prisoners. He urged Huerta to take every precaution to prevent their death except by due process of law. Finally Wilson reported to the state department that Huerta had asked him on February 19 whether Madero and his vice-president should be exiled or confined to a lunatic asylum and that he responded that Huerta ought to do what he thought best for the peace of the country. Knox sent an urgent wire in return that such a consultation placed a responsibility on him for their fate and that the department hoped that the prisoners were not being subject to cruel treatment. Despite the urging of fellow diplomats, his own government, the Madero family, friends of the prisoners, and concerned people to use his influence to protect Madero and Pino

---

[10] Berta Ulloa, *La revolución intervenida: relaciones diplomáticas entre México y Estados Unidos (1910–1914)* (México: El Colegio de México, 1971), pp. 53–55, and Kenneth J. Grieb, *The United States and Huerta* (Lincoln: University of Nebraska Press, 1969), pp. 36–37, argue that the Taft administration was prepared to recognize the Huerta regime if an agreement could be reached over claims.

Suárez, Wilson took no further steps to save them. On the night of February 22, 1913 Madero and Pino Suárez were assassinated. Given Wilson's penchant to see what he wanted to see, it is conceivable that he simply could not credit his champion Huerta with the foul deed of murder. In later years he claimed that he did not realize that the prisoners were in danger. Whatever the truth, Wilson must share largely in the blame for the deaths of Madero and Pino Suárez, if only because of criminal negligence.[11]

III

Woodrow Wilson of the Democratic Party was elected president of the United States in November 1912 in a three-cornered race with Theodore Roosevelt running on the Progressive Party platform and William H. Taft seeking reelection as a Republican. The issues were largely those of domestic reform, and although Wilson won only 42 percent of the popular vote, he could hardly be considered a minority president on the issues, since the program of his principal contender, Roosevelt, was scarcely distinguishable from his own. With the political tides running so strongly for domestic change, it is not surprising that Wilson devoted little attention to foreign affairs in his campaign and none at all in his inaugural address. Moreover, within the foreign policy field, Latin America had never much attracted his attention. In his public writings and personal papers he made few remarks of any importance about the area. In some essays that he wrote between 1889 and 1901 he said in passing that the people of Latin America had apparently not developed the proper character and the experience necessary for democratic government. However, in his *History of the American People* (1902) he branded Polk's conquest of Mexican territory in the War of 1846 an "inexcusable aggression." Despite his overriding concern with domestic problems, Wilson's administration is most widely remembered for his foreign policy ventures, and his first term primarily for his Mexican relations.

---

[11] For a review of the latest findings see Cole Blasier, "The United States and Madero," *Journal of Latin American Studies* Vol. IV (November 1972), Part 2, pp. 207–231.

Much of Wilson's foreign policy can be explained only by his personal beliefs and attitudes. Brought up in stern Southern Presbyterian surroundings, Wilson never lost a certain puritanical approach to life that he adapted to politics. He sought "truth," and once having determined that he had found it, would rarely change his mind on any issue, political or other. Believing too in strong presidential leadership, his attitude toward truth made it extremely difficult for Wilson to compromise differences. In fact he tended to be intolerant of criticism and frequently believed that opposition to him resulted either from an ignorance of the facts or from the defense of narrow personal interests. With this sense of moral righteousness he attempted to conduct foreign policy and international affairs in the same way that he conducted domestic politics, that is, to strong-arm measures through the opposition, whether it be Congress, a dictator, a foreign minister, or the British government. As a consequence Wilson rather often acted as his own secretary of state since he mistrusted the pacifistic William Jennings Bryan on the one hand and the conservative corps of foreign service officers on the other. Despite his inexperience in foreign affairs, Wilson was not slow to develop a policy toward Latin America, primarily the circum-Caribbean area. On March 11, 1913, he stated that just government must always rest on the consent of the governed and that his administration would show no sympathy toward those who seized power to advance their own interests and ambitions. By introducing moral considerations, that is, a "legitimacy doctrine," into United States recognition policy in so blunt and straightforward a manner, Wilson not only abandoned tradition but launched the nation on the perilous course of establishing itself theoretically as the guardian of the political morals of all other states.[12] While previous administrations had at times used a legitimacy doctrine to delay recognition, the action was normally a thinly disguised excuse to extract some tangible

---

[12] Grieb, *op. cit.*, p. 44, points out Wilson's inconsistency in applying his legitimacy doctrine, for example, in recognizing certain Peruvian and Chinese regimes that seized power by force and even murder, and suggests that Wilson's strict application of his policy toward Mexico may have been influenced by his concerns over stability in Central America, particularly in Panama because of the Canal.

concrete concessions. The negotiations over the recognition of Díaz from 1876 to 1878 illustrates this point. But Wilson did not bargain, especially with those Mexican leaders of whom he disapproved.

For the Mexican "people" Wilson had sympathy, idealistic hopes, goodwill, and a large measure of misunderstanding. He regarded Mexicans as Americans, but perhaps not quite as advanced economically and politically. Despite some earlier statements about Latin American characteristics he believed that Mexico was ready for democracy, United States style, and that free elections and adherence to constitutional procedures would solve its problems. With his penchant for personal problem solving and with Mexico his first major international problem, Wilson virtually alone conducted United States relations with Mexico, however unprepared he may have been. He bypassed normal diplomatic channels by using a host of special agents or personal representatives and by keeping negotiations in his own hands. Wilson personally wrote almost every major dispatch to Mexico between 1913 and 1915.[13]

Upon taking office on March 4, 1913, Wilson was advised both by his assistant secretary for Latin America and by his ambassador in Mexico, Henry Lane Wilson, to recognize the Huerta regime. Even if Wilson had not himself considered the regime immoral or had contemplated a new approach to United States foreign policy, he might well have delayed recognition because of the shock the American public was expressing through its newspapers over the assassination of Madero and Pino Suárez. Ambassador Wilson himself was attacked in the United States press for his alleged role in the events of February, and President Wilson's own determination not to support wicked governments as demonstrated in his March 11 speech clearly forecast the policy that was to follow. Some official United States government statements gave the impression that the United States intended to recognize Huerta although not at that time, but Wilson's first statement directly on the subject in April said that it was some way off and might never happen.

---

[13] For a review of Wilson's attitudes about Mexico see Bemis, *op. cit.*, pp. 168–169, and Cline, *op. cit.*, pp. 139–141.

He added that the de facto government might be recognized as the Provisional Government after it had established peace and demonstrated that it could run the republic. United States policy thereafter was to withhold recognition until the fighting stopped and constitutional elections could be held throughout the country. Secretary of State Bryan closely coordinated his own dispatches with those of the president. He inquired of the ambassador in Mexico about the popular support that Huerta enjoyed and about the possibilities of achieving peace. He counseled the Ambassador to urge mediation and concessions on Huerta to achieve that peace. Huerta's response was a hardening of his own position. Early in May he told Ambassador Wilson that he considered the United States refusal to recognize his government as susceptible to an unfriendly interpretation. As a veiled threat he also informed him that Mexico was not ready to settle the claims discussions that had been underway. A few days later Huerta issued a statement that only routine negotiations would be handled with the United States Embassy. This move resulted only in the alienation of the ambassador and had no impact in Washington.

In the meantime President Wilson began to widen his contacts in Mexico. In mid-April he had requested William Bayard Hale to go to Mexico and report on events there for him. At the same time the president continued to press the embassy to get Huerta moving to set up concrete conditions that would restore peace and justice. In specific terms this meant the holding of elections, the guarantee of an amnesty, and the observance by Huerta of "his original promise not to be a candidate." President Wilson offered the good auspices of the United States as a mediator between Huerta's forces and those of his enemies. The problem with this United States demand was that the Pact of the Citadel had never promised specifically the holding of elections, that Huerta had never ruled himself out as constitutional president, and finally the enemies of Huerta had never indicated any desire for mediation—and Wilson had never attempted to ascertain their sentiments in this respect. As added pressure, President Wilson permitted the United States-Mexican Arbitration Treaty to lapse in late June. In the midst of these events Hale made his report from Mexico. He contended that the ambassador bore a large share of the responsibility for the *Decena Trágica* and that the government that retained him also shared that guilt. Shortly thereafter Wilson suggested the ambassador's recall. Secretary Bryan ordered him home by mid-July, and in August Henry Lane Wilson was dismissed from the service.

President Wilson further increased the pressure on Huerta. Besides recognition, one of his earliest concerns was the licensing of arms under the Congressional Resolution of 1912. Since he remained indecisive for several months, arms continued to pass both to Huerta and to his enemies. As Wilson perceived that Huerta was not responding positively to his conditions for recognition, he announced in mid-July that Huerta had refused to establish conditions for peace and to hold constitutional elections, which was not true. At the same time Wilson initiated a slowdown in arms sales to Huerta and in late August finally cut them off entirely. During the summer he also appointed another unofficial representative, John Lind, former governor of Minnesota.[14] Some United States newspapers reported that Lind had instructions to secure Huerta's resignation, but his orders were not so bluntly stated. His terms included the assurances that the United States had no intention to intervene militarily in Mexican affairs, but that the United States sought a peaceful solution to the Mexican strife through an armistice, the establishment of a provisional government, the retirement of Huerta from the presidency, constitutional elections with the participation of all parties, and the assurance of Huerta that he would accept the elections results. When Lind arrived at Veracruz he conferred both with Hale and with Admiral Fletcher, the commander of the United States naval squadron in the area. The Mexican government protested his arrival on a warship and made some difficulties about the propriety of his accreditation. Despite these irritants, the Mexican secretary of foreign affairs, Federico Gamboa, received Lind and conversations began about mid-August.

---

[14] On the Lind mission, see George M. Stephenson, *John Lind of Minnesota* (Minneapolis, The University of Minnesota Press, 1935).

The appointment of Gamboa to the department of foreign affairs in August signified that Huerta had adopted a policy of evasion to replace his previous confrontation tactics. Gamboa, as strongly anti-United States as his predecessor, was difficult to deal with, as Lind reported. In reply to Lind's proposals, Gamboa responded with sharp rejection. He argued that friendship and peaceful relations, of which Lind spoke, could be demonstrated by the United States through recognition, and that without official recognition, the Mexican government could not consider the proposals. He also rejected negotiating with the regime's armed opponents who called themselves "constitutionalists," but whom the Huerta government labeled bandits. Lind's counterresponse was that Wilson did not contemplate recognition under existing circumstances. Lind then informed Wilson that Huerta needed money, and proposed a loan. With Wilson's approval, Lind offered the help of the United States government in arranging a loan for Mexico if Huerta agreed to an armistice and prompt elections. Lind's peremptory action in demanding a response the same day the note was delivered and his hasty departure for Veracruz when his time limit expired served only to enrage the Mexican government. Gamboa, in a reply more bitter and sarcastic than his first response, regarded the offer of a loan as a bribe. He brushed off the threat of intervention or of recognition of his enemies since a U.S. Senate resolution on intervention had been overwhelmingly defeated by the Democrats on Wilson's orders, and the "constitutionalists" had not even formed a government. In that same letter, sent to Lind in Veracruz, the Minister noted, however, that the law barred Huerta from standing as presidential candidate in any election to be held. Lind interpreted this latter statement as an agreement to United States terms, and on August 27 wired Bryan to this effect. Bryan, and Wilson too, accepted this interpretation and ordered Lind to stay in Mexico. With this information Wilson made his first major public statement on Mexico, going before Congress to explain his policy. He argued that patience had been necessary but that by offering to mediate the trouble the United States had done its duty. The next step he said was up to Huerta, that is, to resign. Since some fighting might continue, he urged United States citizens to leave the country, but he promised protection for those who remained. And finally he announced that the United States would stay neutral by embargoing arms to all contenders.

The relaxation of tensions that followed this last interchange proved only the calm before the storm. Huerta did call for elections for October 26, and talked of turning the government over to a constitutional successor. The embassy reported, on the other hand, that despite these public statements, the government was making preparations to rig the elections. Then in late September the "constitutionalists" in the north won several victories on the battlefield and their supporters in the Congress tried to force changes in Huerta's cabinet. Feeling his power slipping away, Huerta took drastic action. On October 9 he called a cabinet meeting in his home, and there one of his supporters recommended closing Congress. The other members of the cabinet opposed the move, but Huerta approved the idea and drew up a list of deputies to be arrested. That evening when Congress met, the government threw troops around the legislative hall and arrested the proscribed members. President Wilson immediately branded the scattering of Congress an act of bad faith and a violation of constitutional guaranties. He said it destroyed all possibility of fair and free elections and gave notice that neither the elections nor the government elected would be recognized as valid by the United States. Secretary of State Bryan also wired the United States chargé to inform other diplomatic representatives in Mexico that the United States expected their countries to withdraw recognition. In the United States press, the general and immediate reaction was that Huerta had destroyed his constitutional claim to rule. Many editors believed that Wilson's policy had proven correct, but a few, among them the editors of the *Washington Post* and the *New York Times*, argued that the United States should ignore the change and continue its current policy since the coup involved only internal Mexican affairs.

Wilson's response to Huerta's coup elicited no immediate favorable replies from any quarters but dragged him more deeply into the Mexican turmoil. The Mexican government held elections as scheduled on October 26. There was little or no open interference with the balloting, but as Lind reported from

Veracruz, voting was public and very few eligible voters turned out. Moreover the majority, who cast their votes for Huerta, consisted largely of soldiers. Huerta announced that since none of the candidates had received the necessary number of votes under the provisions of the Constitution of 1857, he would continue as provisional president. In the meantime the other powers, whom Wilson had requested to withdraw recognition, gave at most noncommittal replies and Huerta continued as a consequence to receive money and arms from Europe. In response Wilson prepared a blistering memorandum to the powers and planned to dispatch it after the elections. He changed his mind, however, and delivered the essence of the document in a major policy speech at Mobile, Alabama on October 27, the day after the elections. Although his speech referred to Latin America and the powers in general, it was clearly directed to Great Britain and the Huerta government. He warned that economic concessions granted by Latin American countries to old world powers were harmful and that businessmen had handicapped the development of Latin America. He insisted further that old world powers based their foreign policies on sordid material interests that retarded the growth of political liberty. The United States, on the contrary, wanted to assist Latin America on terms of honor and equality, desired to protect Latin America from these overseas pressures, and had no territorial designs. Much of the speech was pure rhetoric, since Wilson did not, and had no intention to, establish any sort of agency or institution to grant aid to Latin America. Neither did he contemplate any specific acts of retaliation against the European powers. Instead, the speech was a sharp warning to Europe to limit its financial stake in the Western Hemisphere. The speech caused some consternation within the State Department itself, and the counselor of the department pointed out to the president that the United States often based its foreign policies on the same sordid motives that he attributed to the Europeans.

United States policy became still more aggressive. Wilson was determined that Huerta resign. During the fall of 1913 he apparently reached an understanding with the British that in return for administration support to equalize toll rates through the nearly completed Panama Canal, Great Britain would follow the United States lead on Mexico. Although the evidence for this understanding is not firm, the fact remains that after the United States secret demand for Huerta's retirement on November 1, the British began to swing behind the United States position. In a circular telegram to United States foreign missions, Wilson instructed his representatives to make known confidentially to foreign governments not only that Huerta must retire but that the United States must use such measures as necessary to force his retirement. The instruction also stated that the United States would not recognize acts of the Huerta government and invited the powers to impress upon Huerta the need to retire. Following this request the British ambassador led a group of European diplomats in urging Huerta to resign. He refused, probably with the knowledge that some of the powers were not really opposed to him.

The European continental powers regarded Wilson's policy as impractical and idealistic. The continued disorder in Mexico and the consequent economic disruptions were widely attributed to Wilson both in Europe and in the United States. American investors not only complained about their losses but began to exert pressure through Congress for direct intervention if necessary to restore order. Nationalist elements within the Republican Party also demanded that Wilson take drastic measures. Lind once more returned to Mexico City. He was not well received and acted badly. He talked of intervention and even believed that many Mexicans would welcome it. He directed the United States chargé to deliver an ultimatum to Huerta to dismiss his illegally elected Congress. Assuming that Huerta would ignore the ultimatum, Lind returned to Veracruz. He then urged Wilson to get rid of Huerta through civil war, that is, by opening the frontier to arms exports to the "constitutionalists" and by setting up a naval blockade, and if it failed, to use armed intervention. Wilson was not ready yet for such a policy, and Lind finally left Mexico in January 1914. Despite the threats and the pressures, at the end of 1913 Huerta was probably as strong politically within Mexico as he ever was. His government took a position of national resistance to the American threat, and by posing as a defender of national interests, Huerta was able to win considerable support. As the danger of intervention increased, many Mexicans rallied around him as a symbol of national independence.

In the meantime, within weeks of Huerta's coup against Madero, several armed uprisings in northern Mexico denounced the new regime. The most important of these politically was led by the governor of Coahuila, Venustiano Carranza, an aging landowner of modest means, a former Senator under Díaz, a former Reyista, and at the end a follower of Madero. Cold, haughty, arrogant, and intolerant of opposition or criticism, he was to be a mean match for the equally self-righteous Woodrow Wilson. While Carranza was initiating his revolt and proclaiming himself First Chief of the Constitutionalist Armies, similar uprisings were occurring in the other northern states of Sonora and Chihuahua. In Sonora, Alvaro Obregón rose to prominence in the midst of several very able military and political leaders, and in Chihuahua former bandit, muleteer, and revolutionary follower of Madero gunned his way to power with a band of like-minded desperadoes. His name was Doroteo Arango, better known as Pancho Villa. During the spring and summer of 1913 Obregón and Villa both formally acknowledged Carranza as First Chief, but while Obregón became eventually Carranza's military chief, Villa never in fact submitted himself to the First Chief's command. In the United States the emergence of a viable opposition (soon to be called the "constitutionalists") offered an alternative for both the populace and the government to support in place of the Huerta government, which virtually all rejected for being based on murder and tyranny.[15]

The first phase of the negotiations between the United States and Carranza took place in the fall and winter of 1913–1914. In September Carranza left Pablo González as military commander in Coahuila and crossed the mountains to Sonora. There on the border at Nogales on October 17 he formed a provisional government and appointed a cabinet. Wilson sent William Bayard Hale as his personal agent to negotiate with him. Hale

---

[15] For a concise account of the revolutionary politics of this period, see Lyle C. Brown, "The Politics of Armed Struggle in the Mexican Revolution, 1913–1915" in James W. Wilkie and Albert L. Michaels (eds.), *Revolution in Mexico: Years of Upheaval, 1910–1940* (New York: Knopf, 1969), pp. 60–72.

informed Carranza of United States opposition to Huerta, Wilson's contemplated lifting of the arms embargo, and the disinterest of the United States in territorial annexation. Carranza displayed little interest in Hale's points. What he wanted was unconditional United States recognition, no armistice, no participation in Huerta's election, and no United States mediation between Huerta and the constitutionalists. Wilson, however, was not yet willing to recognize Carranza because Carranza's victory over Huerta was far from assured, and his rejection of United States offers of assistance portended future difficulties. Moreover, after the United States had settled its problems with Great Britain, Wilson announced that his government would take all necessary measures to protect not only American but other foreign lives and property in Mexico. However, when Pancho Villa killed a British citizen, Carranza would not permit the United States to send an investigatory committee. He informed Wilson that the United States could protect its own but could not represent all the foreign powers in Mexico. Wilson announced a policy of watchful waiting.

During the winter of 1913–1914 the president of the United States for the first time began to see Mexican problems in more than just political terms. The man responsible for the education of Woodrow Wilson was Luis Cabrera, Carranza's representative in Washington. Cabrera eloquently expounded the ideals of the constitutionalists and convincingly presented the serious economic and social afflictions of his country. In particular he persuaded Wilson of the need for land reform. After his conversations with Cabrera, Wilson ordered the Secretary of the Treasury to wink at arms shipments to the constitutionalists, and on February 3, he formally removed the arms embargo.

Despite these moves Huerta continued to hold his own, Carranza remained stubborn in his own demands, and Wilson became still more frustrated. The explosion came in April. Early in 1914 United States warships began patrolling the Mexican Gulf Coast but undertook no blockade. The ships did call at various Mexican ports from time to time to purchase supplies. On April 9, the *U.S.S. Dolphin*, at anchor off Tampico, sent a whaleboat ashore with an officer (the paymaster) and seven men to purchase gasoline. As they were loading the supplies, a group of Mexican soldiers arrested them for trespassing in a forbidden area. The men were held for about one hour when they were released from arrest by superior authorities. They were delayed from leaving the dock for a short period of time but were finally released with an apology from the commanding officer of the area, General Ignacio Morelos Zaragoza. The commander of the United States fleet, Rear Admiral Henry T. Mayo, was not satisfied with this response. That same afternoon he demanded of General Zaragoza a written apology, court martial of the arresting officer, and a 21-gun salute to the American flag. The response to the demand and the salute were both to be carried out by 6:00 p.m. the following day. At that point the affair was carried by the chargé at the United States embassy to Huerta himself who offered an oral apology and promised an investigation of the conduct of the arresting officer. Wilson and the State Department supported the navy demands. For the next several days communications dragged on between the two governments without resolution. Then on April 14 Wilson announced that he was going to make a strong naval demonstration against Huerta and ordered all available ships from the Atlantic fleet to Tampico.

Neither Wilson nor Huerta wanted an armed confrontation, but their understanding of national honor and dignity led them to a catastrophe. Despite his plans for a naval demonstration Wilson ordered his naval commanders to refrain from hostilities, and his chargé in Mexico City approached Huerta with a conciliatory attitude. The chargé pointed out that, according to custom, in return for saluting the United States flag, an American battery would honor the Mexican flag with a 21-gun salute. Possibly out of fear that the United States would not honor its part of the bargain, Huerta wanted both salutes fired simultaneously. The United States would not deviate from established procedures, and Huerta would not bow to United States demands. A second impasse was reached. On April 18 Wilson sent his last ultimatum to fire the salute by noon of the following day or he (Wilson) would take the matter before Congress. Huerta made one last effort by suggesting that the United States government sign a protocol promising to return the salute. Wilson brushed that aside with little consideration. There the matter rested, and Wilson reported his view of the situation to a joint session of Congress on April 20, and requested authorization to use force against Mexico.[16] On that same day the United States consul at Veracruz reported that the steamer *Ypiranga* of the Hamburg-American line was due in port from Germany on the 21st with 200 machine guns and 15,000,000 cartridges and that Huerta had sufficient railway equipment to move them out rapidly to his forces. After a brief consultation with several members of his cabinet, Wilson gave orders to occupy Veracruz, ostensibly to intercept the munitions. United States personnel in Mexico were alerted in the early hours of April 21 and instructed to do everything necessary to protect United States citizens. The navy received its final orders to land troops at 8:30 a.m., and the occupation began about 11:30 a.m. The *Ypiranga* arrived an hour later and was temporarily detained. The German ship was later released, steamed out of Veracruz, docked at Puerto México, and unloaded its munitions, which Huerta then obtained. In the meantime United States forces met stiff resistance from Mexican naval cadets and civilians in Veracruz. When the fighting ended the United States had lost 19 killed and 71 wounded; the Mexicans had lost about 200 killed and 300 wounded, many of them civilian noncombatants.[17]

Having maneuvered himself into the occupation of Veracruz by a combination of personal stubbornness over a trivial incident, of moral self-righteousness about a dictator, and of a misunderstanding of Mexican nationalist attitudes, Wilson found himself tangled in a web that he did not know how to break out of. Not only was he appalled and unnerved when he learned of the extent of the fighting and the casualties, but he was disheartened by accusations of imperialism and interventionism, both of which he condemned. He desired to withdraw from Veracruz as quickly as possible, but no easy solution presented itself. The occupation did not topple Huerta, and a precipitous

---

[16] The House granted the authorization that same day and the Senate two days later, that is, after the troops had landed at Veracruz.

[17] The Veracruz "incident" is well told in Robert E. Quirk, *An Affair of Honor: Woodrow Wilson and the Occupation of Veracruz* (New York: McGraw-Hill, 1964).

withdrawal might only strengthen his political position and damage the prestige of the United States and Wilson's own moral stance. From this embarrassing situation the governments of Argentina, Brazil, and Chile rescued Wilson. Their representatives in Washington jointly offered their good offices to mediate the dispute. Both Wilson and Huerta accepted, and Carranza accepted "in principle." Niagara Falls, Ontario was selected as the meeting place.

In a confidential memorandum to the mediators Wilson made it clear that he expected to control the outcome. He emphasized that he wanted Huerta eliminated and a single provisional government established that would immediately elect a permanent government according to the Mexican constitution. Prior to the formal meetings the mediators asked for an armistice between Carranza and Huerta, and a strict arms embargo by the United States on both sides. Huerta and Carranza had both accepted the mediation reluctantly, and Carranza refused outright to send a delegation to Niagara Falls when he perceived that the conference meant to treat the Mexican political situation broadly, rather than the more narrow problem of United States evacuation of Veracruz. The Constitutionalists were beginning to win militarily, and Wilson in effect supported Carranza by delaying to call the group together in the hope of a decisive constitutionalist victory. The Mediation Conference formally opened on May 18. It could make no progress. The United States delegates had no powers to compromise, and Wilson would permit no discussion of the original dispute—the arrest of the sailors and the salute to the flag. He permitted only a discussion of the settlement of Mexico's internal problems. Although Wilson insisted that a new provisional government take over power from Huerta and that the provisional government be composed of Constitutionalists, Carranza still would not cooperate. He could not accept that a conference dominated by the president of the United States and held on foreign soil could determine Mexico's fate. To save face the mediators in late June drew up a protocol calling on the contending parties to establish a provisional government that would pledge a general amnesty and the holding of free elections. Such a government would be recognized by the United States and the ABC powers (Argentina, Brazil, and

Chile) and the United States would pledge that it sought no indemnity. Wilson only grudgingly permitted the United States delegates to sign, and the Constitutionalists refused to cooperate in any way. Except perhaps for avoiding further United States intervention in Mexico, the conference accomplished nothing. It failed to remove Huerta, establish peace in Mexico, provide for the holding of elections, or arrange United States withdrawal from Veracruz. It simply provided a forum for discussions while the principal course of events was being decided by the contest of arms. In the face of financial bankruptcy and military defeat, Huerta finally resigned on July 15, less than two weeks after the conference adjourned.[18]

Wilson had rid himself of Huerta, but at an enormous cost of harmonious relationships not only with Mexico but with much of the rest of Latin America. Mexican historians, publicists, and journalists have never forgotton nor forgiven the Veracruz occupation of 1914. As late as the 1950s it was considered politically damaging to have cooperated in any way with the occupation authorities even indirectly or to the benefit of the citizens of Veracruz. Such charges were leveled by his political opponents against the official party's presidential candidate, Adolfo Ruiz Cortines in 1952. In fact most Mexican writers have shown greater bitterness over Veracruz than over the War of 1846. One writer has suggested that while the material losses were far greater in the latter conflict, the motives were open and understandable, while in the former incident the imperialist motives were cloaked in morality and righteousness. While the scorn of Mexicans for Wilson's hypocrisy, as they perceived it, cannot be denied, it also appears that the nature of the imperialism differed substantially between 1846 and 1914. In the earlier period Americans were expanding physically across the country and seizing territory; in the latter period they were expanding financially, economically, politically, and culturally, and seizing not pieces of territory but underlying control of whole political systems. President Polk and General Scott did not care what sort of government they had to deal with in Mexico, although they may have had some personal preferences, while Wilson,

---

[18] Grieb, *op. cit.*, pp. 159–177.

who wanted no territory, insisted on a specific type of government, if not specific men to run it. He wanted to teach Latin Americans, he said at one time, to elect good men to public office. It was this attitude that so enraged Carranza, it was this attitude that for a short time strengthened Huerta as a resistor of United States aggression, and it was this attitude that contributed so greatly to the anti-United States nationalism that arose in Mexico during the Revolution. Significantly, Mexicans could easily assume that Wilson had virtually unanimous support in the United States. Young adventurers jammed the army recruiting offices, and newspapers of many political complexions supported Wilson's actions. In fact some Republican-oriented papers criticized Wilson for not marching on Mexico City, and were supported by jingoes, Republicans searching for an issue, and certain business interests. The opposition to Wilson's policies was less vocal. Pacifists, missionaries, socialists, YMCA officers, most of the diplomatic corps, and even some business interests opposed the intervention. Edward Doheny, representing United States oil and gas interests, telegraphed Wilson his opposition on the grounds that it would benefit British and other foreign interests. One indication of widespread popular apprehension was the general rejoicing when Wilson and Huerta accepted the mediation of the ABC powers and it became clear that war would not result. The best that can be said for Wilson is that his own motives were pure. He did desire to see popular and democratic rule in Mexico, he did see Huerta as a murderer and usurper, he had no desire to annex Mexico or to rule the country, and he did want to force the Mexicans to play fair according to their own laws and constitution. On the other hand, he did not understand Mexican national sensitivities or in fact the implications of his actions for Mexican internal politics or for future U.S.-Mexican relations.

IV

Huerta's resignation did not end Wilson's travail over Mexico. He still held Veracruz and could not evacuate with dignity. He had originally believed that Carranza and the Constitutionalists would welcome overt United States assistance. Wilson was very wrong, because Carranza viewed the Huerta affair as a conflict

between the United States and a usurper. Conceiving his cause
as the symbol of Mexican nationalism in its resistance to foreign
pressures, he took the position that Wilson was not the one to
say what was best for the Mexican people. With that premise,
he refused to accept aid from the United States if the price were
intervention. Furthermore, Wilson expected Carranza to call elections and to establish a representative, democratic government.
But Carranza had no intention of risking loss of control by opening up the political system to elections, parties, and factions. He
wished to continue his informal extralegal rule without benefit
of congress, courts, and judges. He wanted no incumbrances in
dealing not only with remaining Huertistas but also with the
opposing Zapata and Villa elements, all anti-Huerta and all revolutionary but, in fact, independent and mutually suspicious of
each other. By the end of August not only was it clear that Carranza was not preparing to call elections for the immediate
future, but that he believed elections were an internal domestic
matter, not a proper subject for discussion with the United
.States. Carranza wanted to discuss with Wilson only the evacuation of Veracruz.

In contrast to Carranza, Pancho Villa became openly conciliatory toward the United States, particularly as his relations with
Carranza deteriorated. Just after the occupation he told George
Carothers, another special agent, that the United States could
keep Veracruz and as far as he was concerned "hold it so tight
that not even water could get in to Huerta." He also said that he
would not permit that "drunkard" to draw him into war with
his friends. In response to these friendly gestures Wilson began
to look to Villa as the new leader of Mexico. The flamboyant
chieftain enjoyed a favorable press in the United States, and
beyond giving every indication of a willingness to accept United
States guidance, his public statements seemed to make him a
champion of agrarian and other social reforms. Despite this
rapprochement during the summer of 1914, there is no evidence
that Wilson seriously considered recognizing Villa as the government of Mexico. He did, however, toy with the idea of supporting Felipe Angeles, one of Villa's generals, as a candidate for the
provisional presidency.

When Huerta resigned in mid-July, the forces of Villa and

Carranza raced for the capital. Under the leadership of Alvaro Obregón, those of Carranza won out, and occupied Mexico City in early August. Obregón then hurried north to conciliate Villa in the hope of preventing open warfare. They reached an agreement that Carranza would not stand for president in the coming elections, but that he would remain at the head of the Revolution until the elections were held. Carranza countered by proposing the holding of a convention in Mexico City. Villa requested that it be held in neutral territory, and both sides finally agreed upon Aguascalientes. The convention opened in October. Villa promptly violated the agreement of neutrality by throwing his troops into the city. Carranza ignored the meeting, claiming that it was simply a Villista gathering. The convention nominated General Eulalio Gutiérrez as provisional president, but since he had no troops of his own, Gutiérrez had to depend on Villa. Carranza now openly repudiated the convention, and Obregón returned to Mexico City. As Villa began to march on the capital in mid-November Carranza withdrew to Veracruz. Upon his heels came Zapata, and Villa's forces finally arrived in Mexico City in December.

Internal conflict in Mexico brought United States forces to Veracruz, and internal conflict permitted them to depart under Wilsonian conditions. With Huerta's fall, Wilson became extremely anxious to terminate the Veracruz embarrassment. In addition to criticism in the United States and Mexico, he also had to consider the effects on the United States of the spreading conflict in Europe. After war broke out in August, the pressures increased. Despite the sense of urgency to retire from the city, the United States government planned for an orderly withdrawal in cooperation with Mexican officials in Carranza's camp. When Carranza called for a meeting of revolutionary chieftains and leaders in convention to discuss the question of elections, Wilson's hopes for a peaceful solution rose, and he instructed the State Department to begin negotiations for evacuation. In mid-September the United States informed Carranza of its intentions and requested him to name an official to take over the customs house and other offices. Carranza named the governor of Veracruz state to the post. Some delays ensued. United States officers in Veracruz wanted several Mexican officials to work directly with their United States counterparts to smooth over the transfer. The commanding general also reported his concerns about threats from the Constitutionalists to punish collaborators or former Huerta supporters. When approached on these matters neither Carranza nor the governor of Veracruz showed any interest in cooperating with United States authorities or making any sort of guarantees. At this point Wilson ordered a halt in evacuation proceedings and announced a continuation of the occupation until Carranza gave such guarantees. Carranza refused to comply since his position remained that the United States had no right to be there in the first place. The Aguascalientes Convention meeting in October and dominated by Villa's followers, however, ordered him to concede. Carranza refused to issue the decrees in defiance of the Convention, and Wilson remained unmovable. Privately, however, the Mexican official in charge of the office of foreign relations informed United States representatives that there would be no reprisals on persons and no attempts to collect back taxes and duties. He explained that Carranza could not make a public statement for political reasons. Wilson still would not concede. The military situation changed in early November with Villa and Zapata allied against Carranza and Obregón. The former had the larger and better equipped armies, and some of Carranza's forces deserted. In the face of his untenable position in central Mexico Carranza had to evacuate the capital and seek a new base. The logical city was Veracruz, and Carranza was now ready to negotiate. Within two days he had made all the guarantees that Wilson demanded. Wilson then ordered evacuation plans once more to get underway, but made it clear that he was not surrendering the city to any particular faction of the Revolution.[19] The troops started embarkation on November 23, and Constitutionalist forces moved in swiftly and orderly with no serious incidents with United States personnel. Despite his promises, however, Carranza quickly began to take reprisals on all those who had cooperated with the United States authorities; even teachers and policemen were fired from their jobs.

---

[19]Arthur S. Link, *Wilson: The Struggle for Neutrality, 1914–1915* (Princeton: Princeton University Press, 1960), pp. 262–263.

With the settlement of the Veracruz embroglio and the outbreak of World War I in Europe, Wilson began to turn his attention more and more overseas. He never forgot the Mexican "problem," but he became more inclined to conduct relations through regular diplomatic channels. From time to time, however, his personal touch may be discerned. From November 1914 to June 1915 relations between the United States and Mexico were not so much amicable as they were low-keyed. Various business interests both in Mexico and in the United States clamored for action including United States intervention, but Wilson generally ignored them. In Mexico Carranza struggled for supremacy against Villa and Zapata and lesser challengers. If Wilson had a policy during these months, it was still to seek a constitutional solution to Mexico's political problems. Specifically he hoped to see Carranza step down from power, the selection of a provisional government, and the holding of elections. In the meantime the civil war dragged on.

The critical battle came at Celaya in April when Villa's cavalry was mowed down by Obregón's entrenched infantry. Retreating north Villa was decisively defeated again at Silao on June 1. His losses had been heavy, and although he was never driven from the field, he ceased to be a major threat to Carranza. At the same time Zapata was confined to Morelos, and less important rebels were contained or eliminated. The cost of Carranza's victories were enormous in terms of deaths, suffering, and destruction.

For all his stubbornness and narrowness of outlook, Wilson was also a true humanitarian. He had been horrified by the casualties at Veracruz because he expected United States troops to be greeted as liberators. He was just as horrified at the slaughter of Mexican by Mexican. Wilson was no pacifist as his attitude toward the World War clearly indicates, but he was revolted by what he perceived to be senseless or criminal killings over the quest for personal power. Toward the end of May 1915 Wilson once more took a personal interest in the Mexican scene to try to bring the civil war to an end. There is some evidence that he contemplated intervention, but apparently was dissuaded by a report of Judge Duval West who had just returned from Mexico. West argued that most Mexicans would strongly oppose United States intervention and urged Wilson to seek to discover and support a legal successor to Madero. He also suggested that Wilson try to reconcile the warring factions. On June 2 the United States government delivered a note to the Carranza government (and simultaneously released it to the press) disavowing any intention of interfering in Mexican affairs but insisting that the United States could not stand by while Mexico fell into complete chaos. He urged the factions to unite under some program to end the fighting within a short time or the United States government would be "constrained to decide what means should be employed . . . in order to help Mexico save herself and serve her people." As threatening as the note sounded, it represented a softened version of an original draft. The reaction in Mexico was mixed. Mexico City newspapers and many political leaders throughout the country expected an armed invasion from the United States and some military forces were alerted. Zapata in his hills of Morelos scorned the threat. The political leaders of the convention acquiesced in Wilson's demand by removing their "provisional president" to seek an accommodation with Carranza's Constitutionalists. Carranza, however, receiving the news on June 6 of the great victory of his forces at Silao, knew that the Villa and the Convention forces no longer posed a serious threat. He did not deign to respond at all. On June 11 Carranza issued a manifesto to the Mexican people (and a copy was sent to Robert Lansing, the new United States secretary of state) proclaiming his right to the presidency and requesting early recognition from the United States. Once again Wilson seems to have misread events in Mexico. Despite the Constitutionalist string of victories through the spring and summer over Villa's forces, Wilson continued his attempts to eliminate Carranza from the presidency in order to achieve peace. His efforts were completely ineffectual and by mid-August Wilson apparently came to accept the inevitable.

In the meantime several Latin American powers had been meeting in an attempt to reach an agreement on recognizing a government in Mexico. When Wilson publicized his June 2 note to Carranza, the Argentine ambassador suggested to Secretary of State Bryan that the United States and the ABC powers coordinate their recognition policies. Wilson immediately accepted the offer because of its unilateral approach. The Latin

American representatives, eventually including Bolivia, Guatemala, and Uruguay, invited the various factions to submit to mediation. By the end of August all groups had replied affirmatively except Carranza, who did not respond until September 10. By that date Villa had been bottled up in Chihuahua and Zapata confined to Morelos. With this development Lansing espoused supporting Carranza outright although the Latin American group objected. The United States then requested Carranza to pledge himself to protect foreign lives and property and to comply with the duties and responsibilities as normally understood under international law. Carranza took the pledge without objection or delay. The participating Latin American states, followed immediately by the United States, recognized the Carranza regime as the de facto government of Mexico on October 19, 1915. At the same time President Wilson embargoed the shipment of arms to all groups in Mexico except the recognized government.[20]

A brief period of harmony followed recognition. Carranza responded affirmatively to a State Department note requesting the opening of talks on outstanding problems, including claims. He asked for and received permission to move troops across Texas, New Mexico, and Arizona to reinforce his garrison at Agua Prieta across from Douglas, Arizona. In October 1915 Villa completely surrounded Agua Prieta with his forces. The town was important because Villa had lost all contact with the outside world both by land and sea. Carranza's men poured into the town, and United States troops dug in across the border in Douglas. The attack came on November 1 and Villa suffered a bloody and disastrous repulse. He retreated from the area, rested a few days, and then turned south and attacked Hermosillo. After another overwhelming defeat some of Villa's units began to desert.

Despite his military disasters, Villa was still a regional force to contend with. Bitter at Wilson for abandoning him by recognizing Carranza and enforcing the arms embargo, he sought revenge on his two enemies. On January 10, 1916 a group of armed men led by a Villista colonel stopped a train at Santa

---

[20] Robert E. Quirk, *The Mexican Revolution, 1914–1915. The Convention of Aguascalientes* (Bloomington: Indiana University Press, 1960), pp. 253–283.

Ysabel, a cattle-loading station some miles west of Chihuahua station. They forced a party of 17 United States citizens (mining officials, engineers, and technicians) and their Mexican assistants off the train. They robbed the Mexicans and killed all but one of the Americans, mutilating the corpses. The Americans were in the area under Carranza's protection to open a mine. A popular uproar ensued in the United States, but Wilson refrained from threatening the Mexican government. Carranza promised to punish the perpetrators of the massacre, but he could not spare sufficient troops for an adequate combing of the vast areas of Chihuahua. The rest of the country was still far from pacified. He needed his troops not only to keep order in many cities but also to fight a large scale Yaqui Indian uprising and the continuing Zapatista rebellion in Morelos. Wilson remained patient in the face of continuing pressure in the United States, particularly with a congressional resolution of March 7 that called for armed intervention to protect United States citizens.

Although Villa's personal responsibility for the Santa Ysabel attack has not been definitely established, his leadership of a raid on an American border town, probably for personal reasons, forced Wilson's hand. Among the many border communities was the insignificant town of Columbus, New Mexico. In the predawn hours of March 9, a detachment of Mexican raiders under Villa's direct command attacked the town after careful planning and reconnoitering. Although the attack came as a surprise, the local inhabitants and garrison reacted quickly and drove off the invaders after a firefight lasting for several hours. Seventeen soldiers and civilians were killed while the raiders lost about 100 men and considerable equipment.[21] The raid actually constituted a minor incident, but combined with the long-simmering disputes between the two countries, the killings at Santa Ysabel, and the congressional resolution of two days before, Wilson felt

---

[21]James A. Sandos, "German Involvement in Northern Mexico, 1915–1916: A New Look at the Columbus Raid," *The Hispanic American Historical Review*, Vol. L (February 1970), No. 1, pp. 70–88, argues persuasively that while the Santa Ysabel affair bore all the marks of revenge, the Columbus raid avoided the brutalities and bestialities of the former. He presents good evidence that Villa hoped to gain redress from a bank and a merchant house that he believed had cheated him. Sandos is less persuasive on the German involvement.

compelled to take stern measures in an election year. On the evening of March 10, he ordered General Funston at San Antonio to send troops to Mexico to capture Villa. Until internal order was restored in Mexico several years later United States troops from that time did not hesitate to cross the border in pursuit of raiders.[22]

V

While not as sanguine as in 1914 concerning Mexican reactions, Wilson like most people in the United States still believed that United States forces would be welcomed by Carranza to track down a dangerous troublemaker. And for a while Carranza showed some understanding and cooperation. United States officials, however, never clearly appreciated the depth of Mexican hatred and suspicion of the United States, nor the fear of most Mexicans that the United States was awaiting only a favorable opportunity to seize more territory. The more responsible elements in the United States dismissed the clamorings and wild statements of United States jingoists and interventionists while the Mexican populace took them as representative of popular and official attitudes. Carranza feared United States armed invasion more than Villa's attacks. When word came to him of the Columbus raid, he ordered his commander at Veracruz to resist an expected United States marine landing. On March 11 he instructed his representative in Washington to inform the state department that his government should not be blamed for Villa's attack, and that the raid did not justify an invasion even if only to capture Villa. He suggested a renewal of the type of agreement made in the Diaz' years during the Apache wars, that is, reciprocal border crossings of armed forces in hot pursuit. Lansing immediately responded by giving Carranza the right to send troops cross the border on the assumption that Carranza would grant the same privilege. But Carranza's message referred to future raids not the recent attack on Columbus or a present pursuit of Villa. United States troops crossed the border March 15 under the command of General John Pershing.

For the first few weeks tensions and frictions between the

[22] C. C. Clendenen, *The United States and Pancho Villa: A Study in Unconventional Diplomacy* (Ithaca: Cornell University Press, 1961).

United States and Mexico both at the seats of government and in the military arena remained at a rather low level. Then, as United States forces entered the city of Parral, the hostility of the Mexicans became plainly evident. Carranza's troops and the local inhabitants attacked the Americans with stones and bullets, driving them from the town, killing two and wounding six. With Wilson's orders not to clash with Carranza forces, the Americans did not counterattack, but continued their frustrating task of chasing Villa over Mexico's northern wastes. On numerous occasions the United States troops encountered Villista bands and usually bested them. Villa, however, always escaped. By the end of May most of Villa's forces had been disrupted and scattered, and although Villa himself remained free, local Mexican authorities and people as well as Carranza began to demand that the Americans return across the border. During June tensions grew severely, and many Mexican groups, not all Villistas, raided United States territory. Then on June 21 a short but vicious firefight erupted at Carrizal between Carranza troops and United States forces. Both sides suffered about 25 percent casualties. War became a real possibility with popular passions aroused on both sides. Wilson mobilized the national guard and demanded release of prisoners taken at Carrizal. The Carranza government recognized the danger and released them June 30. Wilson did not desire a showdown either, and ordered Pershing to draw his forces into a fairly tight perimeter around Casas Grandes and Colonia Dublán. Then Carranza on July 4 suggested negotiation or mediation. In a prompt answer, the United States agreed to negotiate directly. The immediate crisis ended.[23]

Commissioners from both governments met at New London, Connecticut from September 6, 1916 to January 15, 1917 to negotiate the withdrawal of United States troops and the settlement of the question of protection for United States citizens. At first Luis Cabrera, representing Mexico, made a single demand for unconditional withdrawal of all United States forces. The United States commissioners insisted on some sort of security guarantee for the border. The talks dragged on until finally a

[23] Arthur S. Link, *Wilson: Confusions and Crises 1915–1916* (Princeton: Princeton University Press, 1964), pp. 195–221 and 280–318.

compromise was reached. Carranza, however, repudiated the formula for withdrawal and the meetings broke up acrimoniously on January 15, 1917. Wilson, however, was determined to push matters no further. The dispute with Germany was growing more bitter, and he wanted to free both his troops and his attention for what he conceived to be the more serious conflict. Moreover his own commissioners advised him to withdraw the troops, reestablish full relations with Mexico, and patrol the border vigorously against raiders. In late January he decided to withdraw unilaterally and on February 5, the last trooper crossed back into the United States at Columbus, New Mexico, where it had all started. Carranza had made his position stick.

Despite his stubbornness in terms of Mexican nationalism, Carranza was not a dreamer, but a practical politician, not a romantic but a pragmatist who clearly understood the limits of his position. As the war in Europe dragged on and the United States became more involved, the Germans sought assistance in various quarters. During 1916 the Kaiser's government granted full recognition to Carranza, and some Germans enlisted in his army; in November Carranza formally suggested Mexican-German cooperation, "going so far as to offer submarine bases to the Germans." The German government declined the proposal, but certain elements in the foreign office remained impressed with the possibilities opened by an alliance with Mexico.[24] In January 1917 the German Foreign Minister, Arthur Zimmerman, instructed the German minister to Mexico that, in the event of war between Germany and the United States, he should offer Mexico the return of her lost territories in exchange for a German-Mexican alliance. The minister was also to urge Carranza to negotiate peace between Germany and Japan and to help form an alliance of the three powers. On February 15 he was instructed to proceed immediately with the proposal. When the Zimmerman telegram came to light, Carranza would not respond satisfactorily to Washington's request to repudiate the German offer, but neither did he give the Germans satisfaction. Apparently he did not rebuff them bluntly, but it also appears

---

[24] Arthur S. Link, *Wilson: Campaigns for Progressivism and Peace 1916–1917*, (Princeton: Princeton University Press, 1965), p. 434.

that he did not entertain serious thoughts of entering into a German alliance.[25]

In the midst of these military and diplomatic developments, Carranza decided that the moment had arrived to begin the process of restoring constitutional order. With his victories over Villa and Zapata giving him control of most the country, he returned to Mexico City in April 1916 and two months later called for municipal elections, to be held in September, as the first step in his political program. Next he convoked a constitutional convention to consider a draft of a new constitution that would incorporate all reforms thus far instituted only by decree. Although Carranza tried to control the outcome of these elections, he was far from successful particularly in the choosing of delegates to the convention. Although the old conservatives were not represented, almost every shade of revolutionary doctrine, even Zapatismo, had its spokesman. As a result, the moderate draft that Carranza supported was substantially altered and the final product for more radical than Carranza desired. Those sections most strenuously debated included Articles 3, 5, and 130 on education, forced labor, and the role of the clergy. In addition two other articles, 27 and 123, introduced wholly new concepts into Mexican constitutional law, and almost from their inception embroiled the country in debates with the great powers, especially the United States. Article 123 constituted virtually the outline of a labor code. It included wages and hours regulations, protection of children and women in the work force, provisions for health and safety measures, and procedures for settling labor-management disputes. One scholar has summed it up this way: it "constituted the most enlightened statement of labor protective principles in the world to that date."[26] Article 27 appeared still more radical to the capitalist world. It subordinated property rights to societal needs. Drawing on this concept the article then provided for the expropriation of latifundia and the creation of small landholdings, placed all waters,

---

[25] Barbara W. Tuchman, *The Zimmermann Telegram* (New York: Macmillan, 1966), pp. 146–147, 152–153, and 188–189.

[26] Charles C. Cumberland, *Mexican Revolution: The Constitutionalist Years* (Austin: University of Texas Press, 1972), p. 347.

rivers, and lakes under the national patrimony, gave the national government ownership of all subsoil resources (including petroleum), and imposed restrictions on foreign economic operations in the country. Despite bitter debate over specific points, the delegates overwhelmingly supported these radical measures and, after two months of work, adopted the new constitution February 5, 1917. The next day Carranza announced presidential and congressional elections for early March, and by the provisions of the constitution itself, the new regime would take office May 1. With Mexico on the road to "constitutionalism," President Wilson regularized diplomatic relations by naming Henry P. Fletcher as ambassador in February and by extending de jure recognition in September.

VI

For the next four years no major crises troubled United States-Mexican relations, although no conflicts reached a final settlement. The governments of both countries were involved in problems that they perceived to be of greater consequence than their mutual relations. Wilson committed United States resources and manpower to the war in Europe, and Carranza focused his attention on consolidating his political position within Mexico. Villa's fortunes fluctuated within the northern region until his main forces finally disbanded in 1919. Zapata remained a thorn in the side until his assassination that same year. Economic dislocations and minor uprisings kept Carranza constantly on the alert for domestic turmoil and limited his interest in foreign affairs so long as no immediate threat of invasion materialized. As the Mexican elections of 1920 approached, Carranza gave clear signs that he had no intention of relinquishing power. He named as his personal choice of successor to the presidency his ambassador in Washington, Ignacio Bonillas. By 1920, however, Carranza's one-time military chief, Alvaro Obregón aspired to the office, supported by a formidable organized and popular following. The new Mexican labor organization saw in him its best hope of fulfilling some of the promises of the Revolution. When Carranza insisted on imposing Bonillas, a clique of northern chiefs, headed by Obregón, Plutarco Elías Calles, and Adolfo de la Huerta, rose in revolt. Within a month Carranza fled from

Mexico City, but he was assassinated before he could escape the country. An interim government bribed Villa to keep the peace, the remaining Zapatistas were pacified by promises of land, and Obregón, after the promised elections, became constitutional president in November. Wilson during these years threw all of his energies first into winning the European war and then into confirming the peace through his sponsorship of a worldwide organization, the League of Nations. After participating in the Versailles peace conference, he returned to the United States to persuade his countrymen to enter the League. He met strong and determined resistance, and in an effort to overcome it embarked on a nationwide speaking tour in September 1919. In the course of his *gira* he suffered a stroke, and for many weeks was confined to his bed; for over seven months he did not meet with his cabinet. Public opinion became confused by the political turmoil that resulted, and when the treaty of peace, including provision for the United States to join the League, came before the Senate, it failed to win the necessary two-thirds majority. At the general elections in November 1920, Wilsonian internationalism was rejected overwhelmingly by the voters, who elected Warren G. Harding, the Republican candidate, as president.

Despite the lack of major crises in Mexican-United States relations, no problems were solved during these years. The oil controversy, in many ways symbolic of the revolution vs. the status quo, flared briefly and then receded, but had to await almost 25 years for a final settlement. Mutual raids and unauthorized crossings of the border continued but in decreasing numbers. Finally Mexican fears of armed intervention and United States talk of forceful solutions to outstanding controversies pervaded all discussions and negotiations.

The most serious problem facing the Carranza and Wilson regimes in their closing years remained the question of foreign property rights in revolutionary Mexico. Many United States citizens claimed damages from ad hoc confiscations or violence, while others protested, as confiscatory, Article 27 of the Constitution of 1917, specifically those provisions that proclaimed the rights of villagers to land and the ownership of subsurface products by the state. The latter affected petroleum rights at the very moment that Mexican production was rising rapidly and becoming increasingly important to Allied forces in World War I.

Although Carranza's political instincts remained basically conservative, on the question of nationalism he was essentially radical. He strongly supported the constitutional provisions that claimed subsoil wealth as state property and also those that placed restrictions on foreign enterprises. In this position he (as spokesman for the Revolution) challenged two of the basic concepts of the capitalist world: the right of private property and the sanctity of contracts. The oil company executives, supported in large part by United States officialdom, met the challenge head-on. In principle there could be no compromise but, in practice, both sides demonstrated a measure of flexibility whatever the rhetoric of the moment. In April 1917 Carranza decreed a 10 percent tax on oil production. In June he refused to grant drilling permits on leases acquired after February 5, the date of the publication of the Constitution, although the Constitution of 1917 did not go into effect until May 1. Finally in February 1918 Carranza issued a sweeping decree that levied a royalty tax, claimed uncaptured oil as state property, and required registration of titles and special government-issued drilling permits for all leases including those acquired prior to February 5, 1917. Only wells already in production remained unaffected.[27]

Oil company officers and most United States officials concerned with Mexican affairs considered these regulations unreasonable if not confiscatory. The Wilson administration, now confronted with the war in Europe, laid down general guidelines that while the State Department should attempt to protect United States property it should avoid the risk of armed conflict, maintain oil shipments to the allied fleets, and as far as possible postpone a settlement of the basic dispute until after the war. The oil companies opted for a hard-line approach and found some support in second echelon State Department officials. Ambassador Henry P. Fletcher, supported by Colonel Edward M. House (Wilson's personal adviser), held to a soft-line particularly on the tax issue, with the result that the "Mexican Prob-

---

[27] *Ibid.*, pp. 392–395.

lem" remained relatively quiet although unresolved throughout the war years.[28] Carranza gave assurances that general confiscation was not contemplated, compromised on the question of registering titles, and finally issued "provisional" drilling permits in January 1920 when it appeared that production might decline. The oil companies paid the taxes under protest, increased their investments, and boosted production.[29] An uneasy balance prevailed.

At the close of the World War a vociferous minority in the United States demanded intervention in Mexico. Republican Party leaders renewed their attacks on Wilson for his failure to protect United States lives and property. Even within the administration Secretary of State Robert Lansing and Ambassador Fletcher believed that the time had come for a definite settlement. Oil company executives agreed, some advocating armed intervention. Continuing disputes over drilling permits became further complicated for Lansing by the Mexican imprisonment of a United States consul, William Jenkins, and by the incapacitation of President Wilson in October. Although careful to avoid an open break with Mexico, Lansing seemed to be moving toward a military settlement. In early December Senator Albert Fall, a Republican spokesman for various oil interests, introduced a resolution supporting a militant stance by the State Department and calling on the president to break diplomatic relations. At this point Lansing retreated, persuading Senate leaders to delay action so as not to endanger negotiations over the Jenkins case. After the Jenkins case was settled, Lansing and Fletcher attempted to persuade Wilson to take a firm stand on the issue of property rights, and by the end of the year they were openly stressing the desirability of breaking diplomatic relations. Wilson refused to follow this course, and when the

---

[28] Robert Freeman Smith, *The United States and Revolutionary Nationalism in Mexico, 1916–1932* (Chicago: The University of Chicago Press, 1972), pp. 94–99.

[29] Lorenzo Meyer, *México y Estados Unidos en el conflicto petrolero (1917–1942)* (México: El Colegio de México, 1968), p. 20 points out that the decade of the revolution (1911–1921) constituted the golden age of Mexican production. Mexico achieved its highest production in history in 1921, when it ranked second only to the United States in output.

oilmen and Carranza patched up a temporary truce in January 1920, the threat of a diplomatic break and armed intervention evaporated. Ambassador Fletcher resigned in disgruntlement over the lack of a final solution and Wilson dismissed Lansing for exceeding the administration guidelines.

Whatever the improbability of United States armed intervention in Mexico in 1918 and 1919, most Mexican leaders believed it to be a distinct possibility. Too many incursions had already occurred for the rhetoric to be taken lightly. Even Zapata isolated in his strongholds in Morelos came to fear that his alternatives would be a surrender either to Carranza or to the United States. Consequently late in 1918 his agents made inquiries on whether France could be counted on to restrain the United States or whether the Allied forces in concert would assist Mexico in the face of a United States threat.[30] Carranza, as noted above, always remained flexible on specific applications of Article 27, however adamant he remained in principle. He regarded armed intervention not only as a threat to him personally but to the whole revolutionary concept of Mexican nationalism.

Finally, unauthorized and illegal border crossings continued as minor irritants. Raids from Mexico into the border states of Texas, Arizona, and New Mexico continued with some frequency. Confidential instructions emanated from Washington to the commander of United States troops on the frontier to pursue raiders and attempt to capture and destroy them, but not to remain more than three days nor to penetrate more than 60 miles into Mexico. If United States forces met Mexican government troops, they were to pass on to them their information concerning the raiders and return to the United States. Carranza continued his protests. In June 1919 in his last major undertaking Villa moved on the town of Juárez across the Rio Grande from El Paso, Texas. Following his usual custom he attacked early in the morning, and while he did not overwhelm the defenders he could not be driven off. Fighting continued into the following day (June 16) with some shots falling into El Paso. The United States commander thereupon decided to move against Villa and

---

[30] John Womack, *Zapata and the Mexican Revolution* (New York: Knopf, 1969), pp. 179–180, 299–300, and 311–312.

so informed the Carrancista commander. United States forces attacked Villa the morning of June 17. Although Villa eluded the trap, his forces were largely dispersed, and his army in effect ceased to exist. The battle of Juárez constituted the last major invasion of Mexico by United States forces, although minor incursions continued in pursuit of bandit raiders. Throughout Carranza protested.

After a decade of revolution, Mexican-United States relations could never again return to a status quo ante. Although no major controversies had been definitively settled when the Carranza and Wilson administrations ended, the Mexican revolutionary leadership was virtually unanimous in its adherence to the principles of Article 27 that established national jurisdiction over all resources, foreign and domestic, past or present, within the country. Just as vehemently, United States leaders whether Republican or Democrat, business or political, insisted on the inviolability of contracts and the right to private property. They may have varied on specific issues and on tactics, but Senator Fall and President Wilson both consistently opposed the principles implied in Article 27.

For the first time in the modern industrial age a weak, underdeveloped, and economically penetrated state insisted on modifying if not abolishing its dependence on a highly industrialized, militarily powerful overlord. The struggle over drilling permits, registration of land titles, and salutes to the flag involved not only economic and political conflicts of interest but, more fundamentally, ideological and theoretical differences that defied compromise at the basic level. Economically the revolutionary leadership was determined to gain control over the petroleum industry not only for the material rewards that would accrue but, more importantly, for the control that it would give them over this vital resource, one of the core elements in the country's drive for economic modernization. Mexicans not foreigners, for good or ill, would make the major decisions in the economic development of the country, decisions that would influence virtually every realm of national life. For the same reason Carranza (and Huerta too) insisted so stubbornly in resisting Wilson's efforts to control constitutional and political developments in the country, sometimes at fearful costs. By 1920 the principle of national control over national life had been stated and sustained. However vigorously United States leaders rejected it, they were not able to make the Mexicans retract, although some compromises were reached on implementing devices. The struggle would continue while painfully and slowly a new relationship emerged.

CHAPTER VI

The Land and Oil Controversies: 1920–1945

WOODROW WILSON, LIKE TAFT BEFORE HIM, bequeathed to his successor the problem of recognizing a new Mexican regime. In the United States election campaign of 1920 both political parties pledged to deny recognition to the Obregón government until a specific agreement had been reached to arbitrate claims for damages and losses incurred by United States citizens primarily during the Revolution.

Obregón, on the other hand, anxiously sought recognition from the United States. Coming to power by coup d'etat and burdened with the suspicion of the assassination of his predecessor, Obregón needed an early ratification of his position both to solidify his domestic political situation and to assure his international status. These purposes were intimately linked because international recognition, especially by the United States, would ease his access to foreign loans that would strengthen him at home. And with Europe devastated by World War I the United States remained virtually the only source for major borrowings. The critical issues revolved about Article 27 and Article 123 of the Constitution of 1917. The former stipulated that subsoil rights resided in the state while the latter limited business rights by establishing the most advanced labor code of the day. As we have noted above, these socialistic and revolutionary concepts (some of pre-Marxian origin) ran directly counter to laissez-faire capitalistic doctrines of individual rights in private property and the sanctity of contracts. The United States government had complained that the Constitution and implementing legislation constituted ex post facto laws, a type of legislation condemned in the United States. These contrary positions were difficult to reconcile.

I

Once the new Obregón administration settled into office, the United States government again attempted to reach a definitive settlement on the claims problems, particularly the question of oil rights. Because of the continuing policy shifts of the Carranza regime, both the Harding and Wilson administrations were reluctant to accept verbal assurances from Obregón that Article 27 would not be rigidly enforced. In fact the Harding administration initially demanded a treaty, not a private promise or even an executive agreement on the matter in return for recognition of the Obregón government. Secretary of State Charles Evans Hughes argued that even if Obregón adhered strictly to such an understanding there was nothing to bind his successor. Obregón refused to sign a treaty, and for some months negotiations remained stalemated. In an effort to break the impasse Obregón prevailed on the Mexican Supreme Court in September 1921 to enunciate the doctrine that if the owners of oil properties had performed some "positive act" to develop their leases before the Constitution went into effect, their holdings would be secure. In other words, new oil leases would come under national control, but old grants would not. By May 1922 the Court had handed down five such decisions, thereby making the ruling binding on lower courts as precedent. Secretary of State Hughes tried to hold out for a treaty, but the affair had become such a cause célèbre that Obregón would have committed political suicide had he agreed to a treaty.

In the meantime political and business pressures in the United States had been building in behalf of recognition of the Mexican government. Some of the smaller oil companies favored a prompt settlement of differences and resented attempts by the major companies to dominate the negotiations as well as the industry itself. In addition various local chambers of commerce and business groups, particularly those with export interests, began to agitate for a normalization of relations. Even some large industrialists and several border state governors joined the campaign.[1] Most important, however, was the bondholders' association that feared Mexican repudiation of the debt if a political settlement could not be reached.

---

[1] Robert Freeman Smith, *op. cit.*, pp. 195–203.

Claims made by the holders of Mexican government bonds were recognized as falling in a different category of indebtedness from claims for confiscation or damages. Neither the United States nor the European governments insisted on arbitration for such claims. The United States government had never become involved in placing the bonds directly or indirectly, and the Second Hague Convention of 1907 had forbidden the use of force to collect such debts. Nevertheless the United States government was not totally uninterested in the affair, and contact was maintained with several representatives of banking interests, particularly with Thomas W. Lamont of J. P. Morgan and Company. In fact, the International Committee of Bankers on Mexico, for which Lamont became chief negotiator, was apparently founded as a result of discussions held at the State Department between the financiers and the diplomats. Moreover the Department requested that the Committee accept the policy of the United States as the "dominating influence in the operations of the group."[2] In June 1922 the Mexican government reached an agreement (Lamont-De la Huerta) with the bondholders to recognize $500 million of debts, including the railroad bonds, and to establish procedures for its payment.[3] Although the debt agreement did not produce the desired effects, a loan and formal recognition of Mexico by the United States, it did have a major impact on judgments in the department of state. Secretary Hughes began to retreat from his insistence on a treaty, and the Chief of the Division of Mexican Affairs counseled moderation and compromise. Obregón, for his part, perceived that his Doctrine of Positive Acts was an insufficient guarantee for Hughes and proposed bilateral talks on the whole range of Mexican-United States problems. Hughes readily accepted.

Each country named two commissioners to review jointly outstanding disputes and to report their findings to their respective governments. The commissioners met in quarters on Bucareli

---

[2] *Ibid.*, p. 129.

[3] Bazant, *op. cit.*, pp. 235–237. Most of this bonded indebtness dated from the Díaz period. The Madero government borrowed $20 million from a New York banking firm. Huerta borrowed $30 million from German and Swiss bankers to pay off the New York loan. Carranza and subsequent revolutionary governments recognized the debt but not Huerta's other borrowings. Carranza was unable to float any bond issues.

Street in Mexico City between May and August 1923 and succeeded in reaching some limited agreements. In an "extra-official
pact" (simply the signing of the minutes of the conference by
the four commissioners), the Mexicans on the agrarian issue
pledged their government to pay cash for expropriated property
in excess of 1755 hectares (in effect not to seize more than 1755
hectares of any holdings). The Americans agreed to receive bonds
in place of cash for expropriated properties up to 1755 hectares.
On oil the Mexican commissioners reiterated that they could
sign no treaty. In a "gentleman's agreement," however, they
pledged Mexico's adherence to the Doctrine of Positive Acts.
Finally, both sides agreed by formal conventions to the establishment of two claims commissions: a regular commission for the
settlement of the older more routine claims that had accumulated since the last agreement in 1868 and a special commission
to handle the more serious revolutionary claims.

For Obregón and his supporters the Bucareli Agreements, as
the settlements were called, paid off handsomely. In return for
"paper guarantees and legal debating points,"[4] he gained solid
political and economic advantages. With the successful conclusion of the Bucareli conference and the previous agreement on
the bonds, the new Coolidge administration recognized Obregón
de jure. Improved commercial relations and greater political stability strengthened the regime and enabled it to meet a severe
political crisis late in 1923. With Obregón's term ending in 1924,
the president had begun to consider his successor. Two candidates, both long-time supporters and followers, were preeminent.
They were Adolfo de la Huerta, the provisional president in
1920 and Obregón's Secretary of the Treasury, and Plutarco
Elías Calles, Secretary of Government in Obregón's cabinet.
These men represented the right wing and the left wing, respec-
tively, of the revolutionary ruling groups in the country. Obregón
chose Calles as the stronger of the two, but the choice led to a
severe split in the governing coalition, a split that produced a

---

[4] Robert Freeman Smith, *op. cit.*, p. 233. Many Mexicans, of course, do not
agree with the interpretation, and denounce Obregón for yielding to
United States pressure. For a particularly strong and well-argued different
interpretation see Antonio Gómez Robledo, *The Bucareli Agreements and
International Law*, translated by Salomón de la Selva (Mexico: The
National University of Mexico Press, 1940).

brief but bloody civil war during the winter of 1923–1924. When the revolt broke out, the United States government supplied Obregón with arms and munitions on a long-term credit basis from stocks in United States arsenals, and kept a tight embargo on any type of arms shipments by private firms. After several months of hard fighting the Obregón forces prevailed, and Calles was duly elected and inaugurated president in the summer of 1924.

The new president, although strongly nationalist and bitterly anticlerical,[5] was a moderate social revolutionary like his predecessors Carranza and Obregón. He sought to control foreign investment, to enforce the anticlerical provisions of the Constitution, to strengthen the power of the central government over semiautonomous political leaders and military chieftains, and to continue land distribution without disrupting production. He also gave strong support to urban labor organizations, but he appears to have been motivated more by a desire to build a power base than to improve the lot of the working man. Labor organizations were tightly controlled through a leadership tied to the president. Workers' demands were kept modest, and labor leaders were sacrificed for disloyalty or just for expediency.

When Obregón was assassinated in 1928 on the eve of his succession to the presidency for a second term, Calles called all the major political and military chiefs into convention to found a new political party. Partly because of his great prestige, and partly because of widespread fear of a renewal of revolutionary violence, Calles was able to prevail upon the convention to found the type of party and to name the type of provisional president that he (Calles) could control. Over the next six years and with three different presidents Calles remained the *Jefe Máximo*, using the now official party as a holding company to control the

---

[5] Early in 1926 Calles ordered the arrest and deportation of all foreign clergy and the enforcement of any constitutional provisions that prohibited Church ownership of real estate, Church operation of schools, and Church-sponsored communal societies (religious orders). Protesting bishops were exiled, and the bishops placed the country under interdict. See M. Elizabeth Ann Rice, *The Diplomatic Relations Between the United States and Mexico, as Affected by the Struggle for Religious Liberty in Mexico, 1925–1929* (Washington, D.C.: The Catholic University of America Press, 1959), pp. 58–68 and 88–90.

Mexican political system. Various reform measures ebbed and flowed, but the main thrust of these years was a slowing of reforms, a consolidation of power at the national level, and the clear emergence of a new elite.

Rocky, but not stormy, Mexican-United States relations characterized the early Calles era, and calm prevailed during the later years. A new bondholders' agreement (Pani-Lamont), negotiated in 1925, separated the railroad from the bonded indebtedness to improve debt service, but payments remained irregular and uncertain. More seriously, in December 1925 Calles pushed through the Mexican Congress a Petroleum Law and an Alien Land Law, the first comprehensive enabling legislation to Article 27 since the adoption of the Constitution. The former limited to 50 years the possession of oil properties acquired before 1917. The law violated the gentleman's agreement reached in the Bucarreli talks, and strong protests were voiced by the United States press and the recently arrived ambassador, James R. Sheffield. Relations became even more troubled when Mexico began to supply arms to Nicaraguan revolutionists while the United States government was supporting the incumbent Nicaraguan regime. Elements of the press and public, especially those representing threatened United States property owners, again began to demand intervention. The oil interests in particular tried to build up support for intervention, but President Coolidge proved more conciliatory. Moreover, the general mood of the United States by the late 1920s was to disengage from armed occupations in the Caribbean, not to expand them. On January 25, 1927, consequently, the Senate of the United States unanimously passed a resolution for continuing arbitration. Interventionist sentiment quieted immediately. Frustrated in, and criticized for, his efforts to support United States property interests in Mexico, Ambassador Sheffield submitted his resignation in July. In Sheffield's place Coolidge appointed to Mexico an old college friend, Dwight Morrow, a prominent banker and a partner in J. P. Morgan. Morrow was instructed to reach a peaceful solution, and Coolidge and Calles discussed mutual problems by telephone.[6]

---

[6] Bemis, *op. cit.*, pp. 217–218.

The Mexican government and people viewed Morrow with suspicion upon his arrival mainly because of his business connections. Partly because of his personality and partly because of intentions to deal fairly and sympathetically with Mexico's problems, Morrow quickly overcame much of the initial hostility manifested toward him. Small gestures, such as living in a Mexican-style house and sponsoring goodwill visits by aviator Charles Lindbergh and comedian Will Rogers, won him praise and even trust. He quickly established excellent personal and diplomatic relations with Calles, and in November 1927 suggested to the president that the renewed oil controversy might be settled by a judicial decision reaffirming the Doctrine of Positive Acts in a currently pending suit. Nine days later the Mexican Supreme Court so declared in the case of the Mexican Petroleum Company. In December, Calles recommended amending the Petroleum Law to conform with the court's ruling. Congress complied and the revision came into force early in January. Several remaining points of uncertainty were clarified by an exchange of notes, and new regulations, drawn up in conformity with the amendments, were devised in informal talks between the embassy and the Mexican government. The negotiators used the language of the Bucareli agreements whenever possible. Upon formalization of the amended regulations in March, the state department declared that all future questions on oil should be left to the Mexican courts. This settlement, in which the Mexican government regularized the rules of the petroleum game and the United States government recognized Mexican sovereignty on the oil issue, stood until 1938.[7]

On the religious question, which had assumed serious pro-

---

[7] Meyer, *México y Estados Unidos*, p. 186, sees 1927 as a major turning point in United States policy on the oil question. He argues that from that time the United States government never again gave unconditional support to the oil companies and that it began to admit the right of the Mexican government to regulate subsoil resources and other property rights; see also Stanley R. Ross, "Dwight Morrow and the Mexican Revolution," *The Hispanic American Historical Review*, Vol. XXXVIII (November 1958), No. 4, pp. 506–528, who argues that Morrow's successful handling of the oil controversy made it possible for him to seek an agreement on the religious question.

portions during 1927, Morrow worked hard but quietly to reach a settlement between the Catholic Church and the government. In April and May 1928 he arranged for John J. Burke, a United States Catholic priest, known for his liberal social views, to confer secretly with Calles to mediate between the exiled Mexican bishops and the government. A year later he arranged a third meeting, this time between two bishops and Provisional President Emilio Portes Gil. As a result of these conciliation efforts, a modus vivendi was reached, .and in June 1929 the bishops lifted the interdict imposed three years earlier; by the end of the year most of the *Cristeros*[8] had laid down their arms.

On a third issue, the settlement of claims, Morrow had little success (nor did Sheffield before him). In fact it appears that he had virtually nothing to do with the claims commissions and apparently exerted little pressure on the Mexican government to come to general terms. He did, however, interest himself in the problem of agrarian expropriations, and "pursued a policy of handling claims on an individual basis." His style was personal, his method informal, his results mixed. Many Mexicans have accused him of responsibility for slowing down the agrarian reform program in the early 1930s, but this position credits him with greater influence over Mexican policy than in fact he enjoyed. While it is true that agrarian expropriations declined, the basic conservatism of Calles must bear the primary responsibility.

After the Bucareli agreements were signed in 1923, Mexico and the United States engaged in some diplomatic fencing in the process of establishing the two claims commissions. Finally in 1925 the two governments agreed upon a Panamanian citizen

---

[8] The term *Cristero* describes those opponents of the Church policy of President Calles who took up arms in defense of Catholic interests with the cry of *Viva Cristo Rey*, "Long Live Christ the King." For a scholarly and vivid account of the religious strife and the United States role therein, see David C. Bailey, "The Cristero Rebellion and the Religious Conflict in Mexico, 1926–1929," Michigan State University, Ph.D. dissertation, 1969. Morrow's Role in the negotiations is minutely detailed in L. Ethan Ellis, "Dwight Morrow and the Church—State Controversy in Mexico," *The Hispanic American Historical Review* Vol. XXXVIII (November 1958), No. 4, pp. 482–505.

as the neutral umpire for the general commission and a Brazilian for the special commission. The groups did not function well and, after the Brazilian umpire disallowed the American claims for the Santa Ysabel massacre, the United States refused to present any further cases to the special commission. The general claims commission did little better. Of almost 2800 United States claims and over 800 Mexican claims presented, the commission had settled only 148 cases when it was finally disbanded in 1934. In the meantime European-Mexican commissions had arrived at a formula for settling the claims at 2.67 percent of face value. In 1934 a Mexican-United States treaty adopted this same formula for special claims, and in 1941 Mexico and the United States signed a convention in which Mexico agreed to pay $40,000,000 for full settlement of all property claims except oil.

II

As the elections of 1934 approached, Calles found himself under increasing pressure to select a candidate who had sympathy for the social and economic promises of the Revolution. The Jefe Máximo responded to the Revolution's left-wing elements by appointing a relatively young man who had a reputation for honesty and reform, Lázaro Cárdenas, governor of Michoacán. Calles also agreed to a so-called Six Year Plan, in emulation of the plans of the Soviet Union, calling for expansion of education, economic growth, and a stepped-up agrarian reform. With this program Calles believed that he had mollified the left and would be able to control the next president and the course of developments. In these expectations he was seriously mistaken because Cárdenas proved to be not only an able politician but a dedicated reformer. Traveling thousands of miles about the country during his election campaign, Cárdenas built up enormous popular and political support by demonstrating sincerity of purpose, an aura of ability, and warmth of personality. Shortly after taking office he began to challenge some of the major policies of the Jefe by pushing agrarian reform and expressing sympathy for striking workers. Behind the scenes he was also quietly building political support among second-level politicians and bureaucrats and making conciliatory gestures toward the Catholics. When the showdown came between

Cárdenas and Calles, the president could demonstrate more strength, and the Jefe eventually went off to exile in the United States. With his way cleared, Cárdenas proceeded not only with a vast agrarian program, but also with plans to reorganize labor, to reform the party, and to nationalize or control certain elements of the economy. Some of these brought renewed conflict with United States economic interests that attempted to solicit assistance from their government for protection.

The decade of the 1930s saw vast changes not only in Mexico but throughout the world including the United States. Reform was in the wind everywhere. In some places it led to revolution of the left as in Mexico, while in others to revolution of the right as in Nazi Germany. In the United States it led to modest reforms to improve living conditions for some of the less fortunate in society. The Great Depression was a major catalyst for change, but the depression did not bring about a United States revolution. However it did bring to office men who had some sympathy for revolutionary change and an understanding for governments that were attempting to improve the lot of city workers and farm laborers. Franklin Roosevelt, elected president of the United States in 1932, brought with him bureaucrats and diplomats with broader vision and perspective than the simple protection of every parcel of United States-owned property abroad or at home. They had some notion of the social utility of property, and while it may not have been as broad as the Mexican concept, it was not an alien idea. Negotiation and compromise were possible in United States-Mexican controversies, and these were sorely needed when the great conflict over oil rights appeared once again in Mexico in the late 1930s.

Throughout the Cárdenas years (1934–1940) Josephus Daniels served as United States ambassador to Mexico. Because he had been secretary of the navy at the time of the Veracruz occupation, he met initial hostility and distrust in Mexico. Like Morrow, he overcame this handicap by a friendly attitude toward Mexican revolutionary aspirations. By no means a revolutionary himself, Daniels always demonstrated sympathy and understanding for change and reform in Mexico even when he did not approve of specific measures carried out nor the methods by which innovations were enforced. Representing the New Deal of Franklin Roosevelt, committed to the nonintervention doctrine of the Good Neighbor Policy, and sympathetic toward nationalism and social reform, Daniels performed a successful balancing act between protecting U.S. interests and respecting Mexican sovereignty. He brought his own brand of liberalism into diplomacy. Although he enthusiastically supported broader commercial ties with Mexico, he counseled the State Department to move cautiously to protect private United States interests, arguing that such narrow views might jeopardize more important interests. He did not conceive his job as including the collection of private debts or the protection of high risk capital that expected large profits. The ambassador rebuffed bankers and businessmen who expected him to serve them. He believed that the United States government should not encourage United States investors to buy Latin American government bonds. On the other hand he frequently used his representational prerogative to speak for Americans who, he believed, had legitimate grievances.

In addition to the normal functions of diplomatic representation, Daniels had to face three major issues that created complications in Mexican-United States relations: a renewal of the church-state conflict, land reform and United States agrarian claims, and lastly the nationalization of oil. Although the oil problem was by far the most serious, prolonged, and potentially dangerous to harmonious relations, the other two initially seemed the more important. Two months before his appointment as ambassador, United States Catholic bishops had protested publicly against what they perceived as persecution of the Catholic Church in Mexico, and the prestigious Jesuit weekly *America* urged the new ambassador to intervene actively to protect religious freedom. Daniel's friend, Father John Burke, who had participated in the earlier compromise effort, reported that the Mexican church-state question was again becoming critical. Burke informed him, however, that the Vatican opposed armed rebellion and the clergy's participation in partisan politics. At the same time, he pointed out, the authorities, particularly state governments, were virtually abolishing religious practice by severely limiting the number of priests permitted in their jurisdictions. Despite these pressures Daniels wanted to stay aloof from the controversy. He made no allusions to it in his opening remarks in Mexico and, in fact, praised the regime for its social reforms when he presented his credentials. As far as Mexican officials were concerned, Daniels got off to a good start, but some editors of the United States Catholic press severely criticized him for implying approval of Mexican church policy.[9]

The Mexican church-state issue was primarily an internal matter and, except for agitation by U.S. Catholics over the plight of their coreligionists in Mexico, would never have constituted a diplomatic question. Unfortunately for Daniels, shortly after the Cárdenas inauguration the Mexican Congress began debate in the fall of 1934 on amendments to the education articles in the constitution. The nature of the debate indicated that government leaders were planning further restrictions on religious education and the introduction of "socialist" education into the public school curriculum; both measures would heighten the fears of Mexican Catholics. In the United States various organized Catholic groups began to demand action to help Mexican Catholics, attacked President Roosevelt for his hands-off policy, and demanded the recall of Ambassador Daniels for a speech he had made the previous July in praise of Mexico's drive for universal education. Daniels' address to students in the United States was interpreted as support of the antireligious nature of Mexican public education. Through the remainder of 1934 the attacks increased in intensity and by the following year manifested themselves in government circles. In January 1935 Senator William E. Borah called for a Senate investigation of religious freedom in Mexico to determine if American rights were in any way being violated. Catholics in the House of Representatives introduced at least four resolutions during the first six months of the year calling for action, and state legislatures in four states, including New York and Illinois, petitioned Washington to take some measures. Finally in July, 250 members of the House of Representatives signed a petition asking for an official investigation of religious rights and facilities of United States Catholics in Mexico. Roosevelt was determined not to

---

[9] E. David Cronon, *Josephus Daniels in Mexico* (Madison: The University of Wisconsin Press, 1960), pp. 85–87.

intervene and quietly shelved the various resolutions and petitions. The administration did not ignore the issue, however. In fact the political pressures within the United States made the administration acutely conscious of the religious problem in Mexico and forced it to abandon its policy of strict abstention from Mexican domestic affairs. The State Department instructed Daniels to approach the Mexican government quietly about American concern. Behind the scenes the ambassador tried to convince the authorities to ease up on religious restrictions, particularly to permit more churches to open. Since Cárdenas himself apparently desired a rapprochement with the Church, and an easing of the more burdensome restrictions imposed in some states, the American representations, carefully handled as they were, caused little or no friction. In May 1936 Daniels persuaded Cárdenas to permit a public funeral procession for Pascual Díaz, the deceased Archbishop of Mexico City.

Agrarian claims proved far more difficult to negotiate than the Church question, and Daniels frequently found himself at odds with official State Department policy. Secretary of State Cordell Hull, a firm believer in private property, insisted that full and prompt payments be made for all properties expropriated from United States citizens in the land reform programs. Daniels opposed this view throughout his tenure despite his representations to the Mexican government in obedience to United States policy directives. Daniels believed it unreasonable for his government to expect that United States landowners would be spared expropriation while Mexican landowners were having their lands taken, and unrealistic to expect full and immediate compensation. He argued that the easiest course for the United States to take was to try to obtain special concessions for persons who had particularly good claims, especially for modest-sized holders who might well have been treated illegally under Mexican law.

After the agreement on special claims in 1934, the embassy attempted to negotiate for the settlement of agrarian claims up to 1927. When it became apparent that no solution could be reached, the embassy and the Mexican government agreed to turn the question over to the General Claims Commission established by the protocol of 1934. At the same time Daniels requested that the Mexican government refrain from further expropriations of United States property until payment had been made for those already taken. The Mexican government refused, and no further progress was made for several years. After the expropriations of oil in 1938 and Mexican promises to pay for the properties taken, the United States again pressed the issue of payment for expropriated lands. This time the Cárdenas government responded more affirmatively, probably in the belief that if its promises on oil were to be accepted it had to make some gesture on the land question. A few weeks after the oil expropriation, Cárdenas offered to make monthly cash payments on the agrarian debt, particularly to small claimants such as the farmers in the Yaqui valley, and to deliver Mexican government bonds to the large landholders. The U.S. State Department objected to this discriminatory practice, but Daniels reminded the Department that the United States itself had previously taken the position that the Yaqui farmers were a special case. He also informed the Department that Mexico could not possibly pay off all the claims in cash. Secretary of State Hull remained unyielding in his demands for payment, and the Mexican government denied that there was any stipulation in international law on "immediate" payment.

The controversy grew more heated. Newspapers in the United States strongly supported Hull, while the Mexican press vigorously attacked him. For a time Mexican government officials remained silent, but on September 1 in his address to Congress, Cárdenas bitterly denounced the United States position as an attempt by the strong to impose its will on the weak. He offered, however, to submit agrarian claims to a two-man commission subject to the ruling of a third impartial arbitrator. For reasons that are not clear, Hull shifted his position and decided to end the acrimonious public exchange. On September 20 he called in the Mexican ambassador and suggested that it might be well to begin quiet oral conversations on the practical details of a settlement based on a mixed claims commission as the Mexican president had offered. In October Cárdenas promised to pay one million dollars per year until the claims were paid off and the State Department quickly accepted. Final settlement was reached on November 19, 1941 when Mexico and the United States signed a comprehensive convention (ratifications exchanged April 2, 1942) whereby Mexico agreed to pay $40 million over 17 years to settle all claims, including the agrarian, but excluding the oil claims, which were settled by a separate agreement. Six million dollars had already been paid on the foreign debts, and the remainder would be paid in annual installments of $2,500,000. With the involvement of the United States in World War II clearly a possibility, and with Mexico far more hostile to Fascist nations than she had been to the Central Powers of World War I, the convention also provided for a reciprocal trade agreement, the stabilization of the exchange rate between the peso and the dollar, an agreement for the United States purchase of Mexican silver, and a U.S. Export-Import Bank loan to Mexico.

More serious than either of the above problems was the dispute over oil rights that arose again in the 1930s. Under the Morrow-Calles formula of 1928, the Mexican government still theoretically owned all subsoil deposits, but the companies in fact faced no real obstacles to the exploitation of their holdings. Within five years about two-thirds of the companies had received confirmatory concessions from the government. In 1934, however, the new regime began to scrutinize the oil titles more strictly, and by the end of the year the government was refusing to issue any more confirmatory concessions. At the same time the government established Petroleos Mexicanos (PEMEX) as a wholly owned and operated government oil company. Officials of the oil companies, becoming very alarmed at these developments, planned to bring former Ambassador J. Reuben Clark to Mexico to appeal to Calles. Daniels refused to become involved in the revived controversy and advised Secretary Hull to forestall Clark's visit if possible. Clark, nonetheless, came to Mexico but accomplished nothing.

Leases, subsoil rights, and PEMEX may have worried oil company officials at the beginning of the Cárdenas administration, but the catalyst that spelled doom for private oil interests in Mexico proved to be not these old issues but a new one: labor organizations and their relationship to the Mexican government. One of the basic reforms of the Cárdenas regime, and often overshadowed by the more spectacular land expropriations, was the reorganization of the labor unions. Although the rights of workers were enshrined in Article 123 of the Constitution of 1917, the Obregón-Calles era witnessed only sporadic labor gains both in organization and in material benefits. Cárdenas determined to increase the number of organized workers, concentrate them into larger and more powerful unions, and integrate them into the official party that Calles founded but that Cárdenas soon controlled. Cárdenas' sympathy for workers' grievances in fact constituted one of the major points of difference with Calles that eventually led to the latter's fall. When Cárdenas broke definitively with the Jefe Máximo in the summer of 1935, labor rallied en masse to Cárdenas.

Troubles started in the oil fields early in 1935 when the workers struck the Huasteca Company, a subsidiary of Jersey Standard, over demands for pay and benefits that the company termed excessive.[10] The strike was eventually settled and did not spread beyond the Tampico area. It was, however, a portent of things to come. The strike had again demonstrated the weaknesses of the labor organizations in the oil fields and at the beginning of the following year, the 21 independent unions, under the urging of Cárdenas, merged into the Petroleum Workers' Union of the Mexican Republic (Sindicato de Trabajadores de Petroleo de la República Mexicana—STPRM); at the same time they joined the Cárdenas-sponsored national labor organization, the Confederation of Mexican Workers (Confederación de Trabajadores Mexicanos—CTM). During the summer the oil workers met in convention to discuss the question of an industrywide contract. They determined upon a wage and fringe-benefit package totaling 65 million pesos annually and demanded control over the hiring and firing of workers. In November they presented the oil companies, some 15 major producers and three shipping firms, with a standard industrywide collective contract that conformed to the Labor Code of 1931. It included, in addition to wage increases and other material benefits, an eight-hour

---

[10] The some 13,000 oil workers were divided into 21 small unions. All had labor contracts, but there was no uniformity from union to union or from employer to employer. All the majors were affiliates of larger British and American corporations. In addition there were a few independents, but these generally were not involved in the controversy.

day, double pay for overtime, strike pay, housing, schools, and paid vacations. The union also insisted on a closed shop and the inclusion of office workers in the union. The companies rejected the proposed contract and the union threatened to strike.

To prevent the collapse of a major industry, Cárdenas intervened.[11] On November 27 he called for a six-month cooling-off period during which negotiations would continue. In response to labor unity, the companies came to grant the principle of an industrywide contract, collective bargaining, and right to some fringe benefits. They objected, however, to the proposed wage increases and remained adamant against including office personnel in the union. The bargaining dragged on inconclusively. Of some 250 items placed on the agenda, only about 20 had been mutually agreed upon by the last day of the truce. The companies complained that the union raised many issues only for propaganda purposes, while the union complained that the companies were not bargaining in good faith.[12] On May 28 the union called a general strike. Initially the public did not express any great sympathy for the strikers, and when the work stoppage began to affect the economy, union officials recognized that they had to win popular support if the strike were to succeed. Consequently, within two weeks the union began legal proceedings to declare the walkout not a "strike" but an "economic conflict" under the terms of the Labor Code. The code defined an "economic conflict" as a general type of labor-management dispute in which the basic elements of an industry have become so unbalanced that an ordinary strike has no effect. In such cases the government must enter the dispute to arbitrate, to conciliate the factions, to make an award that will equalize economic power, and finally to enforce the decision on both sides. The code also established the Federal Board of Arbitration and Conciliation to take charge of "economic conflicts" so

---

[11] Although production was down from the peak years of the early 1920s when Mexico was producing 193 million barrels annually (over 25% of world production), the country was producing 40 million barrels in 1935 and exporting 19 million.

[12] Cline, *op. cit.*, p. 233, a sympathetic observer of the Cárdenas era said of the agenda: "It was filled with far more exaggerated demands for social benefits than bonafide issues which could be compromised."

defined. The union succeeded in its petition, thus forcing the companies to deal with Cárdenas rather than with union officials.

By law the Federal Board appointed a committee of experts to investigate the facts of the case and to make recommendations to the Board for the settlement of the dispute. The committee consisted of two members of the president's cabinet and Jesús Silva Herzog, a professor of economics. Reportedly Silva Herzog carried out the investigation, and on August 3 the committee submitted to the Board a lengthy document on its findings. Basically the committee findings supported the worker's demands. They reported that the companies made enormous profits in Mexico as compared with their profits in the United States, partly they claimed as a result of low wages in Mexico. As the result, the committee argued, the companies could well pay wage increases amounting to about 26 million pesos or about half their excess profits, and provide social benefits and working conditions to conform with the 1931 Labor Code and Article 123 of the Constitution. The companies responded that their total profits amounted to only 18 million pesos, and on August 18 a delegation of oil men conferred at the State Department with the Under Secretary Sumner Welles, an expert on Latin American affairs. A great deal of controversy ensued over the findings of the committee, and when it seemed that the issue had become completely deadlocked, the companies began to remove various surplus funds and property from Mexico. Finally on December 18 the Federal Board of Conciliation and Arbitration announced its own conclusions. In effect, it supported its committee, ordering wages to be raised about 27 percent or about 26,300,000 pesos, the office staff to join the union, the institution of a 40-hour, five-day week, the establishment of pension, vacation, and life insurance programs, and the provision of work clothes and housing (or allowances). The companies appealing for a writ of *amparo*[13] took the case to the Mexican Supreme Court. They claimed that the awards would

---

[13] *Amparo* is the basic legal recourse in Mexico against the violation of one's constitutional rights by the action either of administrative decisions or of laws.

ruin them, particularly since wage increases according to their calculations, would come to 64.5 million pesos and the fringe benefits would add more than 35 million pesos, making a total cost of over 100 million pesos.

While the case was under consideration in the Supreme Court, both sides tried to exert outside leverage. During the controversy the Mexican government had requested United States financial aid through the purchase of Mexican silver. The oil companies tried to use Mexico's request as a lever to bargain, but U.S. Treasury Secretary Henry Morganthau agreed to buy 35 million ounces of Mexican silver on deposit in the United States and to make regular monthly purchases. In addition to the fact that many United States companies worked Mexican silver, Morganthau feared that any rebuff to Mexico would force Cárdenas into barter trade agreements with Germany and Japan, countries toward which the United States was becoming increasingly hostile. In Mexico the labor unions and some sympathetic government officials tried to arouse popular support by couching the conflict in broadly nationalistic and class-warfare terms. A victory for the oil workers would mean a victory for the Mexican workingman, while a victory for the companies meant the continued exploitation of the Mexican people by foreign imperialists. Cárdenas himself entered the fray. In an address to the CTM on February 24 he said that many of Mexico's troubles could be traced directly to the foreign oil companies. He also insisted that they were trying to influence the course of justice by covert economic means, that is, by sudden large bank withdrawals that threatened the fiscal system.

The Supreme Court announced its decision on March 1. It denied the companies' appeal for *amparo* and ordered compliance with the Federal Board's ruling. The Board then set March 7 as the deadline for compliance. Following the Court's decision the companies offered to raise wages by 24 million pesos, and the unions and Cárdenas seemed inclined to accept. Cárdenas even agreed to pledge, as the companies requested, that this was the final and maximum demand. The companies, however, wanted the pledge in writing, but Cárdenas regarded this as "a slur on his personal honor and a grave reflection on the integrity of his administration." Because of the bargaining, the Board extended the deadline to March 15. When the deadline expired the companies bluntly notified the Board that they could not and would not comply. On the following day the Board ruled the companies guilty of *rebeldía* (defiance), an action that made them subject to worker control. Royal Dutch Shell's subsidiary "El Aguila" (which produced two-thirds of Mexico's oil output), worried by the charge of *rebeldía*, met that same day with Cárdenas, who simply suggested that they pay the 26,300,000-peso wage increase. The British consulted with the Americans, but the latter urged them to stand firm. They believed that at most the Mexican government would place their companies under receivership but expected diplomatic intervention to save their properties. Cárdenas, however, determined on a more drastic response, on the evening of March 18, 1938 announced by radio his decision to nationalize the Mexican oil industry.[14]

The United States response to the expropriation decree was mixed. Ambassador Daniels was sorrowful because of the unnecessary bitterness engendered. The companies were outraged, and the State Department took a restrained public posture. Secretary Hull, however, worried about the opportunities presented to Italy, Germany, and Japan if United States-Mexican relations deteriorated, but other advisers at State favored some sort of crackdown. Some persons tried to persuade the Treasury to stop buying silver to force a lowering of world prices. Morganthau at first refused, but under pressure from Hull he stopped buying silver on March 27. On the previous day Hull cabled a stiff protest note to the Mexican government. The cessation of silver purchases was more a gesture than a reality, however. Although the special purchase agreement was cancelled and the direct United States purchase of Mexican silver substantially declined, the United States continued to buy Mexican silver on the open market. The policy placated certain chauvinistic elements and oil company supporters in the United States but failed to intimidate the Mexican government. Perhaps one reason

---

[14] Cline, *op. cit.*, pp. 236–238, gives another version of these events from March 15 to March 18; Meyer, *México y Estados Unidos*, states that Cárdenas had anticipated the possibility of an impasse and had decided on expropriation should it prove necessary. He charged Francisco Múgica to prepare a document to this effect.

Treasury continued to purchase silver was that most of the producers were themselves United States companies that formed a lobby as powerful as the oil interests. Silver producers argued that if they supported punitive measures not only would they be damaged economically but that they might well be expropriated themselves. They also argued that economic punishment of Mexico would result in lowered purchases of a variety of United States goods. Interestingly President Roosevelt remained aloof from the controversy and limited his remarks to statements that Cárdenas' pledge of compensation was satisfactory and that the oilmen should not expect compensation for future anticipated profits.

The companies responded to the expropriation with long and bitter tirades against the Mexican government. They condemned the loss of their properties as outright robbery, and insisted that the oil that Mexico sold had been illegally confiscated and still belonged to the companies. The companies deluged the United States with articles and pamphlets, and slapped liens on Mexican oil cargoes in Europe as stolen goods. They also instituted direct and secondary boycotts on Mexican oil. No non-Mexican tanker or vehicle would move a drop of Mexican petroleum (and Mexico had no vehicles) and no United States firm would supply Mexico with equipment to run the oil industry. Marketing was obviously severely hampered by the boycotts and Mexico's great need of foreign exchange was increased with one of her major exports cut-off.

The British response was more blunt and direct than that of the United States. On April 8, the British foreign office acknowledged a general right of expropriation but denied that in this particular case "the public interest" was involved as the Mexicans claimed. The note implied that the Constitution of 1917 had no right to sanction arbitrary and confiscatory acts and that the Mexican government had transgressed international law. The note also complained that justice had been denied the oil companies because of the rigged nature of the Mexican courts and boards that reviewed the dispute. It ended by demanding the return of El Aguila to its owners.

After the flurry of activity preceding the expropriation, the Mexican counterresponse to the protests remained rather low-key. In answer to Hull's note, the regime reiterated that it was prepared to negotiate compensation for the oil properties, but that it could not make immediate cash payments. In May the Mexicans responded to the British by breaking diplomatic relations. With much of the United States and European markets cut off, the Mexicans turned to the Germans, Italians, and Japanese for oil sales and equipment and for heavy machinery.

Italy supplied tankers. By September 1938 when the Munich crisis broke, Germany was buying one-third of Mexico's oil exports. Despite this increasing dependence on the fascist states, Cárdenas secretly proposed to Roosevelt an inter-American economic boycott against aggressors. In addition to the slack taken up by Italy, Germany, and Japan, the ill effects of the embargo were also softened by the fact that oil sales after expropriation, although reduced, no longer had to support interest and dividend payments to foreign investors. In other words the decline in capital accruing to Mexico from the oil sales was not proportionately as great as the decline in total sales.[15]

Much more serious negotiations followed the expropriations than preceded it. And just as in 1916 and 1917 Carranza profited by the United States' growing involvement in Europe's troubles, so Cárdenas benefited from growing United States concern with new aggressions in Europe and Asia. Of course, the Roosevelt administration, in line with the Good Neighbor Policy, was more inclined to abstain from intervention over economic conflicts. At the same time Roosevelt himself stayed personally aloof from much of the negotiations with Mexico, leaving policy matters to bargaining between some hard-line officials such as Secretary of State Cordell Hull on the one hand and more flexible officials such as Ambassador Josephus Daniels on the other. Hull tended to take a more short-term view, fearing that if the United States capitulated in Mexico over expropriations, United States interests would be jeopardized in other parts of the world. Although he believed that some expropriations might indeed be worthy or necessary, he insisted on "fair, effective, and immediate com-

---

[15] Merrill Rippy, "The Economic Repercussions of Expropriation: Case Study: Mexican Oil," *Inter-American Economic Affairs*, Vol. V (Summer 1951), No. 1, p. 58.

pensation." Ambassador Daniels took the long-term view. He argued that Mexico needed reforms and the United States should be more tolerant and patient.

It was in this political context that the oil companies sought compensation for their losses. They rejected an offer from Cárdenas to market 60 percent of Mexico's oil at discounts in their favor until they recovered the value of their properties. Instead, they demanded full and immediate payment for their property, including the value of the oil remaining in the ground. They maintained this hard-line stance for over three years, fearing to jeopardize their position in other countries should they yield in Mexico. In addition to their boycotts, which they maintained with some success, they prevailed on the state department to stop purchases of Mexican oil for the United States Navy, to encourage Latin American governments to follow the United States lead, to refuse contracts to United States government suppliers that used Mexican oil, and to set 1939 as a base year for import quotas on foreign oil, a year when Mexican oil to the United States was reduced to a trickle. Besides their media campaign to support their position, they warned tourists away from Mexico, berated Mexican gasoline as inferior, and gave moral support to General Saturnino Cedillo's rebellion in 1938. So successful was this campaign in the United States that a press review of the times indicates overwhelming support for the companies and meager reporting of opposite views.

From the beginning, several smaller companies had complained of the no-compromise position of the major companies, and put pressure on them for some kind of settlement. In late 1938 Sinclair, with 25 percent of production and 40 percent of the refining, sent Patrick Hurley to talk with Cárdenas. He returned convinced that settlement was possible. The majors then united in dispatching Donald Richberg early in 1939 to continue explorations for a compromise. Richberg initially asked for $260 million in cash (which included the value of the oil underground), and suggested that if Mexico could not pay, the properties should be returned. Cárdenas refused. Richberg then proposed 50-year leases on the expropriated properties or the establishment of mixed Mexican-United States companies to exploit the oil with the United States companies putting up their expropriated properties as stock. Again Cárdenas refused. After months of conversations the negotiations broke down over the companies continued insistence in claiming the oil in the ground. Even state department intervention could not keep the talks going. Richberg published a full report of the affair, which appeared in January 1940, ánd resigned. Cárdenas was deeply offended at what he regarded as Richberg's breach of confidence.

When it became clear that Richberg had made no progress, Sinclair once more employed Hurley, thus breaking the majors' united front. In new talks Hurley offered Cárdenas an agreement to accept payment in oil and talked of buying substantial Mexican oil in addition. Realistic bargaining finally got underway in February and March of 1940. The talks were proceeding well when Secretary Hull demanded arbitration of the dispute (April 3, 1940), heightening anti-United States sentiment in Mexico. Not only did the Cárdenas administration refuse to arbitrate what it considered a domestic matter, but timed its note to coincide with the announcement of the settlement with Sinclair. The agreement stipulated that the Mexican government would pay Sinclair $8.5 million dollars over a three-year period and would sell 20 million barrels of oil over four years at 25 to 30 cents below market value. (It was estimated that the discount was worth $4.5 to $5.5 million.) In return Sinclair renounced all claims to oil underground.

The Sinclair settlement brought no immediate break in the general deadlock between the Mexican government and the remaining oil companies. Cárdenas apparently had hopes for reaching a settlement through demonstrating a community of interests with the United States vis-à-vis the war in Europe. He had earlier suggested a boycott of aggressors, had supported the Republican cause in the Spanish Civil War, and had offered Mexico as a haven to Spanish refugees when the Franco forces with German and Italian aid had prevailed in 1939. When France and the Low Countries fell to the German invaders in the spring of 1940, coinciding with Mexico's settlement with Sinclair, Cárdenas and other Mexican leaders took a strong anti-German position. Despite great concern in the United States over the course of the war in Europe, the state department hesitated to make any public praise for Mexico's stand, because of the continuing oil dispute. The United States embassy, nonetheless, appealed for a show of appreciation, and Ambassador Daniels, returning from a trip to Washington, carried a personal message of friendship and esteem from Roosevelt. One explanation for the reluctance of the oil companies and the State Department to follow up the Sinclair deal with such praise was that 1940 was an election year in Mexico. Both the companies and the Department hoped that a more amenable administration would succeed Cárdenas; specifically they hoped for a victory by General Juan Andreu Almazán, a revolutionary more in the tradition of Obregón than of Cárdenas. Almazán obviously enjoyed some popular support in the United States and among some leaders of the Democratic Party, but there is no evidence that he received United States financial support. In fact the Roosevelt administration promptly recognized the victory of his opponent, General Manuel Avila Camacho, Cárdenas' personal choice as successor. Moreover, Roosevelt sent his vice-president, Henry Wallace, to head the United States delegation at Camacho's inauguration. The sending of such a high ranking dignitary to a Latin American inauguration constituted an almost unprecedented action.

Wallace's presence at the inauguration marked the public evidence of a determined effort by the United States to repair its ties to Mexico. Somewhat earlier Sumner Welles had approached the Mexican ambassador in Washington for a general settlement. With the war taking a turn for the worse in Europe and threatening to spread into Asia, the Roosevelt administration decided it was time to end the minor bickerings over Mexican petroleum. In January 1941 Roosevelt instructed Daniels to sound out the Mexican government about building naval bases on the Pacific. Daniels reported that Avila Camacho was willing to strengthen Mexican naval and air defenses, but he warned F.D.R. that the United States would have to pay most of the cost because Mexico was too poor. He also advised the president that the lack of a settlement on the oil problem prevented a full rapprochement with Mexico. During the remainder of the year the two countries settled virtually all of their major outstanding problems and began a series of agreements that would bring closer cooperation and collaboration than at any time in their previous history. On April 1 they signed a treaty (ratifications exchanged April 25) that permitted their aircraft to use each others airfields for landing and servicing in transit to other areas. During May and June Mexican officials cooperated with the U.S. embassy in frustrating German activities in Mexico. In July the United States contracted to buy Mexico's production of strategic minerals, and President Avila Camacho implied that Mexico would join the United States in war if the latter were attacked. As noted above, the spring and summer also saw the continuation of discussions that led to a settlement of agrarian and general claims before the end of the year.

Oil remained the chief obstacle to a general settlement, and even the State Department was becoming exasperated with the intransigence of the oil companies. Furthermore, State was embarrassed when *Newsweek* magazine reported a study of oil properties by the interior department that valued the properties at only $13.5 million, including subsoil claims, rather than the $450 million claimed by the companies.[16] In July serious discussions on the oil question began in Washington. By August the negotiators reached a tentative agreement whereby Mexico would pay $9 million down, and the two governments would appoint a team of experts to evaluate the properties. When the news of the proposals leaked out, the alarmed oil company officials again approached the state department for support. Several state department high officials still supported the companies, but the top officials also recognized the need for a settlement in face of the ever gloomier international situation. Late in September Hull pleaded in vain with the companies to cooperate. Becoming impatient, he then instructed the treasury department to review their books and discovered that the companies' own book value closely tallied with the recent low geological appraisals received by the state department. At the beginning of November, Ambassador Daniels, as he was preparing to retire, found Mexican officials extremely disturbed over Hull's contin-

---

[16] The U.S. Department of Commerce in 1938 listed American direct investments in oil at $69 million, and at the end of 1937 the oil companies listed their assets at $60,247,000. Bemis, *op. cit.*, p. 347.

ued reluctance to sign the agreement on oil without the consent of the companies. The companies were still hoping to negotiate a management contract, but the Mexican government squelched this effort in a blunt public refusal. The Mexican embassy in Washington also affirmed that the oil settlement must be included or there would be no general agreement. On November 18 Hull suddenly changed his mind and decided to sign without company consent. Notes were exchanged the following day at the State Department. In addition to the agreement to settle the controversy on the value of the oil properties by a panel of two experts and the general and agrarian claims by a payment of $40 million, the convention provided that the United States purchase up to $25 million of Mexican silver annually, make available credit up to $40 million to stabilize the peso, lend Mexico $30 million through the Export-Import Bank for road building, and negotiate a trade treaty with Mexico. Ratifications were exchanged April 2, 1942.

Only the valuation of the properties blocked the final disposition of the oil conflict. The oil officials were bitter about the settlement, but agreed to cooperate in supplying the information required by the panel of experts. When the investigations got under way, the American member of the team was shocked at the discrepancy between the oil company claims and the facts that they uncovered. Much equipment was obsolete or in disrepair, pipelines were corroded, and the total investment worth much less than the millions claimed. The American and Mexican experts had no difficulty reaching agreement on 75 percent of the award "using standard American valuation practices based on prudent investment theory."[17] The final agreement, reached in April 1942, evaluated the total worth at $23,995,991 with interest at something over $5 million. Of the total, $18,391,641 was awarded to Jersey Standard, an amount that compared favorably both with the company's own book value and estimates made earlier for the State Department. The experts also recommended that one-third the award be paid July 1, 1942 and the remainder in five equal and consecutive annual installments with 3 percent interest. The companies protested once more, but the

---

[17] Cronon, *op. cit.*, p. 269.

state department informed them that it was this amount or nothing. The companies then accepted the award, and with some technical alterations in method and timing of payments, the debt was liquidated in 1949.

A few odds and ends remained. First, President Roosevelt arranged for a resumption of Mexican-British relations as part of the war effort, and in September, 1947 the terms of settlement were finally reached. The Mexican government agreed to pay $81.25 million that with interest over a 15-year period came to about $130 million. Second, several small British and United States companies were exempt from the expropriations in 1938. They were, however, required to sell their output to PEMEX or to market it within Mexico at fixed prices. In 1948 PEMEX bought 40 percent control of Gulf's Mexican holdings and in 1950–1951 bought them outright. In November 1950 it also bought out Abraham Z. Phillips. By July 1952 there were only two small foreign holdings left: the British owned Kermex Oil Fields Company, and the United States operated Charro Oil Company.

III

The break in the oil negotiations in 1940 and the gradual shift in the attitude of the state department toward a settlement prepared the way for cooperation between the United States and Mexico during World War II. In contrast to its neutral position in World War I and its accompanying suspicion and even hostility toward the United States during those years, Mexico sought close working relationships with its northern neighbor as the Second World War began to involve the Western Hemisphere. Cárdenas apparently felt uncomfortable trading with the fascist states and early on sought to reestablish his political and economic links with the United States and Great Britain. Economics obviously played a role, but political ideology cannot be dismissed. After all Cárdenas had long supported the Spanish Republicans against the Spanish Nationalists, who were supplied and equipped by Germany and Italy, and had offered Mexico as a haven for Spanish exiles after the Nationalist victory. His sympathies lay naturally with the democratic states and many of his leftist supporters strengthened that position in 1941 when Hitler attacked the Soviet Union. Only minor rumblings of discontent were to be heard as Mexican-United States relations changed from official correctness to cordiality. Prior to the attack on Pearl Harbor, Mexico cooperated with the blacklisting by the United States in July 1941 of individuals and firms doing business with the fascist powers. The German ambassador received no sympathy when he protested to the Mexican government. The following month Mexico broke off economic relations with Germany by closing Mexican consulates in Germany and by forcing the Germans to close their consulates in Mexico.

Following the entry of the United States into the war, Mexico entered into closer economic, political, and military relations with its northern neighbor than at any time before or since. Basically the United States supplied some technical know-how and training, certain types of machinery and equipment, and of course a modest amount of capital for Mexico's economy and military establishment, while Mexico supplied manpower and raw materials to the United States. Conversations on mutual defense, begun the previous March, led to the creation of a joint United States-Mexican Defense Commission in January 1942 to coordinate military action and to provide for the training of Mexican military personnel in the United States. At the same time the United States entered into a bilateral lend-lease agreement for military equipment to modernize the Mexican forces. Mexico obtained a credit of $40 million with an option of purchasing any article it wished to obtain at a discount of 67 percent. Because of shortages during the war and of higher priorities for other countries, Mexico actually received less than half the authorized amount of equipment in dollar terms, and elected to retain all of it. With the settlement of all outstanding claims, Mexican oil began once more to flow into United States ports, some by way of Mexican tankers. As the Germans stepped up their submarine warfare, they first stopped and warned Mexican ships from trading with the United States. Mexico ignored the warnings, and on May 14 German submarines sank a Mexican tanker and on May 22 attacked another, killing several Mexican citizens on each occasion. A few days later President Avila Camacho convened Congress in extraordinary session and held a conference with his governors and military zone commanders. Despite some division of opinion in the country, Avila Camacho asked Congress for a declaration of war, and on May 30 Congress complied. Mexico signed the United Nations pact in Washington on June 14. The Mexican populace did not enter the war with any noticeable enthusiasm, but there was little opposition.

With Mexico in the war, further official cooperation followed. A Mexican-United States Commission on Economic Cooperation studied the Mexican economy and made recommendations for the increase of Mexican production for the war effort. A railway mission of United States technical experts attempted to assist Mexico with modernization of its lines. Neither of these accomplished very much, and the technical experts became involved in a labor-management dispute in Mexico. Most important of the economic agreements, however, was that concerning the importation of unskilled Mexican labor into the United States to work primarily in agriculture. In August 1942 Mexico and the United States signed a series of agreements that would permit the contracting of about 200,000 Mexican workers (*braceros*). During the war no more than 75,000 braceros were working in United States fields at any one time, and they never represented more than 2 percent of the agricultural labor force. The importance of those agreements lay, however, in the patterns that they established for the continuation of such contracts for almost 20 years after the war ended.

Mexico's entry into the war also brought further military cooperation. Negotiations between the two countries provided for the mutual induction of alien residents into the armed forces of each country. The agreement of course worked in a one-sided manner. Virtually no American citizens were taken into the Mexican army, while some 250,000 Mexicans were inducted in to the U.S. armed forces, of whom 14,000 saw combat, and 1000 were killed.[18] Mexican military forces trained in the United States comprised primarily air force officers and men. By mid-1944 three squadrons had completed initial training in the

---

[18] Johnny M. McCain, "Contract Labor as a Factor in United States-Mexican Relations, 1942–1947" (Austin: unpublished Ph.D., dissertation, University of Texas, 1970), p. 10; Cline, *op. cit.*, p. 276.

United States. In March 1945 Mexico's Squadron 201 embarked for the Philippine Islands and saw action during the last summer of the war.

IV

The interwar years were marked by bitter conflict and gradual adjustment interspersed by brief periods of relative calm and harmony in Mexican-United States relations. Periods of severe strife emerged whenever Mexican revolutionary leaders attempted to implement one or another principle of the Revolution, particularly those involving private property rights. In view of Mexican firmness on principle, of United States reluctance to employ armed force, and of broader Mexican and United States economic interests and needs, both sides made some concessions in practice all along the way. In the end the Mexican government made good its claim to subsoil rights and its insistence on agrarian reform. On the other hand, it paid for its expropriations but again, on the other hand, not in the amount that its claimants demanded. The United States eventually was forced to accept the principles of Article 27, but its citizens received some compensation. The several periods of harmony during these years coincided with the retreat or the retrenchment of revolutionary fervor and action. The Bucareli agreements, the Morrow-Calles accord, and the "turn to the right" after 1940 all inaugurated periods of conciliation and cooperation between the two countries. The period ended surprisingly with an almost definitive solution to all the major outstanding problems and all by compromise: bonded indebtedness, claims, oil, and land. Most importantly by the end of the period, Mexican revolutionary leadership had successfully made the point that internal developments within Mexico would be decided basically by Mexicans in what they determined to be the national interest. Officially the United States government came to accept the principles of nonintervention and self-determination, although it continued to insist on the right to make diplomatic representations in behalf of the interests of its citizens abroad. The period ended with the United States and Mexico as allies in World War II, a situation that would have been virtually inconceivable at the beginning of this period.

Finally Mexico's external dependence, while not abolished, had been substantially modified. Foreign investments had fallen to less than one-quarter of what they had been in 1911. Although the United States still constituted the major foreign market and loomed overwhelmingly powerful militarily, the system of internal production had come largely under national ownership and control.[19] By 1945 Mexican leadership had the sense of security that it controlled the country's destinies as never before.

---

[19] Lorenzo Meyer, "Cambio Político y Dependencia," *Foro Internacional* Vol. XIII (October-December 1972), No. 2, p. 127, presents valuable insights on this at least temporary accomplishment of the revolution.

CHAPTER VII

The Contemporary Era 1945–1970: The Peripheral Issues

DESPITE SOME UNRESOLVED problems and the emergence of occasional irritants in their dealings with each other, the United States and Mexico have enjoyed since World War II the most harmonious relationships and the longest crisisfree era in their history. In fact only the Díaz period compares favorably and that was primarily at the official level and among a very small elite. The peaceful settlement of the oil and land disputes in the early 1940s contributed greatly to this rapprochement, but obviously Mexican internal stability and the United States shift of priorities away from Latin America to other parts of the world also played important roles.

I

For the past 30 years or more Mexico has offered to the world the virtually unique experience of undergoing dramatic economic growth and development accompanied by a high degree of political stability without total repression of civil rights. From a poor, undeveloped, and largely agricultural state in the 1930s, Mexico has become by the opening of the 1970s one of the more industrialized and diversified countries of Latin America, itself the most developed part of the so-called Third World. With an economy growing at a steady average rate of over 6 percent per year, Mexico has achieved a per-capita gross national product of over $500 despite a population growth rate that is one of the highest in the world. To be sure, the wealth and income of the country are not equitably distributed, and Mexico, like most growing economies, has fueled its development by restricting consumption, a process that imposes the greatest relative sacrifices at the lower end of the economic scale. What redistribution has occurred in the past two decades affects the middle range of families, with the top 5 percent showing a relative decrease in its share of income and the middle classes in the 51 to 95 percent group increasing their portion of the national income. It may well be that the lower 30 percent of all families not only did not retain their share of the national income but may in fact have suffered an absolute decline. Furthermore the greatest differential in income is to be found between the rural and urban sectors. The average urban family enjoys an income twice that of the rural family, but the top 5 percent of rural families compares favorably with the top 5 percent of urban families. Despite the great land distribution programs, some families have managed to retain or to acquire large holdings through various subterfuges, and government irrigation and rural credit programs have favored the large private holders over the small subsistence *ejido* farmers. In addition, almost half the rural work force is composed of landless wage earners.[1]

During these same years, Mexico has experienced an unprecedented period of political stability. The last military uprising occurred in 1938, and it proved to be a relatively minor affair that loyal forces easily suppressed. Over the years there have been demonstrations, protests, strikes, and riots, many of them ending in bloody encounters with the police or army. Several political agitators who violated the political rules of the game have been assassinated or imprisoned, but overall most opposition groups have sought change within the system or their greater participation in the system instead of the revolutionary destruction of the system itself. Revolutionists have found little support among the citizenry at large, and extremist groups have been frustrated by lack of popular response, their inability to recruit able leadership, and a constant quarreling among themselves. At the same time the leaders of the new Mexico have demonstrated enormous political ability. Through the official

---

[1] Richard Weisskoff, "Income Distribution and Economic Growth in Puerto Rico, Argentina, and Mexico," *Review of Income and Wealth*, Series 16 (December 1970), No. 4.

political vehicle, now called the Institutional Revolutionary Party (PRI), the heirs of the Revolution have constantly recruited able young men into their ranks, rewarding loyalty, zeal, and ability with appointed and elective offices. Opposition political groups meet less harassment today than 30 years ago, but access to power and public office is not readily available to them, and membership in political parties other than the PRI offers few rewards other than symbolic protest to current policy.

From its inception in 1929, the official party has undergone several changes in title as well as substantial changes in form and organization. Originally established as a holding company for Calles, the Jefe Máximo, and comprised of regional, local, or state groupings under military chiefs or political caciques, it has evolved into a semicorporativist body with regional subdivisions based on the states and territories of the country. This organization is divided into three sectors; the peasant and labor union components make up the bulk of the membership in raw numbers, but the so-called popular sector, with its various subsector elements that can accommodate virtually every conceivable occupational status or any other kind of status, includes the major power holders. In fact, the party is still the holding company that it was in 1929; however, instead of a single jefe exercising power, a group of interrelated politicians, business executives, labor and peasant leaders (usually neither workingmen nor peasants), intellectuals, and other assorted dignitaries determine policy and distribute resources. Within this group, the president of the country is the single most powerful leader, but he cannot exercise the powers of his office arbitrarily or whimsically. The day of the flamboyant national caudillo is over. So too is the day of novel social experimentation and massive redistribution of national wealth, although the rhetoric of the party and national leaders continues to be revolutionary and socialistic. On the other hand the present leaders have not entirely forgotten their heritage. Although the relative gap between rich and poor continues to widen, there has been some distribution of the new wealth to most classes, and there has been a modest extension of welfare benefits to a widening group of people. Educational and medical facilities particularly have been improved and increased, and some of the leaders do appear genuinely concerned for improving the lot of the most disadvantaged, especially of the rural poor.

Three interrelated questions remain about domestic conditions in Mexico that bear on future relations with the United States: Is the Mexican Revolution dead? Has the present regime become another Díaz-like period with a new conservative elite? Is another revolution likely? None of these questions can be answered definitively, although all have been the subject of debate in popular and academic circles both in the United States and Mexico. The Mexican Revolution is over if one considers violence and dramatic redistribution of socio-politico-economic resources as basic elements of revolution; it is still in progress if one can accept incremental change, based on some of the ideals expressed in the more violent and experimental stages of the Revolution, as a continuation of the process begun in 1910. In much the same way one can approach the second question. Undoubtedly a new elite has arisen since 1940, wealth and income are more inequitably distributed in the 1970s than in the 1930s, elections are generally meaningless exercises that exhibit no real competition for public offices, and the regime places far greater emphasis on economic productivity and modernization than it does on social welfare or the equitable distribution of that improved productivity. On the other hand Mexicans enjoy far more civil liberties today than in the late nineteenth century, more people do participate in the fruits of development, and some leaders of the system sincerely acknowledge the problems and are seeking solutions. Most importantly, many leaders are sensitive to serious and widespread complaints that surface, and are concerned to mollify and pacify the discontented, if only to preserve the status quo. At least one lesson has been learned: the danger of not responding in some measure to deep-seated grievances. The example of 1910 has not been forgotten.

But some critics still insist that Mexico cannot escape another period of violence. They argue that the population increase will eventually outrun the ability of the economy to continue growing and that the present inequities and alienation of certain groups will then become more intense and lead to large-scale and more widely supported violence. It is possible. For the present, however, too many necessary ingredients are missing. In addition to the fact that groups with a vested interest in the status quo have expanded in size and numbers since 1940, many other Mexicans are basically hopeful and optimistic about their personal futures and feel a high positive relationship to their society (if not to the political leaders as persons). Moreover, the existing points of opposing tensions within the society crosscut each other in a bewildering maze. For example, there are serious power struggles within the official party as well as between the official party and the "loyal opposition." More importantly there is increasing tension between landless peasants and peasants who hold some land, as well as between peasants and large landholders. At the same time many peasants still have hopes of government assistance in their quest for land. There are also tensions between rural and urban people, Indians and non-Indians, political left and political right, labor and management, the outlying regions and Mexico City, intellectuals and the political establishment. These various conflicts (and some are more serious than others) have not become polarized in any way. Until they do, there can be no substantial challenge to the system, only demands for adjustments *within* the system. And finally no leader has appeared with the necessary qualities of personal attraction, intellectual vigor, and iron determination to pull together the varied elements of discontent into one organized movement. Until some of these conditions are fulfilled, revolution seems unlikely. Violence may occur, and a sharp, sustained downturn in the economy may make it widespread indeed. The more likely outcome may be a collapse of the political system only, with the basic socioeconomic structure maintained through an authoritarian government supported by the military. Violence, if it comes, will undoubtedly involve the United States to some extent, whether revolutionary or counterrevolutionary forces prevail.

II

What of the United States in the postwar era? The war and its aftermath substantially modified and eventually destroyed the Good Neighbor Policy of President Franklin Roosevelt. Not only did the war distract United States attention from Latin America to the power centers in Europe and Asia, but it involved the United States deeply in global affairs. When the conflict ended, United States leaders and people remained fearful about future aggressions and the spread of Communism in its various forms, and interpreted Soviet imperialism as the potential successor to Fascist and Japanese imperialism. In the postwar years the United States took on the role of policeman of the world to stop military aggression and territorial expansion by force whether through armed invasion or by internal subversion. This containment policy led the country to the formation of a series of defensive alliances, beginning in the Western Hemisphere with the Rio Treaty of Reciprocal Assistance of 1947, to which Mexico is a signatory. The Rio Treaty principle of "an attack on one is an attack on all" became the model for the North Atlantic Treaty Organization of 1949. Containment also led the United States to commit troops to Western Europe and Asia, and involved the United States in the Korean conflict in the 1950s and the Vietnam war in the 1960s. In Latin America, through a much broadened interpretation of its anticommunist policy, the United States participated directly or indirectly with military force in the domestic concerns of three states: Guatemala in 1954, Cuba in 1961, and the Dominican Republic in 1965. It also forced the removal of missiles in Cuba in 1962, but that confrontation involved basically the United States and the Soviet Union, with Cuba reduced to an observer and pawn in the international power game.

Although the Guatemalan intervention of 1954 might conveniently be used to mark the end of the Good Neighbor Policy, that policy had actually been seriously modified if not abandoned at least a decade earlier. As World War II was drawing to a close, it became ever more clear that the interests of the United States and of the Latin American states were diverging. The United States was becoming increasingly concerned with the configurations of power on a global scale and interpreting the spread or potential spread of Soviet power and influence as a major threat to peace and security. Most Latin American leaders were far less worried about Russian imperialism and far more concerned with United States political and economic hegemony in the Western Hemisphere. That is, the United States pressed for common action in the military and political fields globally while Latin Americans insisted on a joint attack on economic underdevelopment and disadvantageous trade and financial terms within their own areas. This conflict of interests was highlighted at the Tenth Inter-American Conference at Caracas in 1954 where Secretary of State John Foster Dulles insisted upon the signing of an anti-Communist resolution while most Latin American delegations demanded consideration of their immediate economic needs.

The United States refused to give much consideration to Latin American demands for economic aid until after a hostile, authoritarian, Soviet-allied regime emerged in Cuba. In 1961 the Kennedy administration instituted the Alliance for Progress as an ambitious program for economic development and social reform within democratic political limits. Although the United States committed more funds for economic programs during the early to mid-1960s, the Alliance in its broad aims failed, and with the increasing costs of the Vietnam war and the increasing popular demands for a curtailment of all United States commitments abroad, the funds for Latin America began to decline by the late 1960s. Although some aid has continued, with its present semi-isolationist mood the United States is not inclined to undertake large-scale programs or costly policies in Latin America. It even attempted during 1971 to limit imports by applying a 10 percent surcharge that applied to Latin America and also to the rest of the world to improve its balance of payments. Facing frustration in Vietnam, strident and sometimes violent demands for reform at home, and criticism of its foreign policies from former allies, current United States leaders are inclined to seek accommodations instead of bold new policies in the international field, while they search for means of handling the domestic problems of inflation, racial tensions, urban sprawl, and political corruption.

With stable governments, prosperous economies, predictable policies in their relationships, and mutual protection of each other's major interests, the United States and Mexico have established almost ideal government-to-government relationships, as well as popular contacts and responses that range from the tolerable to the friendly. Some Mexicans dislike Americans personally and collectively, many despise the American political and economic systems, and virtually all respect and distrust United

States military power. Most Americans still know little about Mexicans, many tend to lump them together with other Latin Americans, all of whom they view as inclined to violence and laziness; some regard them as inferior. A few on both sides of the border have mutual respect and admiration for the other. In this climate no bitter, irreconcilable differences have surfaced. Since World War II there have been no problems of recognition, claims, debts, expropriation, or territorial expansion. In fact not one of the major types of problems that had troubled United States-Mexican relations in the past has caused even a ruffle of discontent in the last 30 years. The problems that have arisen would generally concern any two powers of unequal size with contiguous borders. Trade and commerce, communications of things, persons, and ideas, financial transactions, investment policies, and minor boundary disagreements have all been subjects of constant negotiations. Some issues were defined and settled recently, some needed to be constantly negotiated, and some remained irritants that needed to be managed. No problem was ever permitted to disrupt discussions or normal intercourse between the two states.[2]

III

In place of the quarrels and threats of earlier years, border negotiations for the past several decades have involved several agreements on joint projects. Included in a treaty of 1944 on boundary waters (a source of continuing friction) was a provision calling for the construction of dams and irrigation works on the Rio Grande and other rivers. Several such projects have been completed through cooperative efforts, the best-known being the Falcón and Amistad dams on the Rio Grande. In addition various improvements in facilities, roads, and bridges have been made at border crossing points.

During these years the two countries also settled amicably after 100 years of dispute the minor annoyance of conflicting

---

[2] For a good brief review of postwar relations see Lyle C. Brown and James W. Wilkie, "Recent United States-Mexican Relations: Problems Old and New," in *Twentieth Century American Foreign Policy*, edited by John Braeman, Robert H. Brenner, and David Brody, Modern America Series No. 3 (Columbus: Ohio State University Press, 1971), pp. 378–419.

claims to small bits of territory along the Rio Grande. The largest of these land problems was an area known as the Chamizal in the region of El Paso, Texas. The Treaty of Guadalupe Hidalgo in 1848 established the boundary between Mexico and the United States in the middle of the main channel of the Rio Grande. In the next few years commissioners and surveyors carried out the appropriate measurements, and the Gadsden Treaty in 1854 accepted the findings. The Rio Grande has a habit, however, of refusing to remain in its bed. Along much of its course the river banks are subject to erosion and over the years the area surveyed in 1852–1853 no longer marked the main channel of the river. Moreover, torrential rains and floods in the headwaters and tributaries, such as those of 1864, caused sudden major shifts in the river's course. It was these shiftings that led to claims and counterclaims of territory along the river. In 1884 the United States and Mexico agreed that sudden rapid shifts creating new channels would not affect the boundary between the two states, but that gradual shifts through natural erosion would move the boundary by retaining it in the middle of the channel. In 1895 Mexico put forward its first claim to the Chamizal, arguing that the river had shifted rapidly, abandoning one channel and opening another. The United States maintained to the contrary that since the boundary had shifted as the result of the normal processes of erosion and deposition, the land belonged to the United States. In 1910 the countries referred the dispute to an international arbitration commission, composed of a Canadian jurist and two commissioners, one from each disputing country. The Canadian arbiter ruled the following year that the Chamizal should be divided between Mexico and the United States along the course of the river's deepest channel as it had existed in 1864. The United States commissioner, supported by his government, rejected the settlement on the grounds that the 1864 boundary had been obliterated and that the Chamizal must go intact to one or another of the claimants. In the meantime other areas along the river were being exchanged according to a treaty of 1905 that provided for minor boundary changes brought about by erosion. By 1963 over 200 parcels had changed hands involving almost 30,000 acres of land. Finally during the Kennedy administration a definitive settlement was reached. In

August 1963 President Kennedy signed "The Convention for the Solution of the Problem of the Chamizal." The Senate ratified it with only one abstention (from Texas) in December, and Congress appropriated the first money to carry out the treaty the following year. Engineers and technical experts laid the course for the new boundary, returning the Chamizal to Mexico and part of Córdova Island to the United States. In December 1968 Presidents Johnson and Díaz Ordaz set off the dynamite blasts that shifted the river to its new and permanent course.[3] In 1970 in a follow-up treaty (ratified 1971) Mexico and the United States agreed to settle "all existing territorial differences and uncertainties"[4] to restore and maintain the Rio Grande and Colorado River as their national boundaries, and to establish their maritime boundaries in the Pacific Ocean and Gulf of Mexico on the equidistance principle as established at the 1958 Geneva Convention on the territorial sea. The latter boundaries will be drawn to a distance of 12 miles from the coast but will bear no implications for claims to territorial waters or jurisdiction over the sea.

A second problem with a long history of litigation involved the so-called Pious Fund of the Californias. The fund was established in the late seventeenth century to promote Catholic missionary work in the Californias. Benefactors made grants in trust of money and property to the Society of Jesus, the missionary organization in charge of the work. When the Jesuits were expelled from all the Spanish dominions in 1767, the Spanish government took charge of the fund, and the Mexican government

---

[3] For further information on the Chamizal and other border negotiations see Sheldon Liss, *A Century of Disagreement: The Chamizal Conflict, 1864–1964* (Washington: The University Press of Washington, D.C., 1965); Gladys Gregory, *The Chamizal Settlement: A View from El Paso* (El Paso: Texas Western College Press, Southwestern Studies I, 1963); James E. Hill Jr., "El Chamizal: A Century-old Boundary Dispute," *Geographical Review,* Vol. LV (October 1965), No. 4, pp. 510–522; Arthur H. Leibson, "The International Boundary and Water Commission," *Mexican-American Review,* Vol. 35 (September 1967), No. 9, pp. 30–34.

[4] House of Representatives, Committee on Foreign Affairs, "Statement of Joseph F. Friedkin, U.S. Commissioner, International Boundary and Water Commission, United States and Mexico," *Hearing: American-Mexican Boundary Cooperation* (Washington: G.P.O., 1972), p. 9.

took it over after 1821. By agreement between the Church and the government, the first bishop of California was entrusted with the fund in 1840, but Santa Anna had Congress repeal the legislation two years later when the bishop refused to lend the government money from those sources. Late in 1842 Santa Anna had additional legislation passed ordering the properties of the Pious Fund to be sold and the cash paid into the national treasury. That same law obligated the government to pay the missions an annuity equal to 6 percent of the capital value of the fund. When upper California passed to the United States, the church and the state government sought to have Mexico continue the annual payments. An agreement was finally reached in 1877, at a time when Porfirio Díaz was seeking recognition and the settlement of claims and border problems, according to which Mexico paid over $900,000. After further negotiation the Hague Tribunal in 1902 ruled that Mexico should resume the annual payments. These were in fact paid for 10 years until the Revolution disrupted this and other obligations. There the matter rested for several years. In 1931 rumors were circulating, apparently with good foundation, that Mexico was ready to cede the Chamizal in return for a cancellation of the fund debts, but the trade-off never materialized. Finally when the Chamizal itself was settled, Mexican interest arose in settling the Pious Fund. Following indications of the Mexican ambassador in Washington and the payment of the 1966 annuity, serious bargaining began. Mexico stated that it would make annual payments until a lump-sum settlement could be made. The final agreement was signed August 1, 1967 in Mexico City. The proceeds, amounting to almost $720,000, were set up by United States bishops as an endowment for the National Pontifical Seminary in Montezuma, New Mexico, an institution designed to educate young men for the priestly career in Mexico.[5] In May 1972 the seminary closed, and the endowment was transferred to the Mexican bishops to be used to educate men to the priesthood in that country. The library, the staff, and the student body at the time of the closing

---

[5] Francis J. Weber, *The United States Versus Mexico: The Final Settlement of the Pious Fund* (Los Angeles: The Historical Society of Southern California, 1969).

of Montezuma Seminary transferred to Tula in Hidalgo State.

A third problem, this one of recent origin, was also settled in the contemporary era. For the past several centuries states bordering on the seas claimed certain waters as integral parts of the national territory. Most of the Great Powers established three nautical miles as the limit of their jurisdiction although some states claimed more. Within this area of territorial water foreign ships were prohibited except with permission of the claimant. In the twentieth century, however, many countries have enlarged their claims of territorial seas, some to six, nine, 12, or even 200 miles because of a desire to reserve to their own citizens resources on their coasts such as fish and petroleum. In 1935 President Cárdenas established by presidential decree a nine-mile limit for Mexico, and in 1945 President Truman issued a proclamation reserving the resources on and under the continental shelf for the United States. For many years, these actions created no problems between the two countries. The United States continued to observe the three-mile limit for fishing and navigation. In the 1950s, however, the Mexican government became concerned with the increasing number of United States shrimp boats in the Gulf of Mexico fishing inside Mexico's nine-mile claim. During 1953 and 1954 and again during 1956 and 1957 Mexican coastal patrol boats seized several dozen United States vessels, levying fines and confiscating their nets and catch. An informal agreement was reached between Mexico and boat owners of the United States in which the United States fishermen agreed to respect the nine-mile limit and the Mexicans permitted the United States shrimpers to seek shelter in two designated points in stormy weather. The agreement did not work well, and in 1954 the United States Congress passed the Fisherman's Protective Act that reimbursed boat owners for fines and losses incurred while fishing in claimed territorial waters not recognized by the United States. Although the United States government was obligated to pay such fines, an informal agreement was reached with boat owners and operators to respect Mexico's nine-mile limit. Despite occasional seizures the affair seemed settled after 1957.

Although the issue with Mexico was basically settled on a de facto basis, the United States sought some international agreement on territorial water because of continuing serious problems elsewhere, particularly with some South American claims to 200 miles. Two international conferences on the Law of the Sea (1958 and 1960) failed to reach agreement on jurisdiction over resources or navigation. Then in 1966 both Mexico and the United States enacted similar laws extending their respective fishing jurisdictions to 12 miles beyond their shorelines. Following these actions the two countries opened negotiations for the control of foreign fishing between the nine and the 12-mile limits. Within that area traditional fishing by one in the other's zone could continue, but the operators had to obey regulations, and limit the catch to that of the preceding five years. Mexico continued to maintain her nine-mile territorial limits and the United States its three-mile limit. The agreement went into effect January 1, 1968 for five years and was subject to review.[6] In effect what transpired was an agreement to disagree about theoretical claims to territorial waters and compromise the concrete issue of fishing rights. It appears that United States shrimp fishermen will be excluded from Mexican coastal waters within 12 miles of the coast barring a renewal of the treaty. At the same time the United States hopes to reach a more general settlement with a third conference on the sea that opened December 1973.

IV

In an era noted for sweeping changes in science and technology, entirely new types of problems have arisen in international relations that previously either did not exist or did not lend themselves to treatment and negotiation. Among the great powers such problems have included weapons systems, electronic detection (or spy) instruments, and space exploration. None of these affect United States-Mexican relations, because Mexico as a relatively poor state cannot undertake programs of this magnitude. The technical problems that have affected their common interests have involved airline routes, radio and television channels, and

---

[6] U.S. Department of State, "Agreement between the United States of America and the United Mexican States on Traditional Fishing in the Exclusive Fishery Zones Contiguous to the Territorial Seas of Both Countries," *Treaties and Other International Acts*, Series 6359 (Washington, 1968).

disease. Few if any of these problems lend themselves to definitive solutions, especially as technology constantly changes, but they are subject to periodic review and peaceful adjustments (although the bargaining may be long and hard) as long as the general climate between the states is relatively congenial.

Apart from the exchange of information, emergency treatment of individuals, and shipment of vaccines and medical supplies in cases of disaster, Mexican-United States joint programs to control disease have involved animals rather than people. During the summer of 1972 health authorities in the United States expressed alarm at the spread of Venezuelan equine encephalomyelitis through Mexico. Apparently, no measures were taken to control the disease other than to disseminate information about the areas of its outbreak and the issuance of warnings to horse owners to inoculate their animals.

Two livestock diseases, screwworm fly infestation and hoof-and-mouth infection, have caused severe losses to stockmen of both countries since World War II. The former is still troublesome, and outbreaks occur sporadically; the latter has seemingly been eradicated from both countries by joint efforts, but a careful watch is maintained for both diseases by the Mexican-United States Commission for the Prevention of Foot-and-Mouth Disease. During the 1950s United States government-sponsored research developed by means of radiation sterile male screwworm flies. Since the female mates only once, the release of millions of sterile males leads to an enormous reduction in the fly population because the eggs from such a union are infertile. In the late 1950s the fly was virtually eliminated in the eastern United States. Eradication in the Southwest, however, proved impossible because the flies continued to move up from Mexico. In 1962 Mexican authorities agreed to permit United States aircraft to drop sterile flies in northern Mexico from the Gulf to the Pacific. To reduce the cost of this program the United States Congress in 1966 by law authorized the Department of Agriculture to coordinate plans with Mexico to eradicate the fly throughout Mexico by setting up a sterile barrier at the narrow necks of the continent either at the Guatemala-Mexico border or through the Isthmus of Tehuantepec. Finally, in August 1972 after a renewed infestation of serious proportions the United States and Mexico agreed to authorize the United States Department of Agriculture to establish a barrier zone across the Isthmus of Tehuantepec, some 700 miles south of the border.[7]

Costly and troublesome as screwworm fly infestation may be, hoof-and-mouth disease has presented in the past a far greater threat to livestock. Until the development of vaccines in the 1940s, the only methods used to control the disease were to prevent the importation of animals from affected areas, and once the disease occurred to kill and burn all infected animals. Outbreaks of the disease were fairly common both in the United States and Mexico in the early years of the twentieth century, but apparently had been rather well eradicated by 1930 when the two countries entered into an agreement not to import cattle or swine from areas where the disease occurred. Then in 1946 Mexico imported some Zebu bulls from Brazil, and within the year an outbreak of hoof-and-mouth occurred in the state of Veracruz, spreading rapidly to other areas. The United States responded immediately to Mexico's request for aid. Congress authorized the Department of Agriculture to cooperate with the Mexican authorities in controlling the disease and appropriated an initial $9 million to implement the program. The older method of killing and burning infected and even exposed animals was first utilized. Although owners were compensated for their losses, angry protests arose because in many instances the cattle could not be replaced, a particular hardship for the owners of only one or two animals necessary for plowing. Shortly after the program began, the Mexican government informed the United States that continued slaughtering was politically untenable, and persuaded the United States to try the new vaccines on a mass basis. New strains and new techniques were rapidly developed that permitted widespread effective vaccination at moderate cost. Unfortunately the early slaughterings created suspicions in some Mexican circles that United States agents were engaged in systematic reduction of the Mexican herds.[8] In 1954 the program ended with the final eradication of the dis-

---

[7] Brown and Wilkie, *op. cit.*, pp. 384–386; "Mexico-United States Teamplay," *Mexican-American Review* Vol. 35 (October 1967), No. 10, pp. 24–25; *The Austin American*, October 31, 1972.

[8] Luis G. Zorrilla, *Historia de las Relaciones entre México y los Estados Unidos de América, 1800–1958* (México: Editorial Porrúa, 1965), Vol. II, p. 544.

ease. The United States border, closed to Mexican cattle imports during the outbreak, was reopened, and the joint commission has continued its careful monitoring of conditions. There have been no serious occurrences since 1954.[9]

In the field of communications only radio broadcasting has produced substantial friction between the two countries. Both Mexico and the United States signed the international telecommunications convention in Geneva in 1952; prior to this agreement they had long established contacts by telephone, telegraph, and postal systems. Television too presented no difficult problems. As early as 1951 they signed an agreement allocating channels along the border. In 1958 they signed another agreement allocating ultra-high-frequency channels. Both of these basic documents have been modified over the years with little or no dispute. In contrast, radio has produced much controversy. With its long-range effects as compared with the short range of television, radio broadcasting in either country can drown out or disrupt broadcasting in the other with more powerful equipment. As early as 1937 six countries and two dependencies, including Mexico and the United States, signed the North American Regional Broadcasting Agreement (NARBA) to reduce this type of interference. Mexico refused to ratify the agreement until she obtained a bilateral agreement with the United States protecting six Mexican clear channels. Such an accord was reached in 1940 when the United States consented to limit United States stations on these six clear channels only to daytime operations with a maximum power of one kilowatt. Both agreements went into effect in 1941 for five years and were renewed on an interim basis in 1946 for three more years. Although the signatories negotiated a new NARBA in 1950, Mexico did not sign and withdrew from the conference. For the next six years Mexico negotiated for a bilateral agreement with the United States in a series of conferences held in Mexico City and Washington, D.C. Throughout, Mexico's primary aim was to maintain strict limita-

---

[9] For a thorough and scholarly study of the crisis, see Manuel A. Machado, Jr., *An Industry in Crisis: Mexican-United States Cooperation in the Control of Foot-and-Mouth Disease* (Berkeley and Los Angeles: University of California Press, 1968).

tions on the secondary use of her clear channels. Finally in January 1957 an accord effective for five years was reached that provided that each country would retain the same clear channels as agreed on in the 1937 NARBA (plus an additional one for Mexico) with secondary use at night permitted by each country on a very limited number of the other's clear channels. Second, each country could increase the daytime power of its secondary stations on certain clear channels of the other. Affected United States broadcasters objected vehemently to parts of the agreement, especially those that limited daytime operations. Their influence in the Senate apparently accounted for the long delay in ratification, which did not come until 1961. During the course of the treaty new questions arose. Just prior to its expiration, the signatories extended the treaty for another year, but on December 31, 1967 it lapsed because of lack of agreement. After another year of negotiation marked by disagreements over nighttime use of each other's clear channels, a new agreement again for five years was reached late in 1968. In effect United States operators gained longer hours for broadcasting by obtaining permission for predawn broadcasting while the Mexicans protected their stations in the postsunset hours. Agreement was also reached to establish procedures for continuing negotiations and revisions of details in broadcasting arrangements.[10]

Similar to radio broadcasting, air transportation between Mexico and the United States has produced long and complex negotiations. Prior to World War II, no formal governmental agreements existed. Pan American World Airways enjoyed a temporary concession from the Mexican government for two flights, one from Brownsville Texas to Mexico City and the other from Miami to Mérida with an intermediate stop in Havana. With the involvement of the United States in World War II, the Mexican government in 1942 extended Pan American's concession and granted American Airlines a war emergency permit for a flight from San Antonio to Mexico City with a stop at Mon-

---

[10] "Coming U.S.-Mexican talks may solve old problems," *Broadcasting*, Vol. 71 (July 18, 1966), p. 60; "All work and no treaty in Mexico," *Broadcasting*, Vol. 72 (March 20, 1967), p. 77; *U.S. Department of State Bulletin*, Vol. LX (1969), No. 1555, p. 330.

terrey. In addition the Compañía Mexicana de Aviación, an affiliate of Pan American, received permission to fly from Mexico City to Los Angeles with several intermediate stops in Mexico.

Both countries sent delegations to the 1944 Convention on International Civil Aviation, and both ratified the agreement in the summer of 1946. One of the most important provisions of that agreement stipulated that scheduled international air service must have the authorization of the governments of the states involved. Although the two countries began talks as early as 1945 looking to a bilateral air convention, no agreement could be reached for many years, and the United States airlines continued to conduct their business directly with the Mexican government, while the United States government remained an interested observer. Pan American and American continued to be the only successful applicants for flights into Mexico from the United States. In 1952 President Truman tried to break the deadlock by rescinding unused United States certificates to three other airlines for international flights to Mexico, and by directing the State Department to seek an aviation agreement on a government-to-government basis.

Despite earnest efforts and much interest in negotiating a settlement, no agreement could be reached until 1957. The basic differences separating the two governments revolved around not only the specific routes but, more importantly, the level of competition among the carriers. The United States with one of the most advanced airline systems in the world advocated the right of unrestricted airline competition. Mexico with a struggling, hard-pressed system advocated either a division of the traffic or a pooling and division of the profits. Mexico put considerable pressure on the United States to make some concessions when it granted Air France in 1953 a nonstop flight from New York to Mexico City. In mid-1955 American Airlines claimed that Air France revenues from that concession were running over $2 million per year and that it had reduced United States carrier participation in that traffic from 100 percent to 15 percent. Finally in mid-1957 a provisional air agreement was reached by an exchange of notes that granted seven routes to United States carriers and six to Mexican with only one airline assigned to each route by the respective governments. Several routes overlapped, for example, the New York-Washington-Mexico City granted to the United States, and the Mexico City-Washington-New York granted to Mexico. The agreement represented a compromise on both sides. The United States abandoned its position that there be no limits on the frequency of service or on the aircraft capacity on any designated routes while Mexico abandoned its position that there be an absolute monopoly on each route, that flight frequencies be limited, and that profits be pooled. The provisional agreement gave way to a permanent agreement in 1960 that included various regulatory and technical provisions for inspection of aircraft, fees for use of facilities, availability of fuel and spare parts, handling of cargo and mail, and arbitration of disputes. Over the years the agreement has been extended and revised particularly about increasing the number of routes.

A particularly controversial situation arose between 1963 and 1965 as a result of Mexico placing limitations on United States carriers with respect to aircraft capacity and frequency of service. In 1964 an unofficial gentleman's agreement to freeze capacity, frequency, and route designations led to pressure on the Mexican government from hotel operators, municipal authorities, and other tourist interests to establish new flights to Puerto Vallarta and other west coast resorts. When Mexico relaxed some of its restrictions to serve this area with international flights, the United States government protested the action as a violation of the agreement. In renewed negotiations in 1965, Mexico granted concessions on the question of frequency of service, but the United States refused to grant Mexico any further route concessions at that time. One observer implied that in effect Mexico "sold out" its airlines to maintain and increase its tourist trade. In the years that followed both frequency of service and the number of routes have expanded as both tourist and commercial ties between the two countries have increased. One important result of the air agreements has been the ever-increasing share of the Mexican government in the control and ownership of the Mexican airlines. When the private airlines proved incapable of meeting the financial burdens imposed by international competition, the Mexican government began to intervene. Aeronaves de México was taken over by the government in 1959, and two years later Guest Aerovías was absorbed. Companía Mexicana de Aviación, an affiliate of Pan American, but primarily Mexican owned and controlled, fell into deep financial difficulties by the mid 1960s, but it has remained under private control, now entirely Mexican, but with government participation in stock ownership. Airline routes, frequency of service, and aircraft capacity will continue to be sources of controversy and negotiation, but given the past experience of Mexican interest in the United States tourist trade and United States interest in airline economics, the prospects are bright that compromises can be made and the air agreement extended. The United States and Mexico held talks early in 1973 to prepare a new four-year bilateral agreement to replace the present accord that expired June 30.[11]

V

Several problems have not lent themselves to definitive solutions, and by their very nature they will probably require many years of continuing negotiations and adjustments. Most of these problems involve the movement of persons and things across the common borders of the two countries. Although in an earlier age the movement of United States adventurers and landseekers into Mexico led to tensions and eventually to war, today the flow of persons in the opposite direction and the type of person crossing the border is quite different. The Mexican migrant crossing into the United States legally or illegally is normally a poor peasant seeking not land or adventure but simply a job either on the farms and ranches of the Southwest or more recently in the factories and businesses of the large cities. His actions while creating some problems for United States authorities, particularly if he comes illegally, create at best low-level tensions in the international arena, and while the treatment of people crossing the border or the practice of discrimination against Mexicans in parts of the United States have led to criti-

---

[11] For discussion of this controversy, see O. J. Lissitzyn, "Bilateral Agreements on Air Transport," *The Journal of Air Law and Commerce* Vol. XXX (Winter 1964), No. 1, pp. 248–263 and Max Healey, "Revisions to the Mexico-United States Air Transport Agreement, 1965–1970," *The Journal of Air Law and Commerce* Vol. XXXII (Spring 1966), No. 2, pp. 167–194; Anni Jensen, "CAB Seeks Comments on U.S.-Mexican Pact," *Journal of Commerce*, June 7, 1973.

cism and formal complaint from Mexico, none of these situations is likely to produce serious problems in Mexican-United States relations. The movement of materials as well as persons across international boundaries creates the need for constant consideration and adjustment. With Mexico heavily dependent on the United States in terms of trade and investment and with the growth of substantial population and industrial development in the immediate border areas, the movement of goods and services, legal and illegal, needs to be regulated by both countries. As with the movement of persons these activities have at times created difficulties whether it is Mexican farm products competing successfully in the United States market with United States produce or the movement of United States capital into Mexico to take advantage of cheap labor for export of manufactured products assembled in Mexico, or the smuggling of drugs in both directions. Unilateral and heavyhanded measures in tackling these problems have led to hard feelings and irritation, but again to no serious altercations and have stimulated continued negotiation and compromise. More serious than any of the above problems has been the question of the salinity of the waters of the Colorado River as it flows into Mexico. The Colorado is used on both sides of the border for irrigation, but by the time it reaches Mexico its mineral content is so high that Mexico has suffered great crop damage. United States activities to alleviate the danger have produced at best modest results, and Mexican authorities view the problem as one of the more serious in their relations with the United States.

From their earliest contacts Mexico and the United States have been troubled by the crossing of persons over their mutual frontiers. In the early nineteenth century such migrants consisted primarily of United States citizens in search of land and empire in the largely vacant areas to the south and west of their own country. Mexico's efforts to stem the tide or to regulate it in protection of her vast northern territories proved unsuccessful, first with the secession of Texas as an independent state, and then with the loss to the United States of extensive domains as a result of the disastrous war in the 1840s. The new boundaries established by the war did not end the problems, only changed their nature. The conflicts that arose over border crossings for the next 30 years developed from Mexico's inability to establish order on its northern frontier with respect to Indian raiders and bandits. When the dictator, Porfirio Díaz, centralized political control in his own hands, reorganized his armed forces, reduced banditry, and conquered the Indians, such border problems disappeared, and returned only briefly during the Revolution with the raids of Pancho Villa. Today, a third type of border problem confronts the two countries: illegal migrants from Mexico seeking work or better paying jobs in the United States.

For about a century there has been some movement of people northward across the border. Until the late 1920s movements back and forth across the border were virtually unrestricted. Thousands of Mexicans settled permanently in Texas, New, Mexico, Arizona, and California as miners, railway workers, farmers, and farm and ranch hands. Many came as seasonal workers. Between 1910 and 1920 other thousands fled the turmoil of the Mexican Revolution. Since their labor was eagerly sought (and they worked hard for low pay) no one opposed their entry. The United States government suspended the literacy-test requirement of the Immigration Law of 1917 to permit Mexican labor to replace the men called for military duty in World War I. About 73,000 crossed legally and unknown thousands illegally during the next few years. After the war the authorities continued to interpret the law loosely for Mexican migrants with the result that during the 1920s about 1,000,000 entered the United States.[12] Only toward the end of the decade did the flow taper off when the State Department began to interpret the 1917 law more strictly in the face of labor union demands for a quota system for Latin America. Then came the Great Depression. Not only did the migration cease, but it was reversed. It is estimated that about half of the people who came during the 1920s returned to Mexico, most of them destitute. Some went back of their own accord, but many were deported by immigration authorities working with state officials. Jobs held by Mexicans were given to United States citizens, and it was cheaper to send them back to Mexico than to give them relief assistance. The

---

[12] Citizens of all Latin American countries were specifically exempt from the quotas imposed by the Immigration Acts of 1921 and 1924.

people who remained stayed poor and suffered discrimination. Those who returned to Mexico could find no work and no help. The whole affair further embittered many Mexicans against the United States.

Toward the end of the 1930s the United States economy began to revive, and with the coming of World War II and eventual United States entry, the need for increased supplies of food and materials, and the transportation to move them created a demand from farmers and from the railroads for Mexican labor. The United States government acquiesced, but the Mexican government after the unhappy experience of the 1930s, asked for protection and guarantees for its workers. Following some discussion and conversations on the matter, the United States ambassador presented a formal proposal to the Mexican government in June 1942 on the use of contract labor in the United States. The Under Secretary of Foreign Affairs Jaime Torres Bodet responded that Mexico would study the proposal but reminded the ambassador of the problems of the 1930s, especially discrimination in various states over which the United States government had no control. He also pointed out that some groups in Mexico opposed a new migration, while the government itself feared the dissatisfaction of seasonal workers with the lower pay they would receive upon returning to Mexico. Despite these misgivings the two countries reached an agreement, and an exchange of notes on August 4 brought it into effect. The terms of the agreement, incorporating the basic demands of the Mexican government for protection of workers, provided that the United States government would become the legal employer responsible for the well-being of the workers and that the growers and other users of Mexican labor would be subcontractors. It also guaranteed the migrants nondiscriminatory treatment, a minimum wage, transportation, living expenses, and repatriation. It did not establish a set number to enter, leaving the amount to United States needs and Mexican availability at any given time. The agreement remained in effect until December 31, 1947, although organized labor succeeded in having the section on railway labor eliminated in March 1946. Altogether about 350,000 workers entered during the five years of the program. Most came as farm laborers, and most of them worked in California. The program worked reasonably well, although there was constant bickering over the terms of the agreement between the United States and Mexico, and among conflicting groups within both countries. Organized labor in the United States saw the agreement as a means both of depressing wages and of hindering organization of workers. Various Mexican officials and private individuals opposed the program as an affront to national pride, but some employers also saw in it a lever to raise wages in Mexico.[13]

Because United States farmers in the Southwest demanded good cheap labor, Mexican seasonal workers continued to enter the United States. For the next three and a half years the only legal authority for the entrance of Mexican nationals was the Immigration Act of 1917. On the Mexican side, the Mexican government still demanded a contract with certain guarantees for the workers. Now, however, the United States contractor was the individual grower and not the government. The grower was also responsible for recruitment, but he had to have a certificate from the Department of Labor that a labor shortage existed in his area. During this period about 20,000 legally contracted laborers came to the United States, but at least twice that number of "wetbacks" (illegal migrants) also entered. Because of continuing grower pressure and Mexican dissatisfaction with the unregulated program, the United States Congress in July 1951 passed legislation once again authorizing government-to-government contracting for labor. In August a standard work contract was drawn up and an international agreement reached. These three documents with modifications constituted the bracero program that lasted for 13 years. Over 3,000,000 workers entered the United States legally under this program and although wetbacks continued to cross the border, their numbers declined as legal workers became available and the immigration service stepped up its vigilance. Throughout the life of the agreement organized labor in the United States and a variety of groups in Mexico opposed the bracero program as they had opposed all previous contract labor agreements. By the early 1960s, there was growing sentiment in Congress to terminate the program. Although it is obvious that United States organized labor and its allies contributed to the demise of the program,

---

[13] McCain, *op. cit.*, pp. v–viii, 25–32, 335–336, and 344–347.

the major factor appears to have been the increasing mechanization of cotton harvesting in the southwestern United States. In the last two years of the bracero operation (1963 and 1964) less than 190,000 Mexican workers found employment on United States farms and ranches.

What effect did the bracero program have on United States-Mexican relations? For Mexico, contract labor presented a two-edged sword. On the one hand it acknowledged in a formal, official, and public way that Mexico could not adequately take care of its own people. To nationalists, the program represented another aspect of Mexico's dependence on the United States and constantly aroused fears that the nation would be humiliated through the practice of discrimination and racial bias among the employers. Some business and political groups also feared the potential danger of unrest when the returning workers became obliged to accept much lower paying jobs in Mexico. At the same time the short-term benefits were clearly tangible. Thousands of new job opportunities opened up (reaching a peak in the late 1950s of almost half a million annually) with profit remittances in some years reaching $120 million. In 1956 and 1957 these remittances constituted Mexico's third largest source of foreign exchange. To social reformers the bitter taste of the program was somewhat muted by the realization that this income went directly to peasant families, the most deprived economic group in Mexico. As a result of these mixed results, most opposition in Mexico remained pro forma except for certain Catholic leaders who feared for the moral and spiritual well-being of the workers and their families who were separated for months at a time. Serious complaints from Mexicans revolved more around the implementation of the contracts and specific charges of the abuse of Mexicans rather than around the principle of the program itself. In fact when the United States Congress proposed to terminate the program in 1963, the Mexican government requested that it be phased out more gradually to ease the economic impact on Mexico. Acceding to the request Congress passed legislation extending its life for one more year.[14]

In the United States the attacks on the program were the

---

[14] Richard B. Craig, *The Bracero Program: Interest Groups and Foreign Policy* (Austin: The University of Texas Press, 1971) passim.

reverse of those in Mexico. Serious complaints revolved around the very principle of the program rather than around problems of implementation and interpretation of the contracts. Organized labor and groups sympathetic to United States migrants fought to limit and eventually to end the practice. In terms of relations with Mexico the bracero and earlier labor agreements were negotiated in a general atmosphere of harmony. Virtually all of Mexico's demands were met by the United States. On the other hand unpleasant situations occasionally arose partly over misunderstandings but partly, too, over real grievances primarily from the Mexican work force. To assess accurately the labor contract program is to see it not as producing greater harmony in United States-Mexican relations but as a result of the settlement of the severe conflicts over mineral and land rights in the 1930s and early 1940s. Without those previous agreements it appears highly unlikely that Mexico would have entered into formal negotiations to send its workers to the United States whatever the material benefits.

With the termination of the bracero program in 1964 the regulation of Mexican migrants into the United States reverted to the Immigration and Nationality Act of 1952. Under its terms no provision is made for the movement of seasonal workers, but a would-be laborer may apply for a permanent residence visa if he affirms that he has a job and obtains a Labor Department certificate stating that his employment will not adversely affect wages and working conditions in the United States. The law does not demand that he actually live in the United States to obtain such a visa. As of 1968 700,000 Mexican citizens had obtained this document, and estimates on the number who resided in Mexico ranged from 40,000 to 150,000 citizens. In July 1968, however, the Immigration Act was amended to restrict the number of Western Hemisphere immigrants to 120,000 per year; it is estimated that now a Mexican must wait approximately a year to obtain a resident visa following his application.[15]

The end of contract labor and particularly the imposition of Western Hemisphere quotas quickly led to a flood of illegal entrants. While wetbacks were never entirely eliminated, their

---

[15] Homer Bigart, "Unions Deplore Influx of Mexican Laborers Along the Border," *The New York Times*, May 4, 1969, p. 78.

number was much reduced by the early 1960s. At the end of the decade they began to increase rapidly once again, and in 1971 the Immigration Services reported that almost 350,000 Mexicans had been deported for illegal entry. It was estimated that the total number of wetbacks exceeded that figure by several times. Although some alien labor, particularly the visa holder, is still used in farm work to keep wages low and break strikes of organized labor in Texas and California, most wetbacks seem to be scattering through the country, many settling into unskilled jobs in large cities like Chicago and New York. They are then difficult to locate and within time settle down into American life without the opportunity of becoming citizens but with no intention of returning to Mexico. Not surprisingly the vast numbers desiring entry combined with the difficulty of legal migration has led to the development of considerable smuggling along the largely unpatrolled and undermanned border. Often the migrants are bilked of their funds and abandoned. On the United States side, the increasing problem has led to frustration and sometimes harsh treatment of legal border crossers. It is in this area that Mexican-United States relations have become strained with Mexican charges of discourtesy, humiliating searches, rough treatment, and long delays.[16] While undoubtedly such actions have occurred and have caused local discontent, the illegal migration is basically a problem of United States law enforcement and United States interest-group conflict that only marginally touches international relations. A minor furor was created in Mexico in the spring of 1973 when it was reported that United States and Mexican officials were cooperating in transporting captured illegal Mexican migrants deep into the interior of Mexico against their will at their own expense, and then dumping them.[17] The Mexican government generally,

---

[16] "Surge of Illegal Immigrants Across American Borders," *U.S. News and World Report*, January 17, 1972; "Chain Link Curtain Holds Back Hope," *The Austin American*, August 7, 1972, p. 7; see also Denny Walsh, "Justice Officials Find Corruption Rife Among Immigration Aides in Southwest," *The New York Times*, May 21, 1973, who reported the smuggling of aliens and narcotics, the sale of documents, and abuse of immigrants was widely practiced by immigration officials.
[17] "Report on Moving of Aliens from U.S. Stirs Mexico," *The New York Times*, May 4, 1973.

however, makes few representations to United States authorities about the treatment of its citizens, being far more concerned to maintain basically harmonious relations with the United States along the border because of the growing economic importance of the area to Mexico. The Mexicans appear to do little to stem the flow of wetbacks in part because of the enormous costs of effective vigilance. Moreover, there appears to be little popular demand (and therefore little prohibited pressure) in Mexico to impede Mexican working-class people from leaving the country if they desire.

VI

People are not the only border crossers who have created problems. Water does too, particularly the quality of water. The United States and Mexico share three river systems: the small Tijuana near the Pacific Coast, on which there is no agreement, and the Colorado and Rio Grande over which there has been much negotiation, treaty signing, and conflict of interest. Geography has determined that the disputes over the waters of the Rio Grande, the international boundary for 1200 miles, would be settled more or less equitably because both countries, desiring to develop agricultural lands along much of its course, will see to it that quality controls deliver good irrigation water almost to the mouth of the river on the Gulf of Mexico. The Colorado, on the other hand, flowing most of its course through the United States before it empties into the Gulf of California in Mexican territory, has created tensions in Mexican-United States relations for over 70 years.[18] The problem arises from rich farm land on both sides of the border, scarce rainfall, and insufficient river water to irrigate the available lands.[19]

For many years no treaties regulated the use of the waters except for general stipulations about navigation, which were usually meaningless. The treaties ending the Mexican-United

---

[18] The Colorado forms the international boundary for 20 miles before entering Mexico for the last 100 miles of its course.

[19] The average rainfall in the Colorado River basin is only 15 inches per year. This produces an average flow of 15,700,000 acre-feet after evaporation, amounting to only 3 percent of the flow of the Mississippi River. Recorded extremes range from a low of 6,000,000 to a high of 25,000,000 acre-feet.

States war and providing for the purchase of 1853 ignored irrigation usage because so few people lived in these desert areas. In the 1880s, however, dam building accompanying settlement in the upper Rio Grande began to threaten Mexican users below El Paso. After many years of conversations and negotiations, a treaty was finally signed in 1906 guaranteeing Mexico 60,000 acre-feet of Rio Grande water, the amount then being used. In later years Mexicans severely criticized this treaty because it impeded further agricultural expansion on the Mexican side. In the meantime the first use of Colorado River water for irrigation occurred in 1901 when a private United States company constructed a canal from the river (on the Mexican side of the border) to the Imperial Valley in California. The Mexican government raised some questions but did nothing to impede its operations. Then in 1908 the Mexican and United States governments established a joint commission to study the allocation of the waters of both the Colorado and the Rio Grande. Before the commission produced any tangible results, the break of relations with the Huerta government by Woodrow Wilson halted all negotiations. By the time Huerta fell, such critical new controversies had arisen over land and mineral rights that made compromise over water resources impossible. Negotiations bogged down in 1929 when Mexico claimed water in proportion to its irrigable acreage and the United States proposed for Mexico an amount in proportion to past usage as established in the 1906 treaty on the Rio Grande. During the 1930s, however, new pressures were building on both sides to reach an accomodation. Under Cárdenas, Mexico began to construct a series of dams on tributary streams that threatened to divert huge amounts of Rio Grande water to irrigate the lower valley. Texas farmers clamored for protection, but Mexico would negotiate only over both the Colorado and the Rio Grande as a single package. Mexico for its part was more than willing to bargain because the great Hoover Dam and the All-American Canal, then under construction, would soon divert large quantities of Colorado River water to California, Arizona, and Nevada. Although the Colorado River states, especially California, objected to concessions to Mexico, Secretary of State Cordell Hull in 1937 decided to undertake negotiations on both rivers. Bargaining proceeded slowly, but further developments encouraged both

sides to make concessions. United States plans in 1939 to build
diversion canals upstream on the Rio Grande from Mexican
canals pressured Mexico to scale down its demand for Colorado
water, while the coming of World War II pressured the United
States government to override state complaints (particularly of
California) and guarantee Mexico a fairly generous flow of
water. Basic agreements were reached in late 1943 and a treaty
signed on February 3, 1944. Overriding bitter and strenuous
opposition from California, the United States ratified it overwhelmingly in July and the Mexican Senate, with less opposition, unanimously. For the Rio Grande the 1906 treaty remained
in force for the upper basin, and for the lower valley Mexico
guaranteed the United States 350,000 acre-feet. In addition the
new treaty provided for the construction of three major dams,
flood and salt control projects, and the generation of hydro-
electric power. For the Colorado, the United States agreed to
deliver 1,500,000 acre-feet of water to Mexico "from any and all
sources," to increase this to 1,700,000 acre-feet if a surplus became available, and to acquire and retain all works necessary
to deliver this allotment. The treaty also provided that, if a
"drought" occurred in the United States, Mexico's share would
be reduced proportionately to that in the United States.[20]

Despite the importance of the treaty in dealing with a particularly thorny and complex controversy, it must be faulted on
several grounds. First, the negotiators predicated the treaty on
an exaggerated estimate of the flow of the Colorado River,
18,000,000 acre-feet. Given the anticipated needs of the basin
states at 16,000,000 acre-feet, Mexico's allotment of 1,500,000
fell easily within range. In fact, however, the average has proved
out at something under 16,000,000, limiting thereby the availability of water in the United States. Second, no definition was
ever reached for "drought" or determination made as to who
would define and declare a drought. Third, and most critically,
the treaty included no statement on the "quality" of the water
delivered to Mexico. Obviously, a part of the water would be
return flow from water already used in the United States, but
how much and how saline was left unspecified. In the debates

---

[20] Basically, the discussion of the salinity problem to 1965 is adapted from
Norris Hundley, Jr., *Dividing the Waters: A Century of Controversy Between
the United States and Mexico* (Berkeley: University of California Press, 1966).

over ratification, proponents in the two countries argued diametrically opposed positions, but neither side tried to reconcile them, perhaps out of fear of losing the whole treaty. Mexico was pleased with the Rio Grande settlement, and the United States government knew that it could control the Colorado interpretation.

For 17 years the treaty worked reasonably well despite decreasing rain and snow, increased United States usage, and the operation of United States storage facilities. Although the flow into Mexico decreased, the minimum allotment was met, partly through return flow, and no crop damage resulted in Mexico. The mix was still good irrigation water. Then suddenly in 1961 a crisis appeared in the form of an enormous jump in the saline content of the water. The source was the Wellton-Mohawk region of the Gila River valley. The Wellton-Mohawk region contains some good farmland but insufficient water. The Gila River flows intermittently, and groundwater is limited. In 1952 a canal from the Colorado began bringing water to the basin, and for several years the area blossomed. By the end of the decade, however, the basin with little or no drainage was becoming waterlogged and unusable. To solve this problem the government opened a drainage canal in February 1961 running from the irrigated areas to the Gila River channel near its confluence with the Colorado. By the end of the year the saline content rose to 2700 parts per million of water, and Mexico refused to use it. Mexican farmers suffered crop losses and the Mexican government complained to the United States of treaty violation. The United States pointed out that the treaty said nothing of quality and suggested that Mexico was in part responsible for high saline levels in her soil because of poor drainage practices. The arguments dragged on for three years, until in March 1965 the United States agreed to build a bypass channel for Wellton-Mohawk to flow into the Colorado River below Mexico's Morelos Dam, the source of its irrigation water. The dam was completed in November 1965 with the expectation of dropping the saline content to 1500 parts per million. The water so diverted still constituted a part of Mexico's guaranteed 1,500,000 acre-feet.[21]

---

[21] Brown and Wilkie, *op. cit.*, p. 399.

The bypass channel did not solve the problem. Admittedly the salinity content was reduced,[22] but Mexican farmers and political leaders continued to complain about saline damages to crops especially when they mixed some Wellton-Mohawk water with other Colorado River water. If they did not mix in any of the Wellton-Mohawk flow, then obviously the amount of water available did not provide sufficient moisture for all the acreage under cultivation. In his visit to the United States in June 1972, President Luis Echeverría in a hard-hitting talk to a joint session of Congress bitterly protested the unresolved conflict. He called the salinity problem of the Colorado the most critical issue in United States-Mexican relations. In a discussion with President Nixon, Echeverría took the position that Mexico was entitled to the same quality of water as that derived from Imperial Dam, an interpretation of the treaty first voiced by Adolfo Orive Alba, one of the Mexican negotiators, in the debates over ratification in Mexico in 1944.[23] Nixon promised to take action to improve the quality of water allotted to Mexico, and Echeverría in the meantime gave orders to use no more Wellton-Mohawk return flow. In July the Mexico-United States of America Water and Border Commission signed an agreement to replace over half of the Wellton-Mohawk water with more usable water from Yuma-zone wells, thus reducing the saline content of the Colorado to 1140 parts per million. This is a provisional measure until a definitive solution is reached. By the summer of 1973 the United States government had decided to construct a giant desalinazation plant on the lower Colorado River in Arizona.[24]

Some of these "peripheral" issues are serious in their own

---

[22] *Mexican Newsletter* (Mexico, Office of the President) July 31, 1972, No. 17, p. 2 reported the saline content was reduced to less than 1300 parts per million.

[23] Hundley, *op. cit.*, p. 168

[24] *Comercio Exterior de México*, Vol. XVIII (September 1972), No. 9, p. 13. For the text of the Communique issued by the two presidents see *Comercio Exterior de México* Vol. XVIII (July 1972), No. 7, pp. 6 and 36. For brief but excellent accounts of recent negotiations see Richard Salvatierra, "Desalting Plant Would Ease Tensions," *Tucson Daily Citizen*, June 21, 1973 and Burt Schoor, "U.S. Plans World's Biggest Desalting Plant to Clear Colorado River Water for Mexico," *The Wall Street Journal*, June 4, 1973.

right. President Echeverría has called the salinity problem of the Colorado River the most pressing issue in current United States-Mexican relations. Other problems such as the bracero situation cause hard feelings or even minor explosions from time to time. The important factor to be noted, however, is that these issues never cause major crises and that as long as more vital economic and political interests are adjusted harmoniously the lesser issues can be settled or negotiated. In earlier times diplomatic protection was one such issue. One observer remarked that there was a parallel "between the upward and downward curve of American territorial and economic ambitions toward Mexico on the one hand, and the concern with which American officials seemed to regard reported injuries. . . . The same events which, in times of mounting ambitions, took on an aspect of extreme gravity, were at the other times treated as minor misfortunes that might happen in any country."[25] United States major interests in Mexico consist of about $2 billion of investments, a lively trade and commerce in both directions, and a political stability that has guaranteed a political closed door to potentially hostile great powers. For Mexico, major interests consist of access to capital and technology and an export market for its goods. Should these be seriously threatened then the peripheral issues can be expected to become more difficult to handle not because they become more serious in themselves but because the general environment becomes more hostile and compromise more difficult to achieve.

---

[25] Frederick S. Dunn, *The Diplomatic Protection of Americans in Mexico* (New York: Columbia University Press, 1933), p. 8.

CHAPTER VIII

The Contemporary Era 1945–1970: The Central Issues

T WO AREAS OF MAJOR IMPORTANCE becloud Mexican-United States relations in the present era: United States intervention in the internal affairs of Latin American states (at times accompanied by military intervention) and United States penetration of the Mexican economy. Over the first area, Mexico can have little influence beyond a moral stance in opposition to direct and indirect pressures from the United States. Mexico is highly sensitive to such an action because of its own experience in the past with United States armed invasions. Although recent incursions of United States troops in Caribbean countries have been much reduced from an earlier period, there is no guarantee that these events will not be repeated. Mexico demonstrates its independence and disapproval of United States political coercion by taking positions opposed to those of the United States such as a continued recognition of Cuba after 1962, a refusal to sign the Caracas anti-Communist declaration of 1954 that preceded a United States-supported exile invasion of Guatemala, and adamant opposition to an inter-American police force. Related to its concern for United States intervention in Latin America is Mexico's interest in creating a Nuclear Free Zone throughout Latin America. While the United States is broadly sympathetic, it insists on the exclusion of certain areas from the ban, and no compromise seems possible at this time. Whatever the disagreements, however, these matters have never threatened normal economic relations much less a break of diplomatic relations between the two countries. Over the second area, Mexico theoretically enjoys almost unlimited options in restricting, limiting, or even eliminating foreign investments, trade, grants, and loans. In practice, however, the government must move cautiously lest it jeopardize the nation's development program through a flight of capital that would follow any sudden shifts of economic policy toward an extreme nationalist position. Mexico's current leadership, committed to continued economic development, fears that a prolonged stagnation in growth would not only damage the country economically but might well lead to a renewal of political instability. It is this frustration, sense of dependence, and feeling of helplessness in confronting its neighbor, its major trading partner, and its source of needed capital that has prevented a full rapprochement between the two countries. Practical problems can be dealt with on an orderly and relatively unemotional basis, but a constant note of tension, prickliness, and formality underlies most negotiations because of the existing disparities and the dependent aspect of the relationship.[1]

I

During the 1960s a high-ranking official in the Mexican foreign office said that "anything that may occur between the United States and the other countries of Latin America cannot, in the future, be alien to us. Latin American problems have inevitably become essential elements in Mexican foreign affairs."[2] They long have been and still are. Mexico's long and bitter experiences with foreign intervention in her internal affairs, whether military, political, or economic have made the country extremely sensitive to all sorts of external pressures on other countries. And the closer they are to home geographically and the more they involve the United States, against whom Mexicans lodge the most grievances, the more sensitive they become. As a

---

[1] In 1966 Antonio Carrillo Flores, then Secretary of Foreign Relations, clearly indicated that the Mexican government well understood the relationship between internal instability and external intervention. See his "La política exterior de México," *Foro Internacional* Vol. VI (1965–66), pp. 233–246.

[2] Jorge Castañeda, "Revolution and Foreign Policy: Mexico's Experience," in *Latin American International Politics: Ambitions, Capabilities, and the National Interest of Mexico, Brazil, and Argentina*, edited by Carlos Alberto Astiz (Notre Dame: University of Notre Dame Press, 1969), p. 161.

consequence, Mexico has adopted one basic foreign policy principle: the absolute nonintervention of one state in the internal affairs of another. Basically a defense policy that has grown out of Mexico's historical experiences and its dependence on an overwhelmingly powerful neighbor, the nonintervention policy has become deeply ingrained into the consciences of all politically aware Mexican citizens. It is sometimes called "respect for the national sovereignty and the judicial equality of all states" and "the right of self determination of all peoples" to adopt whatever form of government or economic system best suits them. The Mexicans seldom inquire about how these forms come about, that is, whether by military coup, imposition, revolution, or popular elections. To support this position they have adopted a policy of recognizing any government in the Western Hemisphere, however formed, and virtually any government throughout the world.[3] In addition Mexico has voted consistently in international organizations to support a hands-off policy in matters touching the internal affairs of other states.[4]

Beyond the publicly proclaimed doctrine of nonintervention, Mexico has also pursued a general policy of independence in foreign affairs. It has aimed assiduously to avoid an appearance of following the United States lead, but at the same time has refused to tie itself to any other nonhemisphere bloc. On some issues it has joined with other Latin American states in demanding economic assistance from the developed world, in supporting an Inter-American Development Bank, and in adhering to a Latin American Free Trade Association. As one of the major states of Latin America, none of these moves could be interpreted as signifying dependence. In the United Nations, the Mexican delegates condemned the attack of North Korea on the South, and generally opposed the admission of Mao's China,

---

[3] Some major exceptions have included Franco's Spain and Mao's China. Mexico has refused to recognize the Franco government on grounds that foreign powers imposed it on Spain, and until recently continued to recognize Chiang's China probably out of deference to the United States. As the United States position changed on China, Mexico finally shifted to a recognition of the mainland government.

[4] L. Vincent Padgett, *The Mexican Political System* (Boston: Houghton-Mifflin, 1966), p. 152.

but took positions on disarmament, economic aid, colonial territories, admission of new states that showed no consistent East-West voting pattern.[5]

In pursuing its independent foreign policy, Mexico has had relatively little difficulty with the United States. No serious problems arose with Mexico's refusal to consider joining an Inter-American Police Force in the 1960s or to sign a Mutual Security Agreement in the 1950s when the United States adopted a policy of supplying military grant aid to Latin American countries that joined such pacts.[6] Nor were there any major repercussions when Mexico not only refused to sign but sharply criticized as interventionist the 1954 Caracas Resolution, directed against Guatemala, that condemned the infiltration of Communists into Western Hemisphere governments and called for appropriate action under the Rio Treaty. As one observer remarked: "The Mexican position seemed to be that the questionable dangers of Communist aggression did not equal the certain dangers of a United States freed from the restraints of the non-intervention pledge."[7] When intervention did occur in Guatemala a few months later, and then in Cuba in 1961 and the Dominican Republic in 1965, Mexicans protested vehemently. Newspapers ran editorials, leading public figures issued statements, and during the Dominican affair all living ex-Presidents strongly condemned the United States action and praised Mexico's contrasting noninterventionist position.

At the same time that the Mexican government sees to it that

---

[5] John R. Faust and Charles L. Stansifer, "Mexican Foreign Policy in the United Nations: The Advocacy of Moderation in an Era of Revolution," *Southwestern Social Science Quarterly*, Vol. 44 (September 1963), No. 2, pp. 121–129, conclude that a study of roll-call votes in the United Nations reveals that Mexico remained basically independent of either bloc and voted in accord with its basic foreign policy principles.

[6] Mexico has, however, made modest purchases of military equipment over the years: about $650,000 in fiscal 1972 and $2,000,000 in fiscal 1973. At the same time Mexico has accepted on the average less than $100,000 in military grant aid annually, all for training of personnel. See *Foreign Assistance Act of 1972*, Committee on Foreign Relations, U.S. Senate Ninety Second Congress, Second Session, pp. 6 and 11.

[7] J. Lloyd Mecham, *A Survey of United States-Latin American Relations* (Boston: Houghton-Mifflin, 1965), p. 378.

the national position is made absolutely clear, officials refrain from activities that might damage diplomatic or economic relationships with the United States. For example, with respect to the United States armed interventions cited above, government officers themselves made very few official statements on the issue. This subtle kind of compromise has manifested itself even more strikingly during the long conflict between the United States and Cuba since the accession to power of Fidel Castro. At the various meetings of Foreign Ministers called under the auspices of the Organization of American States (OAS) Mexico has refused to condemn Cuba, suspend it from the OAS, break diplomatic relations, or impose an embargo.[8] Throughout, Mexico has insisted that all such measures constituted intervention in the internal affairs of one state by others. Nonetheless, the Mexican government in 1962 roundly condemned the Soviet placement of missiles in Cuba and supported the United States blockade for their removal, at the same time warning the United States to refrain from any invasion of the island. Moreover, diplomatic relations between Mexico and Cuba have remained cool and formal. Travelers using Mexican airlines to Cuba are carefully identified, and the information is turned over to United States and Latin American intelligence services. Mexico has also made it difficult for Cuban books and propaganda to enter the country,[9] and so restricted the Cuba news service Presna Latina, that it finally closed its doors early in 1972.[10]

Related to the above cold war issues, but distinct from them, the Latin American Nuclear Free Zone Treaty of 1967 has created some differences between Mexico and the United States, but these are not of a serious nature. The treaty, first proposed

---

[8] On some of these issues before the OAS, Mexico merely abstained instead of voting against them. Thus she tried to escape the dilemma of being forced either to support a form of intervention or to annoy the United States. On one occasion the Mexican Minister of Foreign Relations spoke of the incompatability of Marxism-Leninism with OAS membership in commenting on Mexico's abstention on the vote to expel Cuba from the organization. See Brown and Wilkie, *op. cit.*, p. 409.

[9] Carlos Alberto Astiz, "Introduction" to Mexico, in Astiz, *op. cit.*, p. 82. See also Mecham, *op. cit.*, p. 378.

[10] *The Miami Herald*, February 6, 1972.

by Brazil in 1962 but pushed to completion largely because of Mexican initiative, prohibits Latin American states from producing, testing, or possessing nuclear weapons in their territories, and forbids the development or installation of such weapons by outside parties. Twenty-two eligible Western Hemisphere states, all but Cuba and Guayana, have signed the treaty and 16 have ratified it (as of September 1971). In addition the sponsors of the treaty have drawn up two protocols, and have invited other powers to sign them. Protocol I calls on countries outside the area of the treaty to uphold the treaty provisions with respect to territories held within the zone, and Protocol II requests the nuclear powers to commit themselves to respect the treaty and not to use or threaten to use nuclear weapons against the treaty signatories. Great Britain and the Netherlands have signed Protocol I, but France and the United States have not. The latter is unwilling to include Puerto Rico and the Virgin Islands in the treaty. Great Britain, the United States, China and France have signed Protocol II, leaving the Soviet Union as the only nuclear power that has taken no action. In signing Protocol II, the United States included a disclaimer to the effect that it did not understand the treaty to restrict "transit" of nuclear weapons in the Western Hemisphere, that is, on board ships passing through the Panama Canal, sailing in claimed territorial waters, or visiting ports. Up to now no Latin American signatory has objected to the United States declaration, and except for the noninclusion of United States territories in the treaty zone, United States-Mexican relations have been untroubled by the treaty during its various stages of negotiations.[11]

II

A second major problem, United States domination of Mexican economic life, has long troubled United States-Mexican

---

[11] Davis R. Robinson, "The Treaty of Tlatelolco and the United States," *American Journal of International Law*, Vol. LXIV (April 1970), No. 2, pp. 283–285 and 294; Committee on Foreign Relations, United States Senate, *Additional Protocol II to the Latin American Nuclear Free Zone Treaty* (Washington, D.C.: U.S. Government Printing Office 1971), pp. 2–6 and 35.

relations. Mexican trade and commerce, although primarily conducted with the United States has created little international tension. Minor complaints are voiced from time to time by one or the other about specific restrictions on entry, unfair competition, or extraordinary (and usually temporary) measures that produce hardship or restraints on particular producers. In the past few years drug smuggling, particularly marijuana, from Mexico has led to some mutual recriminations about responsibility and some mutual harassment of visitors in attempts to stop the traffic. Although tempers flare occasionally over such matters, these difficulties are negotiated on an ad hoc basis and have not seriously marred the generally harmonious commercial relationship between the two countries. Instead, Mexican commercial relations with the United States have created serious internal debate and political conflict within Mexico.

For more than 20 years Mexico and the United States have conducted their international trade without benefit of treaties. The last formal instrument, the Reciprocal Trade Agreement of 1942, expired at the end of 1950. From the beginning neither the Mexican government nor the Mexican business community strongly supported the "free trade" principles of the pact, particularly since Mexico was just beginning to undertake massive programs for economic development. Like all states in the early process of industrialization, Mexico faced the prospect of cheap foreign goods from the developed countries, at first primarily the United States, driving its high-cost infant industries out of business. So long as World War II lasted, Mexico had little to fear since the United States had few products to sell, and Mexican raw materials were much in demand. With the war over, however, accumulated demand in Mexico, especially for manufactured consumer goods, soon began to drain the country of its dollar reserves built up during the war years. Government officials became alarmed at the reverse flow of hard currency, and businessmen, feeling the pressure of competition, began to demand protection for their industries. The United States agreed to some changes in the treaty in 1947, but Mexico remained dissatisfied. By 1948 both parties recognized the inability to compromise their mutually antagonistic interests and principles. By mutual consent, the treaty was terminated. For the same reasons Mexico refused in 1947 to enter the General Agreement on Tariffs and Trade.

Despite the demise of the trade agreement, trade has flourished between Mexico and the United States. Because both countries have used judiciously flexible tariffs, import quotas, and import licensing in regulating their trade, conflict has been held to a minimum. Mexico has relied heavily on licensing to protect its manufacturers,[12] while the United States has used quotas and quality restrictions to protect raw materials like farm products and petroleum in their respective home markets. Moreover, the United States by an informal understanding has extended to Mexico "most-favored-nation" treatment, that is Mexico receives for any export in the United States market the most favorable terms that the United States grants to any third party for that same product. Although the Mexican trade as a percent of total United States world commerce remains a modest four percent (Mexico ranks fifth among United States trading partners), United States trade looms large in Mexican international transactions. Since 1950 the United States percentage of Mexican trade has fluctuated somewhat, but United States purchases during the period 1967–1971 averaged about 70 percent of Mexico's exports and United States sales averaged about 65 percent of Mexico's imports, or about $1.5 billion annually. Mexico's attempts to diversify its markets have met with some small success.[13] Trade with the Latin American Free Trade Asso-

---

[12] Mexico has never used exchange controls and differential exchange rates to regulate imports, a common practice in other parts of Latin America.

[13] Recently the Echeverría administration established a Foreign Trade Institute and some 20 commercial offices around the world to counteract the effects of United States protectionism. In March 1972 President Echeverría traveled to Japan with a group of economists seeking new outlets for Mexico's products. See *The Washington Post*, February 15, 1972, and Francis B. Kent, "Getting Out of the U.S. Shadow: Mexico Seeks to Broaden Its Outlook," *Los Angeles Times*, April 9, 1972; Olga Pellicer de Brody, "Cambios recientes en la Política Exterior de México," *Foro Internacional*, Vol. XIII (October-December 1972), No. 2, pp. 139–154, argues that Echeverría's strategy is to get foreign enterprise to support Mexico's drive for exports by easing up on Mexicanization for foreign firms in the export market.

ciation (LAFTA),[14] Japan, and Western Europe has increased modestly in recent years, but trade with the socialist countries has not fulfilled the promises expected a decade earlier. For the foreseeable future the United States will continue to be Mexico's dominant trading partner.

The nature of Mexican-United States trade patterns since World War II has been conditioned largely by Mexico's drive for import substitution through industrialization. In Mexico, as a result, the kinds and quantities of imports have been a central public issue. Although government interest in increasing its revenues,[15] easing procurement of specific products, encouraging direct foreign investment, and holding down prices has at times conflicted with the basic policy of promoting industrialization, in general a protectionist policy has predominated in theory and practice. Import licenses, instituted in 1944, have become the major tool to regulate imports. First utilized on finished luxury items in 1947, licenses are now required for over 75 percent of all imported items. As soon as the Ministry of Industry and Commerce places an item on the list for licensing, it is rarely removed, and recurrent balance of payment crises and demands by businessmen for protection tend to keep the list growing. In utilizing its other major regulatory tool, the tariff, the Treasury has few rules or criteria as guidelines. Normally the ministry accepts the rates suggested by businessmen unless ministry officials deem them extraordinarily high. In general the rates remain low for raw materials necessary in manufacturing (about 5%) and ascend steeply for finished luxury goods (100%). The price element seldom enters into the decision either of tariff or licensing restrictions, because government officials have believed that industrialization and job crea-

---

[14] Mexican ratification of the LAFTA agreement in 1960 marked a departure from the country's previous policy of avoiding trade agreements. In practice, however, Mexican industries are still well protected in part because LAFTA has not become fully operational, and in part because Mexico enjoys trading advantages with fellow members in the association. In 1971 LAFTA trade accounted for about 6 percent of the total.

[15] In the early 1960s about 25 percent of total government revenue came from import duties.

tion more than compensate for higher prices. On some products where prices appear excessive the government has threatened to open the gates to foreign products, but up to now the threat has not become credible. In the short run this policy met with considerable success. Between 1947 and 1950 imports, particularly in consumer durables like refrigerators, radios, and washing machines, fell 18 percent, as heavy domestic investment displaced the imports, new jobs were created, and supporting industries were expanded. This initial spurt of growth was further propelled by the involvement of the United States in the Korean War, which led to increased demand and higher prices for Mexican exports. With the end of the war in the mid-fifties growth in export earnings began to slow but demand for production goods from raw materials to capital products continued to grow. It was then discovered that restricting imports of such goods was far more difficult than restricting imports of consumer items, because a cut-off of production materials would dampen the industrialization program.[16] Again Mexico was saved in part by a rapid growth of tourism from the United States, and in part by a policy of encouraging foreign investment to overcome the deficits in the balance of trade.

Although the industrialization program has been maintained and economic growth and development has continued, the balance of trade problem has worsened. Despite some fluctuation in annual balance of trade figures the trend since the early 1960s has indicated an ever-growing deficit.[17] During the 1960s and to the present, government policy has been to encourage the development of the export market and the integration of Mexican

---

[16] In 1960 the value of imports was at least 25 percent greater than the value of domestic production, and 83 percent of imports by value consisted of production goods. Raw materials made up 44 percent of imports, and capital goods such as machinery and trucks, 39 percent. See Rafael Izquierdo, "Protectionism in Mexico" in Raymond Vernon (ed.), *Public Policy and Private Enterprise in Mexico,* (Cambridge: Harvard University Press, 1964), pp. 245–246.

[17] Chart is adapted from Saúl Trejo Reyes, "Economic Policy and Export Promotion in Mexico: A New Approach," *Comercio Exterior de México* Vol. XVII (July 1971), No. 7, p. 18, and the "External Sector of the Economy in 1972: A Preliminary Assessment," *Comercio Exterior de México* Vol. XIX (April 1973), No. 4, p. 3.

industries. The latter has been particularly notable in the automobile industry, which has witnessed tightening of requirements that more and more of the components be of Mexican manufacture. In the meantime foreign investment continued to cover some of the deficit, but the government has had to resort to heavier foreign borrowing to achieve a balance in the country's international payments. Debt service has become an increasing burden and while not yet critical, most observers within and outside the Mexican government see foreign investments and borrowings as only temporary palliatives at best, and a reorientation in industrial and trade policies as offering the only long-term hope of escaping a major financial and economic crisis. A Mexican economist recently summed up Mexico's problem by pointing out that while import substitution decreased dependence on consumer imports it increased dependence on intermediate and capital goods; that protectionism increased prices and profits, fostered monopolistic practices, and encouraged capital intensive industries; that the country still suffers unemployment, a growing balance of trade deficit, and an inability to compete on world markets (Table 3).[18]

While Mexico's trade policies have been openly protectionist since World War II, United States policies have been generally oriented toward free trade. Various acts of Congress have authorized the president to conclude reciprocal agreements to lower trade barriers, and the United States has sponsored and

Table 3.   Balance of Trade Deficit 1960–1970 (in U.S. dollars)

Year	Amount	Year	Amount
1960	174,037,000	1967	506,278,000
1961	62,361,000	1968	632,200,000
1962	93,667,000	1969	472,000,000
1963	206,039,000	1970	1,088,000,000
1964	406,466,000	1971	934,000,000
1965	375,271,000	1972	1,123,000,000
1966	296,116,000		

[18] Trejo Reyes, *op. cit.*, p. 19.

joined the General Agreement on Tariffs and Trade (GATT). Recently, however, the United States has suffered not only growing deficits in its balance of payments but, more importantly, deficits in its balance of trade. In order to reduce the steady outflow of dollars (which has already led to two rounds of devaluation) as well as to protect specific United States products adversely affected by foreign competition, the last several administrations have resorted to "voluntary" quotas agreed upon with countries exporting to the United States market, quality controls imposed by the United States, and finally a tariff surcharge in 1971. All of the various actions have affected one or more Mexican imports into the United States.

Responding to United States trade policies in a speech to the Mexican Council of Businessmen in April 1969, Octaviano Campos Salas, then Minister of Industry and Commerce, acknowledged the importance of the United States market for Mexico and requested easier entry for a wider variety of products, particularly manufactured goods. He pointed out that the United States tariff structure discriminated particularly against Mexican manufacturers because the tariff rate rose with the degree of processing but was reduced for products of "high complex technology." Since it would be many years before Mexico would export such goods, he asked the United States unilaterally to reduce or eliminate tariffs on a specific list of products that used low-cost labor and modern machinery such as food products, electronics, some iron and steel products, yarn and fabrics, toys and sporting goods, and certain auto parts. He also complained about seasonal tariffs on fruits and vegetables grown in the northern part of the country for export to the United States market, but reserved his most bitter remarks for United States cotton policy. He noted that while Mexico had cut back cotton production at the request of the United States to halt cotton surpluses, the United States continued to subsidize its cotton exports, thus depressing world prices and cutting deeper into Mexican export earnings. Moreover, Mexico's agreement to impose on itself a "voluntary" quota for cotton textile exports to the United States reduced exports still further. On the other hand, Campos Salas indicated that Mexico was pleased to have a guaranteed quota and favorable price for its sugar entering the United States and expressed the hope that a similar agreement could be reached on cocoa.[19]

Not only Mexico but virtually every state in Latin America had voiced similar complaints during the late 1960s. Most countries were running trade deficits with the United States and were meeting their balance of payments problems only through new foreign investments and heavy borrowings. Mexico's trade deficits with the United States over the past 10 years have averaged from $400 to $450 million, and even the enormous inflow of tourist dollars only modestly offsets it, largely because of an increasing reverse flow of funds caused by Mexican purchases in the United States along the border. In answer to these problems, U.S. Secretary of State William Rogers announced at the meeting of the Organization of American States in Costa Rica in April 1971 that the Nixon administration was going to urge the Congress to extend trade preferences to Latin America. It was reported that the administration would request the removal of all import duties on more than 500 products including almost all manufactured goods except shoes and textiles, which were under severe pressure already from foreign competition. Since Latin America occupies a very low-priority position in the Nixon administration's overall foreign policy structure, these promises were not only left unfulfilled, but in August 1971 the administration imposed a 10 percent surcharge on all imports into the United States. The Latin American states were particularly outraged, and the Mexican ambassador in speeches and interviews pointed out in low key but firm statements the damage that Mexico would suffer. In Mexico City it was reported that a quiet campaign was underway to remove the surcharge.[20] The surcharge was, in fact, removed in December 1971, and the damage to Mexican export earnings was slight. At the same time, however, Mexican officials were further annoyed by the imposition of quality controls in 1971 and 1972 on tomatoes entering the

---

[19] Octaviano Campos Salas, "Mexico's Economic Relations with the United States," *Mexican-American Review* Vol. 37 (July 1969), No. 7, pp. 49–50.
[20] See Kent, *op. cit.; The San Francisco Chronicle*, October 23, 1971; The *Washington Daily News*, November 11, 1971; *The Miami Herald*, October 21, 1971; *The Journal of Commerce*, January 10, 1972.

United States market by the department of agriculture in response to Florida tomato growers who were bringing in bumper crops. Sentiment in Congress was running strong against loosening import restrictions. Farmers and the businessmen were clamoring for more protection and Dante Fascell, Chairman of the House Subcommittee on Inter-American Affairs, and representative from a tomato-growing district in Florida took the position that Mexico should not feel too grieved about its trade deficit since the United States found itself in the same position. On the other hand Mexican grown and processed strawberries constituted one bright spot in the agricultural market. In the late 1960s prices had declined drastically with overproduction and import restrictions, and growers had lost money. With a "voluntary" restraint agreement the market improved and 1972 proved a good year for both growers and processors.[21]

An important aspect of Mexican imports but one more difficult to measure in terms of costs and benefits than goods and ordinary services is technology transfer. Industry depends on technology, and developing countries must largely import theirs because of a lag in scientific and technological development. The costs are usually high. Most of Mexico's technology comes from the United States, and complaints have been raised that much of it has not been adapted well to the smaller Mexican market. Businessmen have not worried about the problem because with Mexico's protectionist policies costs can be passed on to consumers. More important, however, foreign technology imports often carry severe limits on their use, usually by restrictions on exports of products using the technology. A study by the U.N. Trade and Development Board in 1971 reported that of 109 Mexican contracts for patents, trademarks, and unpatented know-how, 104 contained limiting clauses and 53 had absolute prohibitions on export use. Mexicans have also complained that royalties are only a part of the costs, and disguised profits

---

[21] Kent, *op. cit.*, and *The Journal of Commerce* March 29, 1972; also see Hearing before the Subcommittee on Inter-American Affairs of the Committee on Foreign Affairs, House of Representatives, Ninety-Second Congress Second Session, *United States-Mexican Trade Relations* (Washington: Government Printing Office, 1972), pp. 18–26.

(often under the term "technical assistance fees") and the obligation to buy goods from the technology supplier above world prices bears heavily on developing countries.[22] As a consequence the Mexican Congress, on the recommendation of President Echeverría, in the fall of 1972 passed a bill requiring that all contracts embodying agreements on the use of foreign technology be registered with the National Registry for Transfer of Technology. The agency under the law will disapprove contracts that demand payments for technology judged too highly priced or that restrict the use of such technology in ways deemed unreasonable.[23]

The drug traffic has constituted another and particularly troublesome problem in United States-Mexican relations. With the increasing use of marijuana, hallucinogens, and hard drugs in the United States during the 1960s, the Customs Bureau attempted to interdict the illegal flow of these substances into the country. Although millions of dollars of drugs were seized, the traffic assumed such proportions that drugs continued to be readily available in large United States cities. Mexico constituted a major supply base particularly for marijuana. In an attempt to curtail the traffic the Nixon administration, on September 21, 1969, launched Operation Intercept, a program primarily of search techniques at border crossings. Although the Mexican government had been consulted about the proposal, the actual implementation far surpassed Mexican expectations in its rigor. Traffic clogged border towns; tourists and other border crossers experienced long delays; and business on both sides of the border suffered serious losses. Mexico was harder hit than the United States. Within a few days protests arose on all sides in both countries, but particularly in Mexico where Operation Intercept was interpreted as a policy of political coercion. In the face of this rising criticism the Nixon administration abandoned the project on October 11, scarcely three weeks after it was launched with such fanfare.

Operation Cooperation eventually replaced Operation Inter-

---

[22] "Toward a Policy on Transfer of Technology," *Comercio Exterior de México* Vol. VII (October 1971), No. 10, pp. 4–5.

[23] Robert M. Bleiberg, "Killing the Goose?" *Barron's*, November 13, 1972.

cept. In January 1970 Mexico and the United States undertook a joint campaign against the growth and smuggling of opium poppies and marijuana. By early 1972 the authorities were also devoting great attention to the growing use of Latin American countries (including Mexico) as avenues for the heroin and cocaine trade originating in Europe. Canada joined the campaign in March 1972 after drug abuse increased 100 percent in that country over the past year. Mexican officials reported at the same time that over 2000 people had been arrested and various quantities of drugs confiscated. Marijuana continued to loom large in quantity with thousands of fields burned and 146 tons reportedly seized over a 16-month period. The traffic was far from stopped, however, and Mexican army officers asked the United States to tighten its surveillance of suspected dealers who were sending huge sums of money into Mexico.[24] Another facet of the drug trade has involved legitimate pharmaceutical companies. The problem surfaced early in 1972 when the Pennwalt Corporation announced that it was discontinuing its amphetamine operations in Mexico. A new Mexican law had just been passed at the time banning the production and sale of amphetamines in Mexico, reportedly in response to United States pressure. For several years United States officials of the Bureau of Narcotics had been investigating the United States-Mexican trade in amphetamines. They discovered that the product was being exported in bulk to Mexico, and there capsuled and distributed. Most of the distribution went to pharmacies near the United States border, far exceeding the possible demand of the local population. Over an 18-month period it was estimated that some 45 million capsules had been produced in Mexico with 60 to 70 percent reentering the United States illegally. The new law and the closedown of Pennwalt operations in Mexico has supposedly sharply curtailed the traffic in amphetamines.[25]

One final aspect of commercial relations between Mexico and the United States (the so-called border industries) has constituted profitable returns for citizens of both countries. In May 1965 Octaviano Campos Salas, at that time Mexican Minister of

---

[24] *The Washington Post*, March 28, 1972.
[25] *The New York Times*, January 19, 1972 and January 23, 1972.

Industry and Commerce, proposed the establishment of a tariff free zone along the border into which components of various products could be imported without restrictions, assembled by Mexican workers, and then reexported in finished form. He had conceived the idea following a trip to the Far East where the practice had been established successfully for some years. The Mexican government instituted the program in 1966, setting up a zone 12 miles deep along the entire United States border. Over the next six years foreign and domestic investment poured into the area, and working people seeking jobs and good wages (by Mexican standards) quickly followed. By 1973 about 385 firms had invested $800 million, were employing some 44,000 workers, and were producing $40 million dollars annually in goods. The influx of internal migrants on the Mexican side of the border increased the population 77 percent over 10 years to a total of about 2.2 million equaling the residents of the United States side. At the present northwestern Mexico enjoys the highest minimum daily wage in the country, surpassing even Mexico City. In the border industries, now the largest foreign assembly line of United States components for reexport to this country, most employees are women. All the goods produced are labor-intensive and concentrated heavily in electronics, textiles, and pharmaceuticals. Recent diversification has included food processing and packaging, scrapping of railroad cars, and assembly of musical instruments. The most efficient type of operation consists of the "twin plant" concept in which products are initially processed on the United States side, sent to Mexico for labor-intensive work, and reexported to the United States for final finishing, inspection, packaging, and distribution.

Of all the groups involved and interested in these operations, only United States organized labor has opposed the project, claiming that cheap Mexican labor is depriving United States workers of jobs. During 1971–1972 legislation was introduced into Congress to impose tariffs on the full value of the products reentering the United States (rather than only on the value added), an action that would effectively curtail the whole program. Mexican officials, labor leaders, and businessmen have protested the proposal on the grounds that the closing of the border plants would help United States labor only marginally.

They further pointed out that the border industries by creating more prosperous conditions in northern Mexico actually helped the United States balance of payments because Mexican border residents purchase most of their consumer items in the United States to the amount of about $800 million annually.[26] The bill was not enacted in the 92nd Congress of the United States, but the controversy will probably continue between United States labor and other interested parties.

Far more troublesome than commercial relations has been United States participation in the Mexican economy. Such participation has consisted of two main types: the holding of Mexican government bonds and short-term notes of indebtedness, and direct private investment in economic enterprises within the country. The former created tension and conflict from the late years of the Díaz dictatorship to the final settlement of the old debts in the 1940s. New indebtedness of this type has created no international difficulties in recent years, but Mexican government officials, economists, and some business groups have become greatly concerned with the burden that these impose on the general economy. A circular problem has been created because loans are needed on a constant basis to fuel the Mexican economy; the repayment of interest and principal becomes more costly; and the economy must continue its upward spiral to pay off the debts, provide jobs for a rapidly growing population, and meet the expectations of a people whose aspirations for a better life in the material sense threaten to outpace the performance of the economy. Foreign private investments have created more direct problems of an international nature. Like loans, foreign investments have also been perceived as necessary to assist economic growth and to ease balance of payments problems. They also impose costs in terms of profit remittances and royal-

---

[26] See the following for further details: "Export-Oriented Assembly Plants," *Comercio Exterior de México*, Vol. XVII (May 1971), No. 5, pp. 2–3; *The Journal of Commerce*, January 11, 1972 and June 7, 1973; *The New York Times*, January 31, 1972; Hearing before the Subcommittee on Inter-American Affairs of the Committee on Foreign Affairs, House of Representatives, Ninety-Second Congress, Second Session, *United States-Mexican Trade Relations*. (Washington: Government Printing Office, 1972), pp. 26–30.

ties but, more importantly, potential control over vital sectors of the economy by foreign entrepreneurs. The profit motive of the investor often does not correspond to national interests for economic diversification, the creation of export markets, and selective restrictions on imports. The government faces not only the delicate task of compromising very real conflicts of interest between the country's needs for economic growth and development and the investors' need for profit, but also the rising criticism of nationalists, some of whom object to foreign investments on economic grounds of competition while others oppose it on ideological grounds of nationalism. Thus far successive Mexican governments since 1940 have succeeded in keeping domestic criticism to a moderate level while retaining sufficient confidence abroad in the economy to keep investments pouring in and loans easily obtainable.

With its credit reestablished Mexico again resorted to international borrowing. During the 1940s the government negotiated almost $400 million in loans, primarily from the U.S. Export-Import Bank, but also from the World Bank (IBRD) and private United States banks. These loans were invested, not in administrative expenses, arms purchases, or the buying out of foreign concessions, but in economic development projects such as highway and railroad construction, electric power plants and irrigation works, and several industrial projects. Such borrowings continued through the 1950s until finally in 1963 and 1964 on three occasions the government placed bonds on the international market in the amount of $100 million. Since that time the Mexican government has continued to rely more on long-term bonded indebtedness rather than on short- or medium-term notes. Although it still offers most of its bonds in the United States market, the government has sought to diversify its sources of credit; in May 1967, for example, it sold the entire issue of $25 million in bonds in Europe.[27]

During the 1960s the foreign debt rose on the average of 15 percent per year, but in the early 1970s attempts were being made at least to reduce the rate of increase. To date this effort has failed. For 1972 the target was set to hold borrowings to

---

[27] Wright, *op. cit.*, pp. 73–92.

$280 million, but the record-breaking trade deficit of over one billion dollars forced the government to borrow almost that amount. It was announced early in the year that Mexico had contracted a loan of $120 million, the largest ever from private sources. Banks in the United States, France, Great Britain, Canada, Switzerland, and Japan participated in a venture to be used by the public sector to expand basic facilities such as oil exploration and production and electric power generation.[28] The Inter-American Development Bank reported that Mexico's foreign debt in 1970 stood at $3.764 billion (U.S.).[29]

While foreign indebtedness has created internal financial problems for Mexico, foreign direct investments have generated international tensions as well. Not only do Mexican business and government leaders worry about balance of payments problems resulting from the outflow of profits and royalty payments, but they (and intellectuals too) have shown increasing concern over the problem of displacement of Mexican entrepreneurs with foreigners and the possibility of foreign control over vital sectors of the economy. Beginning in 1944 and continuing to the present, a series of laws and executive regulations have narrowed and restricted the scope of foreign investors. These however, have not seriously limited the attractiveness of the Mexican arena for continued investments. A booming economy with favorable tax and interest rates, a stable political system, and a fairly predictable set of regulations have assured the individual investor as well as the multinational corporation of a safe harbor for his investment and also a reasonable return on his money. Overall, the climate of general predictability has continued to make Mexico attractive to the foreign investor for more than three decades.[30] Mexican ambivalence toward this boom of foreign investments in the post-World War II era can be easily

---

[28] *The Journal of Commerce*, January 10, 1972.

[29] *Comercio Exterior de México*, Vol. XVIII (September 1972), No. 9, p. 15.

[30] One of the more recent and precise statements of Mexican official views was given by President Díaz Ordaz late in his administration. He said that foreign investments were welcome when they facilitated access to technical advances, when they sought to satisfy unfulfilled needs, and when they did not attempt to operate in fields reserved to Mexicans. He added that they should associate with national capital in minority form, should reinvest some profits, and should not displace or substitute national capital or

understood. On the one hand foreign capital is believed necessary for continued growth, but on the other it is feared for what
it produced in the nineteenth century: foreign domination of the
Mexican economy.

When foreigners once more became interested in Mexico as
an investment area in the late 1950s, the rules under which they
could enter the country differed greatly from those of the time
of Porfirio Díaz. Not only had the railroads and the petroleum
industry been nationalized but the Constitution of 1917, subsequent legislation and executive degrees and, most importantly,
a nationalist climate, imposed restrictions and limitations unknown in the earlier era. Although the constitution permits foreigners to own many types of property in Mexico, Article 27
stipulates that they must formally agree to consider themselves
as Mexican citizens with respect to their property. This so-called
Calvo clause (adopted from the writings of the great Argentine
jurist of the nineteenth century, Carlos Calvo) has been inserted
explicitly in every Mexican statute on business societies in which
foreigners participate. Utilized more forcefully in Mexico than
in any other Latin American country, it provides that in matters
pertaining to property and contracts foreigners place themselves
under the jurisdiction of Mexican laws and tribunals and re-
nounce the diplomatic protection of their own government.
Moreover, under Article 27 foreigners are forbidden to own
lands within 100 kilometers of the border or within 50 kilometers
of the beaches, and foreign business corporations may not own
any lands for agricultural production.

In addition to Article 27 of the constitution, the executive
decree of 1944, based on extraordinary powers conferred on the
president as a wartime measure, provided authorization for the
specific regulation of foreign investment. To enter the Mexican
scene, the would-be investor had first to secure the authorization

---

enterprises already operating. See Campos Salas, *op. cit.*, pp. 53–54. José
Campillo Saenz, Undersecretary of Industry and Commerce reiterated
much the same sentiment, perhaps in somewhat stronger terms in the fall
of 1972. He said that minority capital must be associated with Mexican
capital "on a minority base as a general rule," give preference to Mexicans
in technical and administrative positions, provide advanced technology, and
produce export goods. See "Yes, the Rules of the Game are Being Changed,"
Comercio Exterior de México Vol. XVIII (November 1972), No. 11, pp. 7–11.

of the ministry of foreign relations to incorporate and to acquire certain types of property. The ministry could also at its discretion require that majority control in the company be exercised by Mexican nationals, that is, the 51 percent rule. In 1945 the ministry issued its first list of activities in which the 51 percent rule applied and in subsequent years expanded it. A few items such as mining and petrochemicals joined the list as a result of special legislation but most of the items resulted solely from ministerial decisions. Several items reflected concern over fundamental economic interests but others, such as carbonated beverages and fruit juices, "resulted from pressures brought for the protection of private Mexican interests against foreign competition."[31]

Moreover, in the years after World War II several industries were reserved for state ownership entirely. Besides the petroleum industry, these included electric and nuclear energy, railroads, basic petrochemicals, and telegraph and wireless communications. In addition, other regulations excluded foreigners but not private Mexican capital from radio and television broadcasting, auto transportation, federal highway transportation, domestic air and maritime transportation, gas distribution, and forestry exploitation. Furthermore, credit institutions, insurance companies, and bonding firms had to have at least 75 percent Mexican capital, while exploitation of minerals had to have 51 or 66 percent, depending on circumstances, and production or processing of petrochemical by-products, 60 percent.[32] The regulations as they appeared tended to affect only new industries entering the field, but in some areas legislative encouragement in the form of tax preferences or favorable purchase prices were given to older firms to adopt the 51 percent (or more) rule or to sell out entirely in the basic industries.[33] As a result of these

---

[31] Wright, *op. cit.*, p. 105.

[32] For the most recent list of firms see Campillo Sáenz, *op. cit.*, p. 9.

[33] In August 1971 the Cananea Mining Company sold 51 percent of its stock to a mixed group of public and private Mexican investors under favorable terms. Cananea was the last major mining company without a Mexican majority. Only eight small firms accounting for 1.3 percent of all mining production remain under foreign control. See "Economic Roundup," *Comercio Exterior de México* Vol. XVII (October 1971), No. 10, p. 24.

governmental moves, foreign participation virtually disappeared in the mining industry and electric power generation.

Recently, the government also began to demand that various industries particularly the assembly type undertake "integration" measures. The automobile industry constitutes a case in point. With most auto parts being imported, the government in 1962 demanded that an increasing number of parts be purchased from Mexican producers. A target of 60 percent of the production cost of Mexican manufacture was set for September 1964 but was extended to the end of 1965 at which time most producers were fulfilling the requirement. In 1972 a government decree required the automotive industry to balance all imports with the export of monetary equivalents in spare parts by 1979. The proportion for 1973 was set at 30 percent and scheduled to rise annually.

Finally the Mexican Congress early in 1973 codified these regulatory measures with its Law to Promote Mexican Investment and to Regulate Foreign Investment. Most of the specific limitations on the percentage of ownership permitted to foreigners were enacted into the new legislation. The law, however, contained at least one major additional restriction, that is, the provision that in all new investments foreign ownership may not exceed 49 percent. In addition the law established two new legal bodies to oversee foreign investment: the National Registry of Foreign Investments in the Ministry of Industry and Commerce and the National Commission on Foreign Investment, composed of seven cabinet-level officers. The latter has wide discretion in applying the rules, and it may increase or reduce the amount of foreign participation permissible in areas of economic activity not specifically covered by preexisting regulations.[34]

Because of Mexico's political stability and economic potential, the restrictive legislation has not acted as a deterrent to foreign capital. It may actually have further encouraged such investments by establishing clear and predictable rules of the game that are subject to at most incremental modifications. The restrictions, however, obviously channeled foreign investments in certain clear directions.

---

[34] "Foreign Investment," *Mexican Newsletter*, January 31, 1973, pp. 9–11.

Foreign investments reached their nadir in the 1940s when they were reduced to about $500 million. Various Mexican governments had already eliminated foreigners from petroleum and railroads and had reduced their holdings in other vital areas. United States investments, for example, in mining stood at less than one-half their worth in 1929, in utilities and transportation at less than two-thirds, and in agriculture at less than one-sixth. Only manufacturing demonstrated some growth, but it was small. In 1943 total United States investment stood at less than $300 million from a postrevolutionary height of $700 million in 1929. Despite this absolute reduction of foreign capital, it still accounted for 15 percent of the country's total investment at the opening of this period.

Both Presidents Avila Camacho and Alemán warmly welcomed foreign capital, and from a slow start during the war years (averaging annually $26 million) foreign investments rose to $60 million annually between 1946 and 1952, when the United States share reached $550 million constituting 75 percent of the total. During these years the beginnings of the dramatic change in the nature of these investments also occurred. Whereas in 1940 90 percent of all direct foreign investments still resided in mining, public utilities, and transportation, by 1952 30 percent was in manufacturing with almost 60 percent of new investments entering that field. Although the next two presidents, Ruiz Cortines and López Mateos, did not give the personal kind of encouragement to foreign investors as did their predecessors, the flow hardly reflected the change in attitude. López Mateos did in fact reduce foreign participation in some basic areas such as electric power, petrochemicals, and steel production, and applied the 51 percent rule more widely. Foreign investments dropped in the first year or two of both these administrations, but when the government decisively signaled the limitations of its own actions and the continued protection of foreign capital in remaining activities, the flow increased strongly. By 1964 the traditional areas of investment were rapidly disappearing with manufacturing accounting for over 50 percent of the total. During the past two administrations these trends have persisted. Most worrisome to Mexican leadership in recent years has been a process called "progressive denationalization" in some indus-

tries, that is, the purchase by foreign capital of already successful operations. Obviously such investments tend to gravitate
toward the most dynamic sectors of the economy. In simply
displacing local capital the foreign investment makes almost no
contribution to the national economy and may in fact damage it
through increased profit remittances abroad.

Further restrictions have been applied to foreign capital to
limit this type of activity while the government has worked to
retain a climate favorable to security and profits in other areas.
Most foreign investors have continued to express confidence in
the Mexican political system and economy by their constant
flow of funds into the country although the United States ambassador to Mexico and some business spokesmen expressed
concern about the new restrictive legislation on foreign enterprise that was being proposed in the fall of 1972.[35] During the
1960s annual United States investments averaged $95 million
and by the early 1970s, about $200 million. Although foreigners
were forbidden to engage further in banking or insurance activities and were restrained from buying out Mexican-owned companies, they were encouraged to enter new manufacturing areas
particularly to develop export markets. By the beginning of the
administration of President Echeverría in 1970 total foreign
investments reached approximately $2 billion[36] of which 65 per-
cent was in manufacturing with 90 percent of new investment
going into that field. The United States share at 70 percent, while
still predominant, has been declining relatively as Europe and
Japan have recovered from the destruction of World War II.

This renewed outburst of foreign investment accompanying

---

[35] Marlise Simons, "U.S. Firms Fear Increasing Nationalism in Mexico"
The Washington Post, November 2, 1972. Also see Robert H. McBride
[U.S. Ambassador to Mexico], "Are the Rules of the Game Being
Changed?," *Comercio Exterior de México* Vol. XVIII (November 1972), No.
11, pp. 5–7. In view of long-term trends the whole affair seemed to be a
tempest in a teapot. For a more positive view see the report in the *Houston
Chronicle* "US Capital in Mexico on Increase," May 21, 1973.

[36] One estimate for 1972 placed the total amount near $3 billion; see *The
New York Times*, January 28, 1972. Daniel Szabo, Deputy Assistant Secretary of State for Inter-American Affairs estimated total United States
investment in 1972 at $1.8 billion, Hearing before the Subcommittee on
Inter-American Affairs. . . . , *United States-Mexican Trade Relations*, p. 16.

the Mexican "economic miracle" has produced a growing debate in Mexico in recent years, largely concerning the theme of dependence. One critic observed that "far from attenuating external dependence, political and economic modernization after 1910 has ended by affirming it."[37] Major complaints focus on the degree of foreign involvement in the economy, the types of activities attractive to foreigners, and the costs to Mexico in terms of national control over its resources and economy. In the mid-1960s, one source states, only 34 percent of all industries were totally Mexican owned while 21 percent were totally or mostly foreign controlled. It is also claimed that in 1969 of all United States enterprises in Mexico, 58 percent sold their total product within Mexico while only 9 percent sold 20 percent or more of its product abroad. Finally, since foreign capital has been attracted heavily into manufacturing, it occupies a critical role in general economic development and threatens independent policy decisions by the Mexican leadership.[38] Defenders of the present system point out that much if not most of the public debt is in Mexican hands and that products of foreign investments account for only about 5 percent of total GNP. Furthermore, foreign capital amounts to only about 6 percent of gross fixed private investment, and direct investments plus loans amount to less than 11 percent of total gross investment of the economy. And finally the defenders deny that foreign entrepreneurs or transnational corporations determine major national policies, political or economic. Publicly government officials have taken a middle position. In February 1973, the minister of national patrimony in explaining the new investment law to Congress criticized that segment of foreign enterprise that absorbed Mexican business or invested in nonproductive, internal, or consumption areas such as restaurants, chain stores, or publicity agencies. He also cited figures to the effect that in the period from 1965 to 1968 Mexico suffered a deficit of 5 billion

---

[37] Meyer, "Cambio político y dependencia," p. 138.
[38] For a particularly sharp critique of Mexican economic policy see David Barkin, *Mexico's Albatross: The United States Economy*, paper presented at the Conference on Economic Relations Between Mexico and the United States, The University of Texas at Austin, April 1973.

pesos as the ratio between new investments and profit remittances. At the same time he argued that foreign investment is necessary, although complementary, because it gives access to modern technology and ensures foreign markets when directed to export industries. And finally he sharply conveyed the impression that the administration clearly controlled the situation.[39]

Since successive administrators have stated the necessity of encouraging foreign investment and, at the same time, have continually but gradually introduced restrictions, there is the question of where the pressures originate for ever-tighter limitations. Several sources may be identified, all interrelated in some way with a basic nationalist outlook. Although the arguments may be couched in economic terms (and no one can deny some very real economic and financial problems with both foreign investments and loans) much of the criticism stems primarily from psychopolitical states of mind. Government economists, university professors, novelists, opposition politicians, and business leaders all have at various times pressured the government toward tighter restrictions on foreign capital. Some, particularly among the business groups, have had very concrete interests in terms of competition, but most have also been genuinely concerned about the potential effect of foreign control over basic sectors of the economy. Some few of these critics reject entirely the concept of a role for private foreign capital and, while they admit the need for outside resources, they advocate loans preferably from international lending agencies and secondarily from foreign governments. The Confederación Nacional de Industrias de Transformación (CNIT) a businessmen's organization of relative newcomers has been the most forceful of business groups in demanding strict regulations, but recently even the more conservative Confederation of Chambers of Commerce and the Confederation of Chambers of Industry have supported certain measures limiting foreign capital. The intellectuals on the other hand criticize not only foreign entrepreneurs but the current social and economic systems of Mexico. They attack the govern-

[39] Wright, *op. cit.*, pp. 92-93; "Foreign Investment," *Comercio Exterior de México*, Vol. XIX (March 1973), No. 3, pp. 13–14.

ment and the conservative business associations and maintain close ties with CNIT. The economists finally have directed their attention to more technical problems. They advocate borrowing abroad and buying technology, and are particularly critical of foreign exploitation and export of primary products.[40] With the government moving increasingly in the direction of limitation and restriction, it has come in line with some of the criticisms over foreign investment. Only the hard-line opponents to any form of investment have not been mollified, but in the present state of Mexico's economy it is difficult to see the government moving in any radical new directions.

III

Despite its rapid economic and demographic growth of the last four decades, Mexico is still a small power compared to the United States. Nonetheless relations between these two states have continually improved in terms of their ability to solve conflicts of interest in a general spirit of cooperation and compromise. Notably too, they have been able to agree to disagree on issues without rancor or bitterness.

Several factors may be advanced to explain this situation. From the United States side, Mexico has demonstrated that its policies protect major United States interests. The country's political stability, its determination to conduct its own affairs, its rejection of radical political solutions, and its refusal to use the cold war as leverage against the United States, convinced Washington that there was little to fear on the southern fronier in terms of national security. At the same time, sectors of the United States business community saw great opportunities in Mexico and, although they may have chafed under some of the regulations and complained of some of the nationalist rhetoric, they found the rules of the game predictable and profits not only possible but attractive. Finally in the post-World War II period United States interests have mostly been directed toward Europe and the Far East. The brief revival of interest in Latin America

---

[40] Alexander Böhrisch and Wolfgang König, *La política mexicana sobre inversiones extranjeras* (México: El Colegio de México, 1968), pp. 12–14; Wright, *op. cit.*, p. 53.

marked by the interlude of the Alliance for Progress (1961–1968), almost bypassed Mexico because of the country's thriving economy. No guerrilla warfare in Mexico worried United States policymakers, and the confident Mexican leadership rejected both military assistance agreements and Peace Corps volunteers.

From the Mexican side, there was less satisfaction with the partnership, but no issues emerged that proved serious enough to damage the relationship. The Americans, however reluctantly, had come to accept the Revolution, particularly the aspects that set forth the right of Mexicans to control and regulate the national economy. Under these conditions Mexico City has welcomed United States capital as a complementary tool for the building of the Mexican economy. Mexico has also been pleased with the increasing hordes of American tourists, and the growing prosperity of its border regions. Concerning trade the government has been ambivalent. Although it needs the access to the huge United States market, it complains of trade restrictions that limit its products. Thus far compromises have prevailed, but the Mexicans clearly prefer to reduce their dependence on a single market. On the security issues the Mexicans always display considerable tension when United States armed forces begin to move about the Caribbean. United States interventions in Guatemala (1954), Cuba (1961 and 1962), and the Dominican Republic (1965) understandably made them nervous. Few if any Mexicans seriously believe a United States incursion into their country is likely under present circumstances, but they do not rule out the possibility should the current level of guerrilla activity increase to proportions that would threaten political stability. The lessons of 1914 and 1916 have not been forgotten.

Perhaps the most critical aspect of United States-Mexican relations lies in the area of dependency. And perhaps the fundamental question here is not the precise quantity of dependency but the psychological factor involved. Many Mexicans deeply feel that dependency, deeply resent that perceived relationship, and feel frustrated in attempts to deal with it. It is this combination of feelings about the relationship on the part of many Mexicans that adds tension to virtually all United States-Mexican negotiations. Obviously the feelings are not without foundation.

Mexico, which does not have substantial research and development programs, receives virtually all modern technology from abroad, primarily from the United States. It also conducts most of its commerce with the United States and receives from its northern neighbor the bulk of its imported capital. It does not seem to help Mexican sensitivities to point out the modest contribution of foreign capital to the total economy or the benefits to growth in having access to the United States market. It makes little impression on Mexicans who feel that Mexico's dignity is damaged by the import of used United States machinery to point out that 95 percent of all used United States machinery is sold within the United States itself. In this context, most Mexicans believe that the Cárdenas administration constituted the period of Mexico's greatest independence from foreign control. Nonetheless in 1940 foreign capital accounted for about 15 percent of all investment while today it accounts for not more than 11 percent, with some estimates running as low as 8 percent. It is the perception that counts.

There is no immediate solution to the problem. United States policymakers and businessmen need to be alert not only to the rules by which Mexicans play, but the deeper sensitivities that have created the rules. Slowly the Mexican leadership is gaining in self-confidence and security. Positive attitudes about Mexico's growth and accomplishments are replacing the earlier more negative attitude of hostility to the United States. Only as Mexicans gain more and more a sense of control over their destinies, and Americans become more willing to work in Mexico as minority partners will the tensions decline. Already most issues are being handled on the basis of a matured partnership. Not all problems can be solved, not all conflicts of interest will disappear, but they can be negotiated equitably and peacefully.

CONCLUSION

THE BEHAVIOR OF SMALL STATES in international relations and world politics has recently attracted the attention of scholars impressed with the endurance of weak states in a world of superpowers. Not only have small and even ministates persisted during an era of world empires, but their number has continued to increase. Questions have been raised about how they have managed to retain and secure some degree of freedom, and having obtained a status of political independence, what sort of common political behavior, if any, characterizes them. Although the literature on the subject is not extensive, sufficient work has been produced to permit some cautious generalizations. For our purposes here, we shall be interested in determining to what extent Mexico and the United States have followed patterns of great power-small power relationships observed elsewhere in the world.

Obviously the first problem to be confronted concerns an understanding of what constitutes a small power. No definition fits precisely all countries so described, but most observers speak of national power in military (security) and economic terms. Questions are raised about the relative size of population and territory; the gross national product in absolute and per-capita terms; the size, equipment, and capacity of the armed forces; and the nature of the socioeconomic structure, particularly the degree of industrialization, the diversification of economic activities, the levels of urbanization and education, and the skills of the citizenry. Some observers construe power more narrowly, maintaining that "a Small Power is a state which recognizes that it cannot obtain security primarily by use of its own capabilities and that it must rely fundamentally on the aid of other states, institutions, processes, or developments to do so."[1] Although Mexico has long ranked among the larger states of the world in territory, and in recent years has grown enormously in population (today it is almost as large as France), it must be rated at best as a middle-level state in economic strength and as a small power in military might. In fact in military matters Mexico expressly refuses even to try to play the role of a middle power like Canada.[2]

What then do small powers do in the face of a military threat or economic domination by a neighboring great power? What can they do, if, as claimed, great powers are unwilling "to ascribe to the small state quite the same value and rights that a great nation's leaders ascribe in the most natural way to themselves"?[3] How do the political leaders and ideologists of small nations compensate for their perceived weakness in the face of inflexibility, impatience, disinterest, and even contempt on the part of a powerful neighbor? An awareness of weakness, both in human and strategic terms, it appears, leads to a search for compensation or to an attitude that reduces its importance. Some small states strike a belligerent note, some a moral tone, some a posture of dignity and stubbornness, some an attitude of "sentimental and puritanical withdrawal from a hostile world."[4]

Traditionally, small powers have adopted one or more of several available strategies. First, many have opted for neutrality or nonalignment in struggles among the great powers, attempting to avoid the costs to, and perhaps even the destruction of, the state. Second, some small powers have tried to resist the establishment of hegemony by any single power or group of powers. Most have demonstrated a preference for a balance of

---

[1] Robert L. Rothstein, *Alliances and Small Powers* (New York: Columbia University Press, 1968), p. 29. The quotation is italicized in the original.
[2] Mario Ojeda Gómez, "The Role of Mexico as a Middle Power" in J. King Gordon (ed.), *Canada's Role as a Middle Power* (Toronto: The Canadian Institute of International Affairs, 1966), p. 126.
[3] David Vital, *The Inequality of States: A Study of the Small Power in International Relations* (New York: Oxford University Press, 1967), pp. 36–37.
[4] *Ibid.*, pp. 33–35.

power situation because it gives them greater maneuverability and bargaining ability.[5] Third, some small powers have tried to compensate for weakness by building small but highly trained and well-equipped military forces in the hope of decreasing their attractiveness as targets. Fourth, some small powers have opted for outright military alliances with more powerful states.[6] In most cases where this has occurred, however, the small states have attempted to keep their commitments to a minimum. The Latin American states, for example, regard the Rio Treaty basically as a peacekeeping instrument within the Western Hemisphere, not as a part of the United States alliance system against the Soviet Union.[7]

Finally, most small states have supported international organizations as a means to restrict the great powers and to establish a rough equality of all states.[8] Small states have also pressed for

---

[5] Annette Baker Fox, *The Power of Small States: Diplomacy in World War II* (Chicago: The University of Chicago Press, 1959), p. 187, points out, however, that as Germany and Italy moved to upset the balance of power in the 1930s the small states "[I]nstead of moving to the side of the less powerful and thereby helping to restore the balance,... tended to comply with the demands of the more powerful and thus to accentuate any shifts in the balance of forces caused by changing fortunes of war or prospects of ultimate victory."

[6] Rothstein, *op. cit.*, p. 6 notes in speaking of Europe that a "Small Power intent on changing the existing distribution of benefits could do so only by becoming a satellite of a revisionist Great Power."

[7] Donald E. Neuchterlein, "Small States in Alliances: Iceland, Thailand, Australia," *Orbis*, Vol. XIII (Summer 1969), No. 2, pp. 622–623, argues that small states will tend to enter alliances if 1) a previous neutrality policy failed to protect them, and 2) if the state has not experienced a previous colonial status. The alliance will persist if 1) the large and small state agree on the nature of the threat and 2) if the small state is confident of the willingness of the large state to employ its forces to protect the weaker state. Neuchterlein has little to say of the degree of commitment of the small state to the obligations of the treaty.

[8] Vital, *op. cit.*, pp. 29–31 points out that leaders of small powers react to "the great affairs of the world" in the light of their own regional interests, in part because with smaller resources these are the only problems on which they can assemble the necessary information. The narrow range of interests also means that small states can pursue a more coherent policy, and if their position is exposed and threatened, coherence is even further enhanced.

legal procedures to prohibit the use of force in disputes, the acceptance of compulsory arbitration, and agreements on disarmament and arms control. Their leaders have always insisted on the equality of rights of all states, their dignity, their sovereignty, and their independence. Ironically their search for security through these measures tends to conflict with their insistence on equality in participation in world affairs. Critics of small states have long noted their unwillingness to take sides in conflicts among stronger countries, or to assume risks. When free to choose, most will remain on the sidelines of major power struggles.[9] In sum, the goal of the small state is "how to avoid, mitigate or postpone conflict, and how to resist superior force once conflict has developed."[10] At the same time the most advantageous world situation for small states appears to be a condition of great-power tension and crisis that leads neither to war that may damage or destroy the small state nor to meaningful detente that may reduce the small state to a satellite in a world divided into spheres of influence for the great powers.

Several other factors are necessary for successful resistance of a small state to a great power. Foremost is the presence of internal cohesion and unity among government leaders and people in the small state. Such unity limits the great power's choice of strategy, forcing it to harsher methods than at first contemplated or conversely to modify or even abandon its basic policy.[11] Second, the small state must have the capacity and the will to resist external pressure. In some instances this may necessitate

---

[9] For a fuller discussion of potential strategies for small powers see Rothstein, *op. cit.*, pp. 31–39; Arnold Wolfers, "In Defense of Small Countries," *The Yale Review*, Vol. XXXIII (Winter 1944), pp. 215–220; Fox, *op. cit.*, p. 182; and George Liska, *International Equilibrium; A Theoretical Essay on the Politics and Organization of Security* (Cambridge: Harvard University Press, 1957), pp. 30, 41, 67, and 126; for a challenge to this conventional model see Maurice A. East, "Size and Foreign Policy Behavior: A Test of Two Models," *World Politics*, Vol. XXV (July 1973), No. 4, pp. 556–576, who purports to demonstrate that small states engage in high-risk behavior instead of more cautious, low-risk behavior.

[10] Vital, *op. cit.*, p. 143.

[11] *Ibid.*, p. 144. Liska, *op. cit.*, p. 40, cites eighteenth-century Poland for the worst type of disaster that may befall a state threatened by powerful neighbors and torn apart by internal dissension.

military action but, more importantly, it might involve only the willingness to pay some kind of economic costs.[12] Third, the small state needs to develop a diplomacy of conciliatory language coupled with the art of procrastination and good public relations. In the end, however, a small state is "a consumer rather than a producer of security" and "follows rather than initiates joint action against aggression."[13]

Whatever the precise meaning of "small power" or "middle power," Mexico is unquestionably weaker compared to the United States militarily and economically. It has endured this relationship for more than a century with the gap increasing and with little hope or expectation of finding allies powerful enough to challenge seriously the hegemony of its neighbor anywhere in the Western Hemisphere, much less in the circum-Caribbean area. Mexico, therefore has generally acted like other small powers in similar circumstances by adopting a basically defensive posture and by developing strategies that might reduce its overwhelmingly dependent position. The evidence presented in the preceding chapters clearly demonstrates that Mexico has fallen into behavior patterns that resemble those of states in similar circumstances. At the same time because of the particular geographic configurations of the Western Hemisphere and the kind of hegemony that the United States established, some aspects of Mexican-United States relations are perhaps unique.

Never in its history has Mexico created armed forces with the expectation that they would engage in major combat outside the national territories. Its leaders have never contemplated a

---

[12] Vital, *op. cit.*, pp. 54–55, 99, and 113–114 points out that many small states are highly vulnerable to economic pressure particularly if they must rely on foreign markets, foreign source of capital, and imports from which a great power might cut them off. Moreover, the small state rarely can retaliate. On the other hand for the major power economic coercion is a crude weapon and not appropriate for all conflicts. On the contrary, Marshall R. Singer, *Weak States in a World of Powers: The Dynamics of International Relations* (New York: The Free Press, 1972), argues that in most situations the power of great states rests not on their coercive instruments but, rather, on their powers of attraction, that is, the needs of weak states for markets, technology, capital, skills, and management abilities.

[13] Liska, *op. cit.*, p. 25.

navy of any importance and have generally neglected to develop the science of logistics for sustained combat at great distances. Troops recruited, trained, and equipped on national and provincial levels have been designed either for internal war or for resistance to external aggression. Mexico has never had territorial ambitions to the south, while to the north her major preoccupation has been to hold and develop what she has against an expanding neighbor. Even with the loss of her territories in 1848, there grew little or no serious revanchist sentiment because of domestic conflicts, the vast underpopulated remaining northern territories, and the unquestioned might of the United States.[14] As a consequence, despite deep-seated hostility toward its neighbor, Mexico has never maintained sizeable forces along its frontier, limiting its armed men to law and order agencies, customs officials, and scattered garrisons. The only combat troops that have fought outside the country were a token air squadron in the Philippines during World War II. Mexico has clearly rejected the notion (except for the period prior to 1848) that it could resist aggression by building up modern, conventional military forces. Needless to say, not only has Mexico not contemplated nuclear weapons, but she has been a leader in developing a nuclear free zone in the Western Hemisphere.

On the question of a balance of power in Middle America, Mexico has never really enjoyed the luxury of an option. True enough, in the 1820s some of her political leaders sought economic and political support from Great Britain, while others sought to balance that influence with support from the United States. When the Texas question arose, Mexican leaders requested diplomatic assistance from Great Britain and France, but neither power was sufficiently interested to take the risks of involvement, including the hostility of the United States. When the crunch came finally in 1845, Mexico stood alone. During the 1860s Mexico's major threat to her independence came from Napoleon III of France supported by a minority faction of Mex-

---

[14] How seriously the Germans misread Mexican views during World War I is illustrated by their response to the Zimmermann telegram of 1917. See Barbara Tuchman, *The Zimmermann Telegram* (New York: Macmillan, 1958).

ican Conservatives. Again no foreign help was forthcoming, but even after the United States Civil War ended in 1865 and thousands of United States troops were deployed along the frontier as a threat to the French, the Mexicans requested little assistance from their neighbor and certainly no alliance. The dilemma was that there could be no compromise about expelling the French, but their expulsion would leave the United States once more unchallenged in the region.

Within a few years after the defeat of the French, it began to appear to some Mexican leaders that they had little to fear in the way of further losses of territory. However, with the economic development program begun by Porfirio Díaz, an even greater danger loomed on the horizon, that is, the loss of independence through economic domination. Díaz and his advisers were quick to recognize the problem and tried to resist this kind of United States hegemony by an economic "balance of power" in Mexico. Foreign investments and foreign loans were sought in Europe to counterbalance the flood of United States capital into the country. The drive was only partially successful, and when new difficulties arose during the Revolution over the expropriation, confiscation, and destruction of United States property and property rights in the country, Mexico again had no substantial outside support. A condition somewhat similar to that of the Díaz period is again developing today. For more than 25 years the country has been growing rapidly economically; foreign capital, mostly United States', has contributed importantly to that development. Again Mexican leaders are concerned about United States economic dominance and are seeking ways to circumvent it. Recent administrations have been seeking new markets, new sources of capital, and new products to sell abroad. They have also slowly but consistently been placing tighter restrictions on direct foreign investments in order to establish a new "balance of power" economically to give the country greater control over specific resources and over the economy in general. Like other small states Mexico has opted for a balance of power to give her greater control over her own affairs, but she sees this balance not so much in military or political terms but, instead, in economic terms.

Mexico has also adopted the strategy of nonalignment in

world power struggles. Such a position was irrelevant vis à vis the great powers (as it was for the United States) during the nineteenth century. As the United States became a great power at the turn of the century, Mexico, and in fact all of Latin America, perforce, could no longer remain completely isolated. With communications and transportation technologies shrinking the globe and, particularly, with international ideological forces (whether fascism, communism, or capitalism) seeking political alliances for the leading states supporting these doctrines, all of Latin America became involved to some extent in the conflicts. In the interwar years Mexico's leadership, proclaiming its own brand of socialism and political freedom, abhorred the rise of nazism-fascism and held ambivalent or divided positions both on Soviet communism and United States capitalism. After World War II broke out, Mexico eventually aligned itself with the allies, a move made easy by the entry of both the United States and the Soviet Union into the war against the Axis. Mexico's cooperation in this period with the United States stands in striking contrast to the hostility that marked their relations during World War I. After the Second World War, the momentum of cooperation persisted for a few years. The Pan American system, a loose regional association, was institutionalized under a formal charter to become the Organization of American States while the ideal of collective security became embodied in 1947 in a military alliance known as the Rio Treaty.

Although Mexico has remained a member of the Rio Treaty, a pact designed to stall aggressive military moves against any American state originating from within or without the Western Hemisphere, Mexico like all small states in alliance has attempted to keep her commitments to a minimum. Although Mexican leaders have never expressed doubts about the United States commitment to defend all of the Americas from attack, they have not agreed with those United States leaders who have seen the Soviet Union and the People's Republic of China as immediate threats to the security of the Western Hemisphere. Consequently, Mexico has refused to support United States policies on Cuba, to participate in the policy of containment, or to furnish troops to fight in places like Korea or Vietnam. Mexico, on the contrary, sees the Rio Treaty basically as a peacekeeping instrument for the Western Hemisphere and does participate in conciliation and arbitration measures instituted under its auspices. However, Mexico did support the United States in the demand that Soviet missiles be removed from Cuba in 1962. Mexico, therefore, has behaved generally as other small states in their attempts to sit out great power struggles. Her major departure from this course seemingly was World War II, but her actual involvement remained minimal. Her activities vary perhaps from those of other small states because of her long association with the United States in the Pan American Union-Organization of American States. But this position is at least partially dictated by the inability to escape United States hegemony, and in the hope that in union with other Latin American states, United States power can be curbed.

Finally, Mexico has most closely approximated the behavior patterns of other small states in its attempts to use legal and moral instruments to protect itself. As early as the Díaz period Mexican leaders attempted to gain support for the Calvo and Drago doctrines, both Argentinian in origin. The former holds that foreigners are entitled to the same protection to life, liberty, and property as nationals, but to no more. The doctrine totally rejects the notion of extraterritoriality or any special privileges for foreigners, including diplomatic pressure exerted in their behalf. The latter doctrine, no longer very relevant, states that force should not be used to collect international debts. Both doctrines in one guise or another are major positions of Mexican foreign policy. To these imported policies Mexico has added one of its own: the Estrada Doctrine. Named for Genaro Estrada, Mexican Minister of Foreign Affairs, the doctrine as promulgated in 1930 announced that Mexico would henceforth recognize any new government that came to power, by whatever means, immediately and automatically. The Mexican government also invited all nations especially in the Western Hemisphere to adopt this position on recognition. All three doctrines support the idea of absolute sovereignty, independence, and equality of states with respect to their internal affairs. All three also reflect Mexican concern with real problems in its history of intervention or threatened intervention over contracts, debt collections, and recognition policy. Similarly Mexico has attempted to curb

United States power through international organizations. Mexico joined at their founding the Pan American Union, the League of Nations, and the United Nations, and also many of their subsidiary bodies. In all these functions the Mexican delegates have fought long and hard against colonialism and its disguised form of intervention. Mexico has long rejected the Monroe Doctrine and its various corollaries that proclaim or imply United States hegemony and right of intervention in other American states for whatever reason. Mexico on the other hand has refused to accept any doctrines within these international organizations that smack of any surrender of sovereignty or loss of control over national territory, resources, or people. Various Mexican governments have refused to support an inter-American police force, to send troops on international peacekeeping operations, or to agree to international decisions that could establish territorial waters. In this respect Mexico has acted almost precisely according to the pattern for small states.

What of Mexico's tactics to achieve her goals and develop her strategies? And how can we summarize her successes and failures in facing the overwhelming military might and economic strength of the United States? In general terms it appears that Mexican leaders have only intermittently been willing to pay the costs of a high level of economic and political independence. These costs are (1) the submergence of party, factional, and ideological differences in the face of external threats; (2) economic bootstrap operations to avoid the necessity of large doses of foreign capital; and (3) the establishment of modern military forces as a deterrent to armed incursions. Internal conflict lost Texas in 1836 and contributed greatly to the disasters of the 1840s. The French intervention was as much a civil war as a foreign invasion, and the Revolution, which was accompanied by such high levels of intervention, was fought more among the revolutionaries themselves than between revolutionaries and old-regime supporters. During years of peace and prosperity, whether in Díaz' time or at the present, regimes dedicated to economic growth have permitted high levels of economic penetration. In Díaz' time, it was overwhelming; at the present it is substantial but restrained and limited. No government has opted for a bootstrap operation on the Japanese model with growth and development generated almost entirely out of national resources. Perhaps the social discipline necessary to follow the Japanese model is impossible to enforce in Mexico. Whatever the reason, the Mexicans have conducted their struggle for national independence with a certain unwillingness to pay these potential costs. Certainly they have been wise not to invest in armaments in the twentieth century because it is inconceivable that any level of armed might that they could have attained would have altered United States policies or purposes. In the economic area the picture is mixed. The Díaz period, except perhaps for the railroads, constituted a virtual sellout to foreigners. In the time of Cárdenas great sacrifices were apparently foreshadowed with the oil expropriation, but in the post-Cárdenas era, the new leaders reopened the country to the foreign investor. The degree of foreign control over the economy in recent decades has never, however, approached that of the dictatorship, and the several Mexican administrations since World War II have gradually been restricting the scope of direct foreign investments in the economy. In other words, in economic matters, the government has been trying to string out the costs in low payments over a long time period; in political terms it has maintained internal cohesion by carrot and stick measures to current and potential opponents; and in military matters, it has opted not to compete but to rely on changed conditions within the international system and, more importantly, within the United States, to increase its flexibility and maneuverability in a world over which it has little control.

In reviewing Mexico's historical relations with the United States over the last century and a half, it is apparent that for about the first 50 years, Mexico was primarily concerned with preventing territorial losses and insuring the political independence of the state. For the past 100 years, Mexican leaders have confronted the problem of neocolonialism in the guise of economic dependence. In these struggles Mexico enjoyed the greatest potential for independent actions and decisions when the United States was distracted from hemispheric affairs by grave internal or international problems, when Mexico enjoyed a high level of internal cohesion, and ideally when these two conditions coincided. Conversely, Mexico suffered her greatest losses of territory and independent action when the country was rent by civil strife, when United States attention was drawn to Mexico with few distractions and, most disastrously for Mexico, when these conditions coincided. The latter prevailed to Mexico's enormous loss in the 1830s and 1840s, and to a lesser extent in the first years of the Revolution. The former occurred first during the Díaz period and in varying degrees since 1917. In the first half of the nineteenth century the United States was bent upon territorial expansion and Mexico was the target. Unfortunately for Mexico her defense of her territory was at best half-hearted. While American volunteers flocked to Texas in the 1830s and enthusiastically took up arms in 1846, the Mexican government had difficulty rounding up recruits for defense, and many leaders seemed more eager to battle each other than the invaders. The Revolution by its nature invited some degree of United States interference, but the protracted nature of the conflict and the bidding by some revolutionaries for United States support only added to the turmoil. Conversely, as the United States became more involved in the Great War in Europe, Wilson began to withdraw from the Mexican scene. He recalled the troops chasing Villa and reduced pressure on Carranza for protection to United States property. Also, whenever Mexico could put its own house in order, by whatever methods, United States pressures also dropped. As Díaz consolidated his position in the 1870s and restored order along the border, United States complaints ceased and border incursions were reduced. In the 1920s and after, as again order returned to the country, United States pressures dropped. Even when a confrontation threatened to develop with the oil expropriation in 1938, the United States government did little more than demand fair and prompt payments. The oil companies slapped a boycott on Mexican oil, but with the Mexican people willing to pay the costs of the expropriation, with the United States becoming more and more concerned with developments in Europe, and with internal unity in Mexico, the crisis passed. Following World War II United States attention remained attracted primarily outside the Western Hemisphere. Mexico continued to develop its Revolution according to its internal dynamic. That Mexican leaders opted to open the country to foreign investors was an internal decision. That they have now chosen in the past decade to close the door somewhat is also their choice. If eventually they determine it to the country's best interest to slam it closed, that too will be their decision. If they retain their present cohesion and unity of purpose, they can anticipate little official pressure from the United States government, whatever cries of anguish and economic reprisals are launched by private business enterprises. In other words, if Mexico's leaders desire the maximum freedom of action in a world of unequal powers, they must first keep their own house in order and, second, broaden the base of economic support to reduce the level of dependence on the United States. Finally, they can pray that primary United States international interests do not focus on the Western Hemisphere, much less on them.

Bibliographical Essay

The best single volume history of Mexico in English is T. R. Fehrenbach, *Fire and Blood: A History of Mexico* (New York: Macmillan, 1973). Despite some unevenness in coverage and an occasional tendency to sensationalism, it is on the whole a solid work. One might usefully supplement Fehrenbach with the works of Charles C. Cumberland, *Mexico: The Struggle for Modernity* (New York: Oxford University Press, 1968), which emphasizes social and economic developments, and Roger D. Hansen, *The Politics of Mexican Developments* (Baltimore: The Johns Hopkins Press, 1971), with its emphasis on the recent and contemporary political economy of the country. All of these however, somewhat slight the 90 years between independence and the Revolution.

What there is of published materials on United States-Mexican relations tends to be nationalistic, polemical, or dated. Older works with much useful information, however, include J. Fred Rippy, *The United States and Mexico*, revised edition (New York: Knopf, 1931); James M. Callahan, *American Foreign Policy in Mexican Relations* (New York: Cooper Square, 1967); Frederick Sherwood Dunn, *The Diplomatic Protection of Americans in Mexico* (New York: Columbia University Press, 1933); and Edgar Turlington, *Mexico and Her Foreign Creditors* (New York: Columbia University Press, 1930).

Aspects of United States policy toward Mexico can also be found in two classic, but strongly pro-United States works on general relations with Latin America: Dexter Perkins, *Hands Off: A History of the Monroe Doctrine* (Boston: Little, Brown, 1941) and Samuel F. Bemis, *The Latin American Policy of the*

United States (New York: Harcourt, Brace, 1943). The most recent work, Howard F. Cline, *The United States and Mexico,* revised edition (Cambridge: Harvard University Press, 1963), is limited largely to the era since 1910 and is marred by some carelessness in details and more seriously by a glossing over of the major conflicts of interest between the two countries. For the Mexican side of these relations, one should consult the rather balanced work of Luis G. Zorrilla, *Historia de las relaciones entre México y los Estados Unidos de America, 1800–1958,* 2 volumes (México: Editorial Porrúa, 1965), as well as the strongly anti-United States study of Alberto María Carreño, *La diplomacia extraordinaria entre México y los Estados Unidos, 1789–1947,* 2 volumes (México: Editorial Jus, 1951).

For models of objective and scholarly work on specialized subjects, see Jan Bazant, *Historia de la deuda exterior de México (1823–1946)* (México: El Colegio de México, 1968) and Sheldon B. Liss, *A Century of Disagreement: The Chamizal Conflict, 1864–1964* (Washington, D.C.: The University Press of Washington, D.C., 1965). Clarence C. Clendenen, *Blood on the Border. The United States Army and the Mexican Irregulars* (New York: Macmillan, 1969) is a detailed, fascinating account of the little known as well as the famous border conflicts and disputes. It presumes, however, the rightness of the United States cause in almost all instances.

Scholars have devoted very little attention to the question of mutual attitudes of Mexicans and Americans toward each other. The works that do exist mostly deal with Mexican views of the United States. Two recent books contain considerable information on the subject, although they do not treat the subject directly: John S. Brushwood, *Mexico in its Novel: A Nation's Search for Identity* (Austin: University of Texas Press, 1966) and Frederick C. Turner, *The Dynamic of Mexican Nationalism* (Chapel Hill: University of North Carolina Press, 1968). Two articles by John C. Merrill based on his doctoral dissertation at the University of Iowa treat this problem more directly: "The Image of the United States in Ten Mexican Dailies," *Journalism Quarterly,* Vol. XXXIX (Spring 1962), No. 2, pp. 203–209, and "The United States as seen from Mexico," *Journal of Inter-American Studies,* Vol. V (January 1963), No. 1, pp. 53–66.

Merrill's findings of considerable anti-Americanism among Mexican journalists and other intellectuals who contribute editorials and feature articles to the press are surprisingly counterbalanced by the interesting work of Rafael Segovia among schoolchildren in public and private schools in Mexico, from grades six to nine. In his "Nacionalismo e imagen del mundo exterior en los níños mexicanos," *Foro Internacional*, Vol. XIII (October to December 1972), No. 2, pp. 272–291, Segovia discovered very high positive feelings toward the United States, especially among lower-class children.

Attitudes of Americans toward Mexico have not been so systematically studied. Arthur P. Whitaker, *The United States and the Independence of Latin America, 1800–1830* (New York: Norton, 1964), devotes some attention to United States attitudes toward Latin Americans in general and toward Mexicans specifically. Historically, United States views on Mexico have surfaced as conflicts arose, and may be found in congressional debates and reports, newspaper editorials, soldiers' memoirs and diaries, religious publications, and books and pamphlets of business executives and corporations. More recently they have also appeared in scholarly writings. Except for these writings, United States views and attitudes toward Mexicans tend to be unflattering.

A large body of literature exists on Anglo-Spanish imperial rivalries and the United States inheritance of the British role. In addition to the work of Whitaker cited above, the reader is referred to two more excellent studies by the same author: *The Spanish-American Frontier: 1783–1795* (Lincoln: University of Nebraska Press, 1969) and *The Mississippi Question: 1795–1803* (New York: Appleton-Century, 1934). These may be supplemented by Philip C. Brooks, *Diplomacy and the Borderlands: the Adams-Onís Treaty of 1819* (Berkeley: University of California Press, 1939) and John Rydjord, *Foreign Interest in the Independence of New Spain* (Durham: Duke University Press, 1935). For greater depth on the history of the borderlands see the *Latin American Research Review*, Vol. VII (Summer 1972), No. 2; much of this issue is devoted to excellent bibliographical articles on the area.

For the beginnings of United States relations with independent

Mexico two older works are still valuable: George L. Rives, *The United States and Mexico: 1821–1848*, 2 volumes (New York: Scribner's, 1913) and William R. Manning, *Early Diplomatic Relations between the United States and Mexico* (Baltimore: Johns Hopkins Press, 1916). J. Fred Rippy, *Joel R. Poinsett: Versatile American* (Durham: Duke University Press, 1935) is an overly enthusiastic biography, while Dorothy R. Parton, *The Diplomatic Career of Joel Roberts Poinsett* (Washington, D.C.: The Catholic University of America Press, 1934), while more limited in scope, is more balanced. Poinsett's own *Notes on Mexico, Made in the Autumn of 1822* (Philadelphia: H. C. Carey and I. Lea, 1824) and his rival's, Henry G. Ward, *Mexico in 1827*, 2 volumes (London: H. Colburn, 1828) give a contemporary flavor that no secondary source can match.

Of the substantial periodical literature, see the following three articles. Charles R. Salit, "Anglo American Rivalry in Mexico, 1823–1830," *Revista de Historia de América* (December 1943) No. 16, pp. 65–84, argues that Poinsett failed in his mission not because of his meddling, but because United States policies conflicted with Mexico's interests. J. E. Baur, "Evolution of a Mexican Foreign Trade Policy, 1821–1828," *The Americas*, Vol. XIX (January 1963), No. 3, pp. 225–261, and Norman A. Graebner, "United States Gulf Commerce with Mexico, 1822–1848," *Inter-American Economic Affairs*, Vol. V (Summer 1951), No. 1, pp. 36–51, present well-researched and interesting data on these early economic relations.

A vast literature has been produced by both Mexican and American scholars on the Texas controversy and the War of 1846. The problems of Spanish administrators in Texas are sympathetically treated in Félix D. Almaráz, *Tragic Cavalier: Governor Manuel Salcedo of Texas, 1808–1813* (Austin: The University of Texas Press, 1971), while the point of view of the American frontiersmen pushing into Texas is also sympathetically presented in Eugene C. Barker, *The Life of Stephen F. Austin, Founder of Texas, 1793–1836* (Austin: The Texas State Historical Association, 1949). During his long career Barker published a long list of books and articles on early Texas, among the best of which is *Mexico and Texas: 1821–1835* (New York: Russell and Russell, 1965). An attempt at a balanced appraisal, emphasizing differences in folk customs and ways, is Samuel H. Lowrie, *Culture Conflict in Texas, 1821–1835* (New York: Columbia University Press, 1932). A new work encompassing the most recent scholarship is David Pletcher, *The Diplomacy of Annexation: Texas, Oregon, and the Mexican War* (Columbia: University of Missouri Press, 1973).

The war has produced defenders and accusers of President James K. Polk. The classic defense has long been Justin H. Smith, *The War with Mexico*, 2 volumes (Gloucester, Mass.: Peter Smith, 1963) and the most recent and best attack on Polk is Glenn W. Price, *Origins of the War with Mexico: The Polk-Stockton Intrigue* (Austin: The University of Texas Press, 1967). For a solid, balanced appraisal of Polk one should consult Charles Sellers, *James K. Polk: Continentalist, 1843–1846* (Princeton: Princeton University Press, 1966), the second volume of this biography. The Mexican view is ably presented by Carlos Bosch García, *Historia de las relaciones entre México y los Estados Unidos, 1819–1848* (México: UNAM, 1961) and Vito Alessio Robles, *Coahuila y Texas desde la consumación de la independencia hasta el Tratado de Paz de Guadalupe Hidalgo*, 2 volumes (México: Talleres Gráficos de la Nación, 1945–1946). Finally, for its extensive and annotated bibliography of 766 items, the reader should also consult Seymour V. Connor and Odie B. Faulk, *North America Divided: The Mexican War 1846–1848* (New York: Oxford University Press, 1971).

For the period between the War of 1846 and the Revolution of 1910, unfortunately, there are no general studies in English. The story, however, can be pieced together with a series of works that deal indirectly or segmentally with the era. For the impact of the war on Mexico, Charles A. Hale, "The War with the United States and the Crisis in Mexican Thought," *The Americas*, Vol. XIV (October 1957), No. 2, pp. 153–173, is essential to understand not only the deep suspicion and fear of the United States, but the desperation of the contending factions in Mexico to gain control and unify the country under its particular program and ideology.

Factual accounts of the political struggles in Mexico and their relation to foreign policy issues are well discussed in Walter V. Scholes, *Mexican Politics During the Juárez Regime: 1855–1872*

(Columbia: University of Missouri Press, 1969), and Frank A. Knapp, *The Life of Sebastián Lerdo de Tejada: 1823–1889* (Austin: The University of Texas Press, 1951).

These may be supplemented with J. Fred Rippy, "Diplomacy of the United States and Mexico Regarding the Isthmus of Tehuantepec, 1848–1860," *The Mississippi Valley Historical Review*, Vol. VI (March 1920), No. 4, pp. 503–531, and Robert Ryal Miller, "Matías Romero: Mexican Minister to the United States During the Juárez-Maximilian Era," *The Hispanic American Historical Review*, Vol. XLV (May 1965), No. 2, pp. 228–245. In Spanish, a fine study, José Fuentes Mares, *Juárez y los Estados Unidos* (México: Libro Mex, 1960), gives the kind of overview that is lacking in English. A detailed study of the last successful territorial negotiation at Mexico's expense may be found in Paul N. Garber, *The Gadsden Treaty* (Philadelphia: The University of Pennsylvania Press, 1923).

For the Díaz period one must consult the nine-volume work, Daniel Cosío Villegas (ed.), *Historia moderna de México* (México: Editorial Hermes, 1955–1972), especially those volumes and sections dealing with foreign affairs: Cosío Villegas, *El porfiriato: La vida política exterior*, Part 2 (1963); Luis Nicolau D'Olwer, "Las inversiones extranjeras," *El porfiriato: La vida económica*, Part 2 (1965); and Fernando Rosenzweig, "El comercio exterior," *El porfiriato: La vida económica*, Part 2 (1965).

The early years of Díaz and the United States are well done in Daniel Cosío Villegas, *The United States versus Porfirio Díaz*, translated by Nettie Lee Benson (Lincoln: University of Nebraska Press, 1963). Special aspects of United States relations with the Díaz dictatorship are interestingly and thoroughly explored in David M. Pletcher, *Rails, Mines, and Progress: Seven American Promoters in Mexico, 1867–1911* (Ithaca: Cornell University Press, 1958) and Marvin D. Bernstein, *The Mexican Mining Industry: 1890–1950* (Albany: State University of New York, 1964).

Despite the number of books and articles that have recently poured from the presses, there is still no single volume on United States-Mexican relations during the Revolutionary years, 1910–1920. There are, however, several excellent background works that include substantial sections on international relations as well as studies on specific aspects of revolutionary diplomacy. In the former category are the two first-rate studies of the beginnings of the revolution: Stanley R. Ross, *Francisco I. Madero: Apostle of Mexican Democracy* (New York: Columbia University Press, 1955) and Charles C. Cumberland, *Mexican Revolution: Genesis under Madero* (Austin: University of Texas Press, 1952). These should be followed by Cumberland's *Mexican Revolution: The Constitutionalist Years* (Austin: University of Texas Press, 1972) and Michael C. Meyer, *Huerta, a Political Portrait* (Lincon: University of Nebraska Press, 1972).

Woodrow Wilson's policies toward Mexico are placed in global perspective by the monumental, multivolume study of his life by Arthur S. Link; the author has condensed his study of Wilson's first administration into *Woodrow Wilson and the Progressive Era, 1910–1917* (New York: Harper and Bros., 1954). Two special studies are interestingly and beautifully written: Robert E. Quirk, *The Mexican Revolution, 1914–1915* (Bloomington: Indiana University Press, 1960) and Barbara W. Tuchman, *The Zimmermann Telegram* (New York: Macmillan, 1966).

Special aspects of revolutionary international relations are well documented and researched in the following studies: Peter Calvert, *The Mexican Revolution, 1910–1914. The Diplomacy of Anglo-American Conflict* (Cambridge: Cambridge University Press, 1968); Lowell L. Blaisdell, *The Desert Revolution: Baja California, 1911* (Madison: University of Wisconsin Press, 1962); C. C. Clendenen, *The United States and Pancho Villa: A Study in Unconventional Diplomacy* (Ithaca: Cornell University Press, 1961); Kenneth J. Grieb, *The United States and Huerta* (Lincoln: University of Nebraska Press, 1969); George M. Stephenson, *John Lind of Minnesota* (Minneapolis: The University of Minnesota Press, 1935); and Robert E. Quirk, *An Affair of Honor: Woodrow Wilson and the Occupation of Veracruz* (New York: McGraw-Hill, 1964). Ambassador Henry Lane Wilson published his apologia some years later in *Diplomatic Episodes in Mexico, Belgium, and Chile* (Garden City: Doubleday, Page, 1927), but his memory proved somewhat faulty and his "facts" must be checked.

Works by Mexican authors on the revolution have tended to be highly personal and polemical accounts. The student should consult, however, the scholarly and well-written work of Berta Ulloa, *La revolución intervenida: Relaciones diplomáticas entre*

México y Estados Unidos, 1910–1914 (México: El Colegio de México, 1971). This may be supplemented with the very nationalistic account of Isidro Fabela, *Historia diplomática de la revolución mexicana*, 2 volumes (México: Fondo de Cultura Económica, 1958–1959).

A portion of the periodical literature should be mentioned. Cole Blasier, "The United States and Madero," *Journal of Latin American Studies*, Vol. IV (November 1972), Part 2, pp. 207–231, includes an excellent review of the latest scholarly findings on this controversial period; James A. Sandos, "German Involvement in Northern Mexico, 1915–1916: A New Look at the Columbus Raid," *The Hispanic American Historical Review*, Vol. L (February 1970), No. 1, pp. 70–88, while not convincing about the importance of German involvement, is persuasive in arguing that local, personal grievances shaped Villa's primary motivation instead of the larger political issues; E. J. Berbusse, "Neutrality-diplomacy of the United States and Mexico, 1910–1911," *The Americas*, Vol. XII (January 1956), No. 3, pp. 265–283, usefully outlines the ambiguity of the meaning of neutrality in the United States; and Kenneth J. Grieb, "Standard Oil and the Financing of the Mexican Revolution," *California Historical Society Quarterly*, Vol. XLX (March 1971), No. 1, pp. 59–71, makes a case from circumstantial evidence for involvement of the company, but admits the difficulty of obtaining hard data.

For some marvelous vignettes of Mexican life in the 1920s and 1930s the student should dip into John W. F. Dulles, *Yesterday in Mexico: A Chronicle of the Revolution, 1919–1936* (Austin: University of Texas Press, 1961). A well-argued, critical view of United States policy is presented by Robert Freeman Smith, *The United States and Revolutionary Nationalism in Mexico, 1916–1932* (Chicago: The University of Chicago Press, 1972), while a more sympathetic approach to the Good Neighbor Policy of the 1930s is E. David Cronon, *Josephus Daniels in Mexico* (Madison: The University of Wisconsin Press, 1960). The student may also find interesting the ambassador's reminiscences, Josephus Daniels, *Shirt-Sleeve Diplomat* (Chapel Hill: The University of North Carolina Press, 1947).

Three special studies should be noted. Lorenzo Meyer, *México y Estados Unidos en el conflicto petrolero (1917–1942)* (México: El Colegio de México, 1968), although somewhat slanted in

Mexico's favor, is the best single volume on the petroleum controversy. Also slanted, in favor of the Catholic Church, but still quite good, is Elizabeth Ann Rice's study of United States attitudes toward the religious conflict in Mexico: *The Diplomatic Relations between the United States and Mexico, as Affected by the Struggle for Religious Liberty in Mexico, 1925–1929* (Washington, D.C.: The Catholic University of America Press, 1959). The Mexican side of the Bucareli agreements is given in Antonio Gómez Robledo, *Los convenios de Bucareli ante el derecho internacional* (México: Editorial Polis, 1938).

The key role of Ambassador Dwight Morrow in the late 1920s is outlined in three fine articles: Stanley R. Ross, "Dwight W. Morrow, Ambassador to Mexico," *The Americas*, Vol. XIV (January 1958), No. 3, pp. 273–289; L. Ethan Ellis, "Dwight Morrow and the Church-State Controversy in Mexico," *The Hispanic American Historical Review*, Vol. XXXVIII (November 1958), No. 4, pp. 482–505; and Stanley R. Ross, "Dwight Morrow and the Mexican Revolution," *The Hispanic American Historical Review*, Vol. XXXVIII (November 1958), No. 4, pp. 506–528.

Mexican-United States relations since World War II in their broad outlines may be found in two general works on Mexican politics: L. Vincent Padgett, *The Mexican Political System* (Boston: Houghton-Mifflin, 1966) and Frank Brandenburg, *The Making of Modern Mexico* (Englewood Cliffs: Prentice Hall, 1964). The principles and guidelines of Mexican foreign policy as seen through official and semiofficial documents and statements have been reproduced in Carlos Alberto Astiz (ed.), *Latin American International Politics: Ambitions, Capabilities, and the National Interest of Mexico, Brazil, and Argentina* (Notre Dame: University of Notre Dame Press, 1969).

Here are some key works on some recent and contemporary issues: Richard B. Craig, *The Bracero Program: Interest Groups and Foreign Policy* (Austin: The University of Texas Press, 1971); Norris Hundley, *Dividing the Waters: A Century of Controversy between the United States and Mexico* (Berkeley: The University of California Press, 1966); Manuel A. Machado, *An Industry in Crisis. Mexican-United States Cooperation in the Control of Foot-and-Mouth Disease* (Berkeley: The University of California Press, 1968); Francis J. Weber, *The United States versus Mexico:*

The Final Settlement of the Pious Fund (Los Angeles: Historical Society of Southern California, 1969); Alfonso García Robles, *The Denuclearization of Latin America* (New York: Carnegie Endowment for International Peace, 1967); Alexander Böhrisch and Wolfgang König, *La política mexicana sobre inversiones extranjeras* (México: El Colegio de México, 1968); and Harry K. Wright, *Foreign Enterprise in Mexico: Laws and Policies* (Chapel Hill: The University of North Carolina Press, 1971).

An excellent brief survey of contemporary relations is Lyle C. Brown and James W. Wilkie, "Recent United States-Mexican Relations: Problems Old and New" in John Braeman et al. (eds.), *Twentieth Century American Foreign Policy* (Columbus: Ohio State University Press, 1971). Apart from the standard United States journals on political science, economics, sociology, law, and anthropology, the student is directed to two first-rate Mexican scholarly journals that regularly carry materials concerned with this study: *Foro Internacional* and *Historia Mexicana*. In addition, he should consult for current developments *Mexican Newsletter* from the Office of the President and *Comercio Exterior de México*, a publication of the Banco Nacional de Comercio Exterior. Both of these periodicals are published in English.

Of the recent literature on small-power behavior, four items are singled out for special mention. David Vital, *The Inequality of States: A Study of the Small Power in International Relations* (New York: Oxford University Press, 1967), is an excellent summary of recent findings. Marshall R. Singer, *Weak States in a World of Powers* (New York: The Free Press, 1972), is a more detailed study of large power–small power relations, and is particularly valuable for its attempt to set up methods for analyzing and measuring "dependency," a topic of great current interest in all Latin America as well as in Mexico.

Mario Ojeda Gómez, "The Role of Mexico as a Middle Power," in J. King Gordon (ed.), *Canada's Role as a Middle Power* (Toronto: The Canadian Institute of International Affairs, 1966), is interesting as a semiofficial Mexican statement. And finally, Maurice A. East, "Size and Foreign Policy Behavior: A Test of Two Models," *World Politics*, Vol. XXV (July 1973), No. 4, pp. 556–576, suggests that small states do not necessarily engage in low-risk behavior, but rather in high-risk behavior, in part because of a time lag in perceiving threats to their security.

Index